Warti

A thousand miles

by

J. W. Day

The Long Riders' Guild Press

www.thelongridersguild.com

ISBN: 1-59048-039-2

To the Reader:

The editors and publishers of The Long Riders' Guild Press faced significant technical and financial difficulties in bringing this and the other titles in the Equestrian Travel Classics collection to the light of day.

Though the authors represented in this international series envisioned their stories being shared for generations to come, all too often that was not the case. Sadly, many of the books now being published by The Long Riders' Guild Press were discovered gracing the bookshelves of rare book dealers, adorned with princely prices that placed them out of financial reach of the common reader. The remainder were found lying neglected on the scrap heap of history, their once-proud stories forgotten, their once-glorious covers stained by the toil of time and a host of indifferent previous owners.

However The Long Riders' Guild Press passionately believes that this book, and its literary sisters, remain of global interest and importance. We stand committed, therefore, to bringing our readers the best copy of these classics at the most affordable price. The copy which you now hold may have small blemishes originating from the master text.

We apologize in advance for any defects of this nature.

The Author, J. W. Day, and his friend Jim Rodd prepare to set out on their one thousand mile trip across England on their thoroughbreds.

AUTHOR'S INTRODUCTION

THIS IS THE TALE OF AN AMBLE ON HORSEBACK THROUGH EAST Anglia in war-time. I set out, first, to get well after a serious illness, on the old truth that "the outside of a horse is the best medicine for the inside of a man." And, second, to see what they were doing to revive the land on farms and manors, in parishes and villages, most of which I have known and loved since boyhood.

There were many old friends to be looked up and gossiped with, much inconsequent talk here and there, some few new friends and places to be visited, and a great many old tales to be retold.

The result is not a text-book on farming—there are too many professors and publicists busy at them already and not enough farmers with time on their hands to read them or write them. Nor is it any facile glorification of the hasty, expensive, but none-the-less remarkable work which has been achieved by the Ministry of Agriculture. Nor does it flatter the mushroom bureaucracy which has grown like fungi since the war on the structure of the War Agricultural Executive Committees. They have their own hired trumpeters to publicize their self-conscious good deeds in the Press and in the clotted-cream accents of the B.B.C.

I have simply put down the everyday views of people whom I met and recorded the day-by-day activities I saw. They are unvarnished and, with two exceptions, unaltered.

Altogether I visited more than a hundred farms and estates totalling 164,000 acres and rode just over 1200 miles on horseback in two months. Of all the farmers I met few wanted a long-term extension of control after the war, and *not one* wanted nationalization of the land. More than half said that they preferred to farm under a good squire rather than to own their own farms. All were convinced that Britain can feed herself in bare essentials for all time if need be; few expect that they will get a square deal the moment international trade is open again. But they are most of them philosophers, and nearly all men who love land with that rare, deep love of natural things which is of the essence of the English character.

The plain truth is that most English farmers, more than 80 per cent. of whom farm less than 250 acres, have done a magnificent war-time work. Theirs is the praise first, last, and midmost. Many War Agricultural Committees have also undoubtedly done well. I saw the good results notably in Norfolk, Suffolk, Cambridgeshire, and Huntingdonshire. That is because they have ridden their lands and responsibilities like good horsemen—with a light rein, with sympathy and understanding, leaving it to the horse-sense of the farmers to get the best out of the land. But in some other counties I hear bitter complaints of high-handed action, petty tyranny, evictions at short notice and for little reason; undue favouritism; excessive waste of petrol and machinery; nepotism and jobbery; pretentious ignorance on the part of officials; and, in some cases, downright hardship caused to old men and women.

If control in agriculture is to be exercised after the war—and, personally, I should hate to see a total perpetuation of the breed of rural bureaucrats, with their contradictory orders and meddlesome clerks—I suggest that the Committee system be reorganized broadly on the following points:

(1) That a Court of Appeal be set up to which farmers can appeal against drastic decisions of a Committee.

(2) That in any case no man be dispossessed of his land at less than a year's notice provided he continues to cultivate it properly during that time.

(3) That the working costs and profits (if any) of each Committee be made public.

(4) That a high proportion of the profit (if any) made by a Committee which has taken over derelict or undrained land to farm be remitted at the end of the Committee's tenure to the *owner* of the land to set against the bill which he will be charged for drainage and/or reclamation and cultivation.

(5) That not more than one member of any family be allowed to serve, paid or unpaid, on an Agricultural Executive Committee or on its staff. This will avoid family favouritism.

(6) That no farm of a dispossessed farmer be handed over to a relative or client of any member or employee of a Committee. This would avoid the jobbery which I am convinced goes on in some districts.

So much for the broad principles of a few basic conclusions I have come to after a lifetime spent largely in East Anglia, where my forbears have lived and owned land for four centuries.

If this book brings to the townsman, who is himself almost invariably a villager at heart, some present picture of the steadfast lives, unchanging values, and English fun of our men of the Eastern Counties, and some sense of the shy beauty of our lands, it will have done a little service to those landowners, farmers, and farm labourers who for twenty years faced the economic sand-storm. At the end they made the desert bloom.

J. WENTWORTH DAY

WICKEN, CAMBS.
December 1942

CONTENTS

CHAPTER		PAGE
I.	The Start from Tolleshunt D'Arcy Hall—A Medieval Manor Farm—Decline of the Yeomanry—How 'Cheap Food' killed the Land—The Dereliction of Salcott-cum-Virley—Bargemen and Smugglers—To Saltings and the Sea.	11
II.	A Shooting Idyll of the Marshes—The Passing of Bulls Bars—Tom Mann, Yeoman of Virley Hall—A Squire of the Old Sort—The Man who refused Money—Smugglers and the Roman Ghost—The Drunken Skipper in the Pond—Drowned Islands—The Peldon Rose Parliament.	20
III.	Two Essex Characters—Ted Allen, Adder-catcher and Bull-tamer—His Battle with 'the City Gent'—When the Devil mowed a Field of Hay—How to tame a Bull—Wick Farm and Langenhoe Marsh—The Roman Temple of Fingringhoe and the Mystery of Arch Hall—Follies of 'Committee Farming.'	31
IV.	Bill Wyatt, 'Admiral' of West Mersea—An Elizabethan Philosopher—How he lassoed a Porpoise—"The Little Owd Boy up Street" who was bombed—On London, "That Wicked Owd Hole"—On Women—At Mrs Hone's—On Drink—"Eighteen Thousand Barrels o' Beer in Me Life"—Duck-driving in the Blitz—The Harbour-master of Pin Mill and his Little Way with Germans—On Towns and how they make Monkeys of Men.	42
V.	Linnett, the Saxon Fowler of Bradwell-juxta-Mare—Vigil by the Roman Fort—Gossip at the Victory on Mersea Island—Poaching on Old Hall Marshes—When Bill Wyatt blacked his Face—The Shooting of Swan Mussett—"He's Still Full o' Shot"—"A Head Place for Rum 'Uns"—Salvaging an Uncle from the Mast-head with an Eel-pick—The Gunner who looked like a Hot Cross Bun.	54
VI.	The Little Ways of Foxes—The Fox in the Owl's Nest—Reynard on a Roof—When Sir Claude de Crespigny swam for a Fox—"A Rum Old Day"—Charles James and the Ploughman—On boxing Horses—The Start by Road—To the Heckford Angel and Maldon.	65
VII.	Maldon, the Town of Plough and Sail—Mother of English Poetry—Northey, Isle of Ghosts and Birds—Vikings and Wild Geese—At the Blue Boar, a Medieval Inn—The Seaman and the Bomb—Company at the Jolly Sailor—Old Fowling Days in the *Joseph and Mary*—The Three Claydons—Liquor Smugglers of Osea Island—"'Git up, hoss'," he say.	75
VIII.	The Mechanical Miracle of Fordson Estates—A Visit to Boreham House Farms—Mr Ford's Agricultural Shop Window—Lessons in Practical Farming—The Maxims of Lord Perry—Follies of Bureaucracy—Farm Wages and Income Tax—Loss of the Smack *Teaser*—A Morning's Fishing—Cousin Luke and his Rifle.	84
IX.	Of Mr Lawrence Washington of Maldon—Woodham Mortimer and its Squiresses—The Windy Lands of Dengie—Will Goodchild's Prairie Farm—Marshes down to Corn—When the Devil threw a Man out of his Bed at Midnight on Wallasea Island—Old Mother Redcap on a	

CHAPTER PAGE

Hurdle—Witches of the Islands—The Viking Ghost of Canvey Point—Cattle, Wild Horses, and Conscientious Objectors—A Short-sighted Horse Slaughter Policy—Wild Irish Gangs—"They lived like Hogs and fought like Dogs"—A Yeoman at Home. 98

X. A Wayside Word with Charlie Brown, the King of Limehouse—The Mechanized Monsters of Hatfield—A Bit of Bread and Cheese with Jack Olding—Bulldozers which move Mountains—American Farming comes to England—What the Caterpillar Tractor can do—"The Indivisible Trinity: Landowner, Farmer, and Labourer"—Hannen Swaffer's Definition—Beak, V.C., of Malta—To Easton Lodge—A Vanished Herd of Noble Deer—Hedingham Castle and the Great Yeldham Gaol. 111

XI. By the Roman Road to Cambridge—Where the Godolphin Arabian lies Buried—The Shepherd's Soliloquy—"Yan, Tan, Tethera," and "One-erum, Two-erum, Cock-erum"—Pepys's Inn—Ghosts of Barnwell Priory—Joe Cannon's Cock-fight—Old Callaby's Ratting Parties—Talk at Histon Manor—On Yeomen—The Beginning and Meaning of the Term—The Tyranny of Bureaucracy—Chivers's, the Greatest Fruit Estate in Britain—Natural Manure, Sound Farming. 124

XII. Lord Eltisley's Farms—An Example of Good Landlordism—His Tribute to the Caterpillar Diesel Tractor—Weekly Costings on the Farm—Pigs, Poultry, and Rabbits—On Wages, Prices, Soil Fertility, E.P.T., and Death Duties—The Folly of too many Artificials—"Muck's your Man"—Post-war Peril of Land Exhaustion—"Duties on Land should be paid not on Death but on the Sale of the Estate." 137

XIII. Partridge-shooting at Kimbolton Castle—"The Perfect English Village"—A Home of Sport—Lord Mandeville and Frank Cowlard—The Boar which brought over £1100—Madingley Hall, "A Gem of its Age"—"Capability" Brown's Landscape—Talk at the Three Horseshoes—On old Pigeon and Rabbiting Days—On Foxes and Anti-Sport Cranks—Farewell to the 'Pansies' of Cambridge—Her Value for the Future. 145

XIV. The Last of a Primeval Fen—On "The Company of Adventurers" and the Drainage of the Fens—A Mighty Achievement—Wicken Fen—The "Fen Tigers"—Pout Hall and its Sheep-stealers—The Murder of Peacock—My Wildfowl Sanctuary and Shoot—Bitterns, Montagu's Harriers, the Great White Heron, and Black-necked Grebes—One Thousand Wildfowl a Year—Cattle Egrets and Garganey Teal—Gay Shooting Days—"Swan Mere's Ploughed Up." 154

XV. A Fen Oak One Hundred and Ten Feet Long—The Prehistoric Man in the Peat—Badcock's Hut—"A Supper Mess o' Water-rats"—Village Aristocracies—"The Five Miles from Anywhere : No Hurry"—The Upware Republic—Black Shuck—Henry Cromwell at Spinney Abbey—The Tale of a Five-hundred-acre Fen Farm—Fields which blow away. 169

XVI. Newmarket, the Town of Kings—Felix Leach, the Gamecock in Human Form—The Man from Swaffham—To Euston by Barton Mills—The Vulgarity of Elveden—The Triumph of Euston—Farming on Sandy Land—The Duke of Grafton's Experiments—An Extraordinary Object-lesson in Reclamation—Ten Sacks of Barley to the Acre. 178

XVII. Across the Norfolk Heaths—The Merman's Grave—Singing Ghosts of Thetford—Lord Fisher's Blackcurrants and Asparagus—The Folly of

CHAPTER PAGE

gassing Rabbits—By Ring Mere and Fowl Mere—Chicken-plucking for a Bet—At Swaffham Market—The Seal which drank Beer—The Rich Land of Lincolnshire—Land of the Tractor and Potato—Thompson and Dennis. 186

XVIII. St Peter's Lodge in Marshland—The Monson Greys—Borrow's Tale of Old Shales, the Kingly Horse—A Memory of the Last Norfolk Witch—The Difficulties of the Farming Squire—How we brought the Big Grey out of Norfolk—From Lynn to Hillington—The Valley Village of Hillington. 200

XIX. The King's Farms at Sandringham—Conservatism pays—Six Hundred and Eighty-eight and a Half Brace of Partridges in one Day—To Heacham, Home of the Hackney—Horace Callaby, a Sportsman of the Old Sort—The Heacham Harriers—The Greatest Farmer in all England—High Farming at Westacre High House—Major Birkbeck's Methods—A Ten-thousand-acre Estate—Rare Birds. 212

XX. Holkham, the Home of High Farming—A Forty-three-thousand-acre Estate—Lord Leicester, a John Bull Englishman—Shooting at Ninety-three—High Wind in the East—On Savage Bulls—Sam Bone, the 'Fowler of Wells-next-the-Sea—Old 'Fowling Days—The Gun in the Closet—The Earl and the Queen—When he refused to be Shaved—A Royal Duke put to Flight. 221

XXI. Reclamation of the Holkham Marshes—Seventeen Sacks of Wheat an Acre—Pasturing Beef Cattle on Sea Lavender—Coke of Norfolk and his Work—"The Father of English Farming"—The Quaker at Holkham—Air Raid at Stiffkey—The Sporting Grocer of Holt—And so Home. 234

INDEX 247

ILLUSTRATIONS

PAGE

The Author and Jim Rodd on Master Robert II and Browny Boy *Frontispiece*

"No better start for such a journey than D'Arcy Hall . . . that moated, modest manor" 16

The Peldon Rose 17

Ted Allen 48

'Admiral' Bill Wyatt, Elizabethan Philosopher of Mersea Island 48

Walter Linnett, the Fowler of Bradwell-juxta-Mare 49

Harvest heat-haze over Cornfields by Alresford Creek 64

Holkham Hall 65

On Wallasea Island 65

Rounding up Sheep on Wallasea Island 112

One of Jack Olding's Sixteen-ton Bulldozers pushing a Tree over 113

At Hatfield House 128

Madingley Hall, Cambridgeshire 129

Swan Mere in 1939 192

Swan Mere in 1941 192

The Author shooting Duck on Swan Mere in 1939 193

"We went by Peddar's Way, that ancient road of ghosts, from Castle Acre" 208

The Squire of Sandringham, King George VI 209

CHAPTER I

The happiest man in England rose an hour before the dawn ;
The stars were in the purple, and the mist was on the lawn.
He sang from bed to bathroom—he could only sing *John Peel*—
As he donned his boots and breeches and buckled on his steel.

WILL H. OGILVIE

The Start from Tolleshunt D'Arcy Hall—A Medieval Manor Farm—Decline of the Yeomanry—How 'Cheap Food' killed the Land—The Dereliction of Salcott-cum-Virley—Bargemen and Smugglers—To Saltings and the Sea

CLATTER OF HOOVES AND CREAK OF SADDLE LEATHER SENT THE moorhens scuttering between the apple-trees. They landed with sliding splashes in the moat. The last Saturday of August 1941 was a bland and mellow day on that Essex upland which falls to the glittering Blackwater.

Elms stood bee-murmurous about the sunny meadow where sits Tolleshunt D'Arcy Hall, moat-guarded. As you come in from the road there stands the church—tall, beautiful, and grey. The spire is slender above elms which nurse a rookery. Within, silent in sunlight distilled through stained glass, lies the grim stone figure of John de Boys. The great Norman is magnificent in death. The soaring tower of his unfinished mansion at Layer Marney, across the fields, is as magnificent in its loneliness, rose-red and many-windowed, looking to the sea.

Beside Lord Marney, beneath a lesser panoply of stone, lies the heaped dust which is all that is left of Thomas D'Arcy Wentworth.

I have a great affection across the bridge of centuries for that dapper, quick-brained, twinkling-eyed sprig of the Wentworths, who lived here in this ancient village with his back to the forest and his face to the sea. As we rode over the arched bridge across the moat, its red bricks stained with grey and rusty lichens, blue with sprouting larkspur, I thought of him with his demoniac shock of hair, his tremendous moustaches, his quick ways of thought, and his mastery of a horse. He might have ridden out on such an August morning four hundred years ago, to cast his hawks at partridges in the knee-high stubbles or at young ducks, just on the wing, on the sea marshes at foot of the fields.

Perhaps it was that sentimental tweak of ancestry which made me ride through the meadow, clatter over the bridge across the moat and into the forecourt of D'Arcy Hall, warm in the sun, to take a glass of sherry and a word for the road from my friend Weston Eve before we set out, Jim Rodd and I, on our ride for a thousand miles through the farming lands of England.

That ride really began in '39, when I lay in a white, pictureless room at Windsor, gazing at a blue November sky through leafless twigs. They would be hunting in those Essex woodlands which I love. I could almost smell the sea wind, the damp odour of dying bracken, hear the plop and squish of galloping hooves down a muddy ride, feel the wet kiss of the salty wind blowing off the marshes. There would be black geese sitting in thousands out on the sand-banks and in the swatchways which we had swept for mines. A few days before they had given me forty-eight hours to live. But I was told that afterwards.

Lying there, so weak that I could not stand, I read William Cobbett. The mind followed that robust, ranting, prejudiced old Radical as he rode from shire to shire, his horse's hooves scattering the sandy gravel on Surrey hillsides one week and ploughing hock-deep through the loamy mire of Norfolk the next. Cobbett lived in a time of wars, revolts, and depressions. English mouths went hungry for bread, and English farmers were driven hard. To-day, almost a century later, history has repeated itself. The land, neglected in peace, is wooed in war. If we are not careful it will be jilted again when peace comes on the sombre wings of economic chaos and unemployment.

So I swore that when I was well enough to throw my leg across a horse I would go out on his four feet, with the warm smell of damp hide and the creak of leather to keep me company, through the fields, warm in the harvest sun, and by the badger-haunted lanes and the pheasant-musical woods of the English counties which I love.

It took nine months, three of them an imprisonment of semi-paralysis, before we two set out. There were plenty of people to warn me of rash folly. "You won't get stabling. You'll never find the fodder. You'll lame the horses on the hard high roads. You can never cover the ground in the time. You'll be held up in defence areas—or the Home Guard will shoot you. Anyway, it's a crazy idea—hire a little car and do it more quickly and in more comfort." That was the sort of dissuasive nonsense.

None the less we started. Unlike Cobbett, I took a Daimler

motor horse-box. Cobbett had no tarmac roads to hammer the heart out of his horses. My plan was to go to a centre in each county and then radiate out on horseback each day visiting farms, reclamation areas, forestry blocks, research stations, and the rest.

We averaged fifteen to twenty miles a day on horseback, totalled over a thousand miles by horse, one thousand three hundred and fifty-five by horse-box, and about two hundred by car when being taken round by officials. The longest hack in one day was forty-seven miles. Not once did I fail to find stabling, although we frequently cast up in a village after nightfall, without making arrangements beforehand. We were never short of fodder, and only once did we have to rob a stack by starlight. We had no accidents and cast only one shoe, and that in the last week of the ride.

I was almost continually in defence areas, yet was stopped only once by a sentry. That was at the entrance to an aerodrome. True, I had a Government 'A' pass fixed on the front of the box, but nothing of the sort on the pommel of my saddle.

We took two guns and a rod, a primus stove and pots, snares and a spade, and lived on the country as we went. There were bags of oats and beans in the box and bales of hay on the roof. At a pinch you could always sleep in the box or in a half-cut stack—which I once did under an Essex sea-wall.

We stayed in the castle of a duke one night and slept the next on the knobbly, straw-stuffed palliasse of a village inn beneath a wavy, whitewashed ceiling. The great mansions of England were open to us equally with the houses of yeomen farmers and the welcome of cottage tea-tables.

You could want no better start for such a journey than D'Arcy Hall, its yellow plaster walls scrambled over with honeysuckle, a glimpse through the open door of a stone-paved hall, darkly panelled. Silver candlesticks and gun-barrels gleamed in the shadows. A fox-mask grinned. The old retriever, grey-muzzled, slept on the flags.

The house is L-shaped, with a front door that looks south over an old, low red wall through the brilliant beauties of a little garden, stately with hollyhocks and sunflowers, lit by roses, scented by lavender and tobacco-plant. Beyond, through sun-dappled elms, cattle graze, and a broad sweep of wheat and barley, glowing in the sun, falls to the two-mile-wide estuary where red-sailed barges glide, and the oyster smacks lie at anchor.

The moat, red-walled on the house side, a sloping green bank on the other, runs four-square round house and garden. Lawns sweep to its edge where harebells tremble like dancers in the sun. Apple-trees shade the great dovecot.

The Elizabethans built it with a pretty thought, a dove for each day of the year, for there are three hundred and sixty-five holes. Walnut-trees and blackcurrant bushes, potatoes and strawberry-beds, roses and hollyhocks, honeysuckle and sweet-scented stocks, lettuces and crimson beets—all are enclosed, with the house and its family, within this moat which would still defy man or wolf by night. Roach and rudd swim lazily in its waters. Tomatoes hang against its rose-red wall, their roots mingled with the roots of tall irises. Wild duck swim among the lily-pads with tame ducks and sailing geese and the moorhens, crimson-pated. They feed with the chickens and patter through the kitchen-garden. For though gun-barrels wink in the panelled hall, Weston Eve will allow no shot to be fired at the wild duck, which for generations have nested on this enchanted moat.

It is a pretty commentary that Weston Eve, descendant of generations of yeomen and millers, should still live to-day in the house which his forbears bought two, three, or more centuries ago. For a time the house where Wentworths lived and Eves followed passed to strangers. Twelve years ago Weston Eve left Maldon, the old town red-roofed, huddled upon its ancient hill at the head of the estuary, and bought back the Manor House and farmlands of his ancestors. That is the pretty side of the picture.

There you have the old love of land, the invincible spirit of home and stability which has made the best in English manhood and struck deep with the roots of her history. But Weston Eve, the miller, could not afford to become Weston Eve, the farmer. Farming was too chancy in those days, twelve years ago, for any man who had spent his life building a modest fortune in the town to risk it on the land. So the broad fields that had seen the tall wheat grow when Arthur Young rode meditatively through this granary of England were put down to grass. Barley that had made sound English beer, oats that had fed stout English hunters, root crops that had nurtured the woolly waves of baaing sheep—that muted undertone of the Essex marshes—gave way to grass and dairy herds.

Two men and a boy did the work where half a village had lived behind the plough and the scythe. No longer were good harvest wages paid. The great horn of the "Lord of the Harvest"—the leader of the reapers, elected by the men, who bargained for wages—echoed no more through September dawns to call the men to scythe and sickle. The roaring jollity of the harvest 'horkey' was an old man's memory. The last decorated wain rumbling home, garlanded and flower-decked in the warm dusk, was a sentimental echo for week-ending novelists to write about. Throughout England, in countless villages, the land which had been shining with the corn, nurse of strong men and bouncing country girls, sold its soul to the townsmen's demand for 'Cheaper Food.' Ploughmen and horsemen, shepherds and hedgers, all the skilled men of husbandry, drifted into the greedy bellies of the towns. The smell of an oily rag replaced the enchantment of new-mown hay and the heady scent of cut corn, gold in the sun.

Garage and factory, featureless town street and jerry-built villa, the pub on the corner and the cinema with its huckstering Hollywood values, took the boys and the girls from the apple orchards and the wheat-fields, the broad acres of mangolds and swedes, the enchantment of woods, and the thrilling smell of strong horses labouring in sun and rain.

I thought of these things, the cynical, man-made tragedy of this prostitution of our rural soul, this economic starvation of our farmers and village people, as I sat in the saddle and drank Weston Eve's sherry with an eye on the roofless barn, the decaying thatch, and the ruinous stock-yards, thigh-deep in nettles. He grinned ruefully.

"Pretty awful, isn't it? For God's sake don't go round the other side. It's worse! Only the cowsheds are decent. My old grandfather would have had a fit if he'd seen those buildings in that state. But what could one do in the last twenty years? Farming wasn't worth a candle unless you had an income from somewhere else—and frankly I'm too old to begin at that game all over again. But I've kept the house and garden in decent order, and I wouldn't part with the old place for anything. We Eves are back here now, and we'll die here."

"You were offered a pretty penny for the panelling by some American, weren't you?" I asked.

"Yes. He was crazy about it. Offered me several thousands and would've run it up a bit more, I fancy, if I hadn't told him I wouldn't part. After all, it was here first, so it may as well stay here last. Money's not everything. Come and have a look at it—it's years since you poked your nose inside."

So I dismounted, leaving Master Robert, that gallant, philosophical old hunter with the golden flecks on his bright chestnut coat, munching apples from Miss Hall—"the best woman rabbiter in all Essex.

She's my cousin, you know—runs the house like a picture-book"—and rolling his friendly eye at Mrs Weston Eve, recumbent on her cane chair in the sun, victim of a hunting accident.

The panelling at D'Arcy is probably unique. The lower part, square Elizabethan panelling, with a little linenfold here and there, is topped by a frieze running round all four walls. That frieze shows almost every imaginable incident in the life of a fifteenth-century manor-house, such as this moated hall. There is the lord and his lady; the jester and the falconer; the courser with greyhounds in leash; the ploughman and the broadcaster of seed; the reaper with his sickle and the hoer with his hoe; the dairymaid with her wooden bucket; the cook with knives and capons; the fisherman with his nets, and the apple harvest in the orchards. I doubt if any other small house can show so full a pageant of the everyday rural life of Elizabeth's England. Do you wonder that Weston Eve would not sell this heritage to go to America—"where a lot of strangers would only look at it, and half of 'em wouldn't know what it means. We Eves have grown up with it."

I fancied that the grave, scholarly countenance and the mild eyes of Dr Weston Eve, the great principal of University College Hospital, smiled down approvingly from the picture at the turn of the stairs.

There are plenty of Weston Eves in farming England—strong, sturdy, brown-faced men, intelligent in mind, forthright in principle, with pedigrees longer and more unimpeachable than those of half the industrial aristocracy, upstarts whose blood has been ennobled by cheque-book. Weston Eve is a yeoman, part of that backbone of the village gentry of England, good master to his men, wedded to his land.

But while the Dane and the Belgian, the Yankee farmer and the canned food manufacturer, the French market gardener, the Chinese egg-merchant, the Argentine rancher and the Californian hog-slaughterer were allowed to dump their wheat, beef, eggs, butter, bacon, tomatoes, vegetables, broccoli, tinned milk, and canned foods in an England, 85 per cent. of whose population lives in towns, there was no hope for that indivisible trinity, the landowner, the farmer, and the farm labourer, or for the boy and girl in the village.

Mr Lloyd George began it when, bitterly class-conscious, he launched his 1910 Budget. It broadened the basis of the present crushing scale of death duties. It was designed to suck old money,

D'Arcy Hall

"No better start for such a journey than . . . that moated, modest manor."

Photo Douglas Went, Brightlingsea

The Peldon Rose,
"That ancient inn . . . sits at its cross-roads like an amiable old witch sunning herself."
Photo Douglas Went, Brightlingsea

old values, and old families from the land. It drove new capital and new men away from it.

You cannot own land without capital, which must be put back into the land as soon as land produces a rent, and you cannot farm that land against unfair competition from abroad—unfair because European imports were produced mostly by men whose wages were infinitely lower than those paid in England and whose living conditions were unbelievably worse.

But so long as the townsman got his cheap, devitalized food, he did not care. So long as the politician won his cheaper votes on that false slogan, "Your Food must never cost you more," so long were farmers driven into bankruptcy, farm workers into factories, and the English land, the best in the world, to nettles and "the Scotsman's paradise—a herd of cows and a sea of stinking muck."

But the Weston Eves and their like—men with brains enough to make money outside farming—hung on to their old homes, their almost useless acres, blindly hoping.

The war has brought them hope. They have been cajoled, flattered, bribed, and wooed as never before. They were wooed in the last war, promised a new heaven and a new earth—and let down with a bang two years after it had ended.

That treachery to our own people must never happen again.

Never again must the internationalists, the importers, the economists, the retailers of foreign foods, the foreign canners, and their political hacks, be allowed to rig the market of public opinion at the expense of the farming and village people of England, the backbone of our manhood, the fountain of our vitality. It has been said, and in ninety cases of a hundred it is true, that no townbred family survives with undiminished vitality after three generations in town. They must go back to the land to recoup and revitalize. Not all the pseudo-science nor all the brittle teachings of the little economic theorists and slick 'thinkers' of to-day can disprove that elemental fact.

You do not breed good men or women on tinned meat, canned tomatoes, foreign eggs with a rubber stamp on them, imported bananas with a band round them, or 'breakfast foods,' milled, grilled, baked-up, dried-up, puffed-up, roughed-up, packed in cardboard, kept for months, and sold at the pistol point of publicity campaigns which no intelligent schoolchild would swallow if it paused to think about them.

Food from our own soil, fresh, unspoilt, full of iron and the salts of the earth—English beef, Southdown mutton, new milk, wheat with the grain in it, green vegetables, and fresh fruits—these are the guarantees of health, the aids of the good doctor, the enemies of the quack.

I thought of this decline in our common sense, this twenty-year-old period of national insanity, the Kettering speech, and the cynical immorality of it all, as I rode out of the gates of D'Arcy Hall, that modest, ancient manor, and turned my horse's head down the sweet village street of D'Arcy.

Bland Georgian fronts; white Queen Anne doorways; lath-and-plaster cottages; the square yellow face of the Queen's Head, home of our gay wildfowling parties; the red-brick gracious front of D'Arcy House, where that jovial mistress of detective stories, Margery Allingham, now lives in the house of my dead old friend, Dr J. H. Salter—that grand old sportsman who was hunting at eighty-two, wildfowl-shooting at eighty-eight, and who died at ninety-two, having brought ten thousand Essex babies into the world meanwhile.

We turned down past the post-office, crouching gnome-like under its eaves, past that white-plastered house on the left with the bulging Queen Anne windows—off the road, through the hedge, and at a hand-canter across the stubbles. Ahead the blue arm of Salcott Creek crept snakily into the land, the vast sail of a coasting barge rusty-red against heat-hazy cattle-marshes. Beyond, the creeks and the saltings faded into the haze of the summer sea with Mersea Island lying whale-backed in blue water, the tower of its Saxon church white in the sun above green leaves.

Down in the hollow at the head of that crawling creek lay the twin villages of Salcott-cum-Virley, forgotten by the world. Between them they have perhaps two hundred inhabitants, of whom about a hundred and eighty-five live in Salcott. Salcott has a tiny church, gabled farm-houses hidden in honeysuckle, cottages which stand with their backs almost overhanging the creek, great sheaves of reeds stacked in their gardens. It has, too, ruined barns, broken-down cart-sheds, decayed cottages, lost memories of rich harvests. Salcott is poor, pretty, but forlorn.

The church, squat and grey with a thatched chancel roof, stands, bowered in trees, with its back to the creek, its eastern window looking over the Old Hall Marshes. Now and then a great sailing-barge, bluff-bowed, red-sailed, steals up the creek on a flood tide and makes fast at the Hithe. It may bring bricks, wood or tiles, metal for roads or coal for cottages. Mostly it goes away empty, but in the old days, when half a dozen barges came up the creek in almost as many days, they went deep-laden with corn or high-baled with hay. There is not a marsh farm in all this country of windy levels and crawling creeks which has not, somewhere on its sea-wall, the tumbledown, weed-grown relics of a great landing-stage. Across the saltings you will see the broad green ribbon which marks "the old barge road." In the days of high farming when wheat grew nigh as tall as a man half the produce of these golden Essex acres went by water.

To go "a-bargin'" was as natural for a village boy as it is for a town youngster to enter a factory. They wore ear-rings in their ears because, they said, it improved their sight and kept their heads free of colds. There is a lot in it. They wore red-stocking caps which rolled up over their ears in cold weather and hung gaily down their backs when the sun shone. If they were not washed overboard and drowned they lived to a grand old age. I know more than one barge hand and barge master still going fit and strong "in his eighty."

Even up to the early thirties of this century the beer for the scattered villages and lonely hedgerow pubs of these marsh parishes came "from over in Kent," in a fleet of sailing-barges. That was the grand Shrimp ale, real malt and hops with no chemical nonsense, brewed by the old family brewery of Colonel Russell in Gravesend. It was a great sight to see a score of the brewery barges thrashing up the Blackwater in a smart wind, taking the spray over from stem to stern, red sails close-hauled in the breeze, a red burgee flicking at the mast-head, its white shrimp dancing in the sun. That old family brewery, like most things good and old, has been swallowed up in a vast modern combine. The beer no longer comes by barge; the eyes are denied a gallant sight.

A century ago Salcott was a den of smugglers. Rightforward men "from up in the country," which means a mile or two inland, thought twice before they ventured into this petty kingdom of the lawless which was ruled from afar by a baronet-squire of the old sort, Abdy of Albyns. I doubt if he ever came down to his two-thousand-acre marshland property except to shoot duck and sail the salt water in a beamy old yacht with a gaff topsail.

You might toss up to decide which were the more desperate from the point of view of the revenue men—the Mersea men, the Tollesbury chaps, or the Salcott gang. Each village was self-contained, bitterly jealous of the other, and just as liable to fight among themselves as against the coast-guards.

CHAPTER II

I like the pheasants and feeding things
  Of the unsuspicious morn;
I like the flap of the wood-pigeon's wings
  As she rises from the corn.

I like these things, and I like to ride
  When all the world is in bed,
To the top of the hill where the sky grows wide,
  And where the sun grows red.

I covet not a wider range
  Than these dear manors give;
I take my pleasures without change,
  And as I lived I live.

WILFRED SCAWEN BLUNT, "The Old Squire"

A Shooting Idyll of the Marshes—The Passing of Bulls Bars—Tom Mann, Yeoman of Virley Hall—A Squire of the Old Sort—The Man who refused Money—Smugglers and the Roman Ghost—The Drunken Skipper in the Pond—Drowned Islands—The Peldon Rose Parliament

WHEN I RODE INTO SALCOTT THAT SUNNY AFTERNOON THE corn was golden, the reapers were clacking in the fields, horses strained and shone in the sun, pigeons rose with a clatter from blackened bean-pods, and the sea glittered far at the end of hazy marshes.

Years ago I had the shooting on the Marsh Farm down to the snaky fleet which they call Bulls Bars. With that and Smith's Farm there were maybe five hundred acres, ranging from upland stubble, tussocky meadow, and old, lichened orchards down to a flat green marsh seamed by the reedy fleet, bounded by sea-wall and saltings. It swarmed with rabbits, showed plenty of partridges, an odd pheasant and hare, and in winter was full of duck and snipe. There were enchanted days when two or three of us shot over a hundred rabbits, perhaps ten brace of partridges, an odd cock pheasant or two, a hare or so. We wound up the evening by killing at flight a score of fowl which included mallard, teal, widgeon, shoveller, shell-duck, tufted duck, peewits, curlew, perhaps an odd coot or redshank, and always snipe.

I rode across the marsh in the warm sun to revisit that enchanted fleet where we had sunk beer-barrels on the edge of the water and stood nights in snow and bitter wind waiting for the whistle of wings. In summer the duck nested in the reeds, redshank in the tussocks, and coots and moorhens by the dyke side. In winter the fleet might be forty to a hundred yards in width, according to the rush of water from the land drains in the upper fields.

A hare got up under my horse's feet and went like a bullet for the sea-wall. Curlew rose from the ant-hills, screaming indignation. Across the marsh by the line of the fleetside reeds the gaunt black figure of an excavator reared a long arm stark against the sea horizon.

As we rode nearer I could see the full tale of its work. The fleet had gone. Where had been brown and shining waters thick with kingcups in May, musical with redshank in September, was now a deep gash in the earth. For a mile the scar wound across the marsh to the foot of the upland. It was perhaps six or eight feet deep and twelve or fourteen wide. Great chunks of clay and wedges of earth, brown and knotted with the roots of reeds, had been flung out in a ragged battlement along the edge. That, for a quarter-century to come, meant the end of Bulls Bars fleet as a haunt of duck and a paradise of reed-warblers.

Anywhere in England to-day you can multiply that picture a hundredfold. There will be no more floods on the marsh for winters to come, no more soggy upland fields, no more bullocks hauled out of miry bogs by cart-horses straining at the ropes. It is a great job for the farmer, a loss to the sportsman and naturalist.

We rode back into the village, clattered over the bridge where an Arnesby Brown brook trickles through miniature sea-gates into the creek, and so, past the Sun, to Virley Hall Farm. Tom Mann, of Virley Hall, is an English yeoman who might have stepped straight out of the Middle Ages. His like fought at Agincourt and Waterloo. They were Elizabeth's pride, Cromwell's vanguard, the secret scorners of the Hanoverians. They are timeless, ageless, and irreplaceable.

They have farmed their own land, driven their ploughs, shot their partridges and hares, brewed their own beer, and raised their sons to fear God and fight the first man who asks for it.

"My Tom's up in the bean-field," said Mrs Mann, wiping her hands on her apron. The kitchen behind her was sweet with the heady scent of new-baked bread. A smell of wood ash came from the whitewashed oven. A brace of partridges hung on a nail. The cat washed its face in the sun. I left my horse in the yard, walked through a field of bullocks, climbed a gate into the bean stubble, and there was Tom. With a yellow straw hat, the texture of honeycomb, rammed on the back of his head, shirt-sleeved, sweaty-faced, and leather-belted, he was pitching beans on to a cart. Tom is broad and round, like a muscular barrel, with shrewd, twinkling eyes, an irrepressible tongue, and a mastery of rustic epigram. He would die for his convictions. I walked across the stubble towards the cart.

At twenty yards he stopped pitching, put down his fork, wiped his hands on the seat of his trousers, and walked slowly in greeting.

"Why, that's Mr Wentworth Day. Damn, I see you come across the field, an' I said to meself, 'That's our Charlie come round again. That's the cut of him all right. Happen he wants to offer me some more money. If he do he can keep it in his pocket!'"

Now "our Charlie" among the farmers and labourers, the fishermen and keepers of that corner of Essex, is Mr Charles Round, of Birch Hall. Charles Round is a squire of the old sort. He owns about five thousand acres and lives in a corner of a square, porticoed mansion of a medium size set in a pleasant park. It looks over a lake full of carp and coots. He farms on a substantial scale, administers his estate well, and does a big job of work for the Essex War Agricultural Committee. I doubt if there has been a winter for a hundred years when a Round has not hunted with the East Essex Hounds. Sometimes they have been Masters; this one is the Secretary. The result is that the family knows every farm, field, woodland, village, and marsh, and those who work therein.

His father, old Charles James Round, 'Father' of the House of Commons and one-time owner of Colchester Castle, was "our Jimmy." The son, tall, fiftyish, with a cavalry-cum-foxhunting look about him, is "our Charlie." No English country gentleman could be paid a higher honour.

"Yes, yes," says Tom Mann. "Our Charlie come over here the other day and says to me, 'Tom, me boy, you got some rare heavy land here. You're right down on the heavy land. That'd break a man's heart and three horses' hearts too. You want some 'chinery to break some of this land up for you. Tractors and such. Digger ploughs. But that all runs into money, so if you want some money just you tell me, and I'll fix it. The War Agricultural's got a credit scheme, and they'll fix you some credit.'

"'Squire Round,' I says, 'I don't want any money. There's too much good money sunk in this heavy old land already. Old Abdy, he sunk a mort o' money in these parts, and what did he git for it? That old Lloyd George, that artful old Welsh monkey, he taxed old Abdy till he had to sell. An' I had to buy. Didn't, I'd 'a' had to get out. There's old Abdy's money in this here land now, and Tom Mann's a-goin' to git it out. I don't want any loans—I'll git the food out o' the land by sweat, not by borrowin'.'"

Tom poured out the grievances of the heavy land farmer. Their salvation for the future is the caterpillar Diesel tractor, the single-furrow deep-digger plough, and the three-furrow plough. But it will need a few more of "our Charlies," men trusted and loved locally, to make such sturdy individualists realize that a credit is not a charity.

There was a time when Tom Mann threatened to serve a summons on every single member of a local Council, because he considered they had wasted the taxpayers' money. There was a Government official from Whitehall who had to leave the farm in a hurry, because Tom swore he would let the bull loose on him. There is a noble lord in Norfolk who still chuckles at the memory of how Tom in his last-war soldiering days poached the peer's pheasants and when hauled before his lordship tackled him as man to man and said:

"I'm a bit of a landowner too. An' if you was down my way in Essex, fed up with the bloody Army, and wanted to git down on the marsh and shoot a duck, Tom Mann'd be the one to say, 'Come on, boy, and hev a goo. Any shootin' man is a friend o' mine. But hev a glass o' beer afore you start.'"

The noble lord produced port instead of beer, an invitation to shoot again instead of a prosecution.

Pym and Hampden were merely the Tom Manns of their age, cast in a seigneurial mould.

I walked back to the house with Tom, had a glass of sloe gin, admired a needlework panel he had picked up in Colchester, a Sheraton side table—for Tom has a fine natural love for beautiful things—ate honey and bread-and-butter, and agreed with him that although farming by Committee may be needful in war, it would be a pest and an imposition in peace.

"Winston says, 'Give us the tools, and we'll finish the job,'" said Tom with his mouth full of bread and honey. "I say, an' all us farmin' chaps agree, 'Give us the prices, an' we'll grow the grub.' We'll pay the men fair and git on with the job. But humbug us about with forms and papers, and you'll get as much good out of farmin' as you would out of throshin' an owd moke with an ash stick."

Down the street, hard by the church, in a garden full of twisted apple-trees, crouches a long, low cottage with a red-tiled roof and dormer windows. It blinks in the sun like an old cat stretched among the flowers. I knocked at the door, bent my head, and was asked in to one of those clean, friendly, cottage living-rooms, full of shining mahogany, chintz, and flowers, which would put a modern sardine-tin flat to shame for sheer livable homeliness. The garden, back and front, a quarter-acre in all, was a blaze of pansies.

"So is the 'lotment," said Mrs Cullum, bustling about. "We've grown over an acre of 'em this year. The W.V.S. collect 'em for some sort of war munition. I believe they did tell me they go to America. My husband used to grow a lot of vegetables, as you remember, but we're only growing enough for ourselves now. This pansy crop takes up all my time. There's forever of cottagers growing them for miles round. They do tell me Essex is the head county for growin' 'em. But it's a funny crop for a war.

"We've had a bomb or two but no damage to talk about. Nothing like the earthquake fifty year ago. That shook the roofs off half the housen, and fetched some of the old places right down. We shot a Zeppelin down on Wigborough Marsh last war, and I did think we might have had one or two planes down in Salcott this time, but no—we've got nothing to hang medals on yet 'cept gardens full of pansies. That's a rum war crop for a cut-throatin' old place like this used to be!

"I hear they've had a rare goo over at Mersea, though—scores o' bombs, machine-gun bullets in the owd wummen's kitchens, and German planes shot down all over the marshes like a lot of ducks. I must git on me bicycle one of these days and goo over and hev a look at some o' 'em, if they haven't carted 'em all away."

We rode on, across fields and by narrow roads for five or six miles to that ancient inn, the Peldon Rose, which sits at its cross-roads like an amiable old witch sunning herself. Like all these good old Essex inns it is long and low, framed in hollyhocks and roses, with a high-pitched roof of red shingles, dormer windows, and low ceilings. It has black, adze-hewn timbers, bits of panelling here and there, stone-flagged floors, and a wise smile on its face. You feel that such an inn is as human and as loving as an amiable grandmother who has seen three generations of brawling brats and roisterous youngsters grow to sound manhood and cheerful matronliness. It knows the strength and weaknesses of its many children and loves them for both.

The road from Salcott comes in at the back of this ancient inn which the Royal Commission on Historical Monuments has decreed should never be pulled down. There is a pond at the roadside overhung by old willows. In the old days the smugglers rolled their barrels of gin and brandy up the road from the Strood, the Roman causeway which links Mersea Island with the mainland. The Peldon Rose stands at the junction of the roads, a green in front, the pond beside, marshes and shining creeks to the east, the glittering waters of the Pyefleet to the north, and the long road to Colchester running into the west. The smugglers dumped their barrels in the pond, for it is no ordinary duck-pond. For a century or more its placid waters, alive with ducks and tail-flicking moorhens, concealed a subaqueous well—a great shaft, no wider than eight feet, which went down fifteen or twenty feet below the bed of the pond. A dozen barrels could be lowered silently with ropes under the moon and left there in utter security. The revenue men might drag the pond without bringing a guilty stave or hoop to the surface. When, a few years ago, it was filled in because of its danger to children, a whole tree and a cart-load of bushes were rammed down the shaft.

As we reined in on the green, by a loop-holed, sandbagged machine-gun post, my mind went back ten or fifteen years to that splendid old lady, Mrs Jane Pullen, whom all East Essex knew and loved. For fifty years she was landlady of this ancient inn which Baring-Gould immortalized in *Mehalah*, his grim Victorian melodrama of the marshes. Mrs Pullen, over eighty, was upright as a dart, precise, shrewd, with delicate hands, the feet of a ballet dancer, beautiful white hair, and a collection of truly lovely Chippendale and Sheraton furniture which she treated abominably. She stood pots and kettles on a sideboard which would have fetched a hundred guineas in London, peeled carrots and onions on a table I coveted, and let farm labourers and marshmen in clay-stained corduroys sit goffling their beer on Hepplewhite chairs.

"Time I was a little gal in me grandmother's day, I laid in me bed here at night many a time and heard the smugglin' men roll the barrels up the road and dump 'em in the pond. Father said, 'Turn your face to the wall, gal, close your ears and eyes, and speak no word to any man.' There was a wonderful lot of spirits, lace, and French wines came up the creeks in those days—all through the free-traders. When old Doctor Green that lived in the Strood House died—that would be about the time of the last war—his cellar was full of kegs of brandy and gin. And why not? The barges used to come right up to the bottom of his garden just by that little cottage where Smith, the sea-waller, lives to-day."

Mrs Pullen is dead now, gathered to the angels where she properly belongs, but I recall lovingly her home-made sloe gin, her damson wine, her adders pickled in bottles, her stiff, black, rustling silk dresses, her fearless eye, her wonderful old port, and the twinkle with which she once showed me a dead fox, full of shot, hanging up in the cellar, while the Master, whips, and followers of the Essex and Suffolk foxhounds were drinking sloe gin in the bar parlour next door.

"After me chickens," she grinned. "You couldn't teach him his manners any other way. But there's plenty more where he came from." She gave me a ship carved in a bottle, a rough little schooner of match-stalks and cotton. "Bein' as you're my best young man in my old age and that was given me by my first sweetheart when I was a gal. A handsome young sailor from East Mersea with a fine eye and black hair. He wore a broad-brimmed Spanish hat what he picked up foreign, and he carved that little old ship with his shut-knife—for me. Do you take good care of it, or I'll haunt ye!"

She believed in ghosts, devoutly and firmly. There is a ghost, the spirit of a Roman centurion who, so they say, walks from Mersea Island to the mainland across the Strood between the glimmering tides, by moonlight. He haunts the Ray Island, that eerie houseless island of bleached grasses and bent thorn-trees which splits the creek. Mrs Pullen would tell how she walked from Mersea by moonlight one night. As she walked the footsteps of an unseen man followed, ringing hard and clear on the still night air. She looked over her shoulder. No man was in sight. The road, the island, and the creeks were plain in the silver light. In the middle of the Strood she met a farmer walking home from the inn. He, too, heard the footsteps.

"He bopped down in the moonlight and looked along the road," she told me. "He never saw a thing. But the footsteps kept comin' all on. Then he turned and run like a hare. He left me all alone in the moonlight. And I walked home to the Rose and never quickened a step, although that old feller kept a-marchin' all on behind me. He never stopped till I got to me door and lifted the latch."

To-day Ivan Pullen, fifth of his line, is landlord of the Rose, farmer of his marshland acres, commander of the Home Guard which, with rifle, machine-gun, bomb, and bayonet, would die in the last ditch of this lonely outpost of the eastern marshes.

There is more than a hint of the Dutch painters' interiors about the inside of the Peldon Rose. Square yellow flags in the low-ceiled entrance passage; half a dozen dead rabbits swinging from hooks and banging your head; a pair of mallard and a bright chestnut and white shell-duck hanging up with a leash of partridges behind the bar; pickled onions in jars; port wine in dusty demijohns; a ham and a harvester's barrel hanging side by side; a pair of hunting-horns winking on the shelf beside pewter candlesticks and bottles of sloe gin. A gun stood in one corner. A bowl of roses splashed deep pools of colour in the surface of a beautiful old oak table. The wide brick fireplace with its iron basket grate was purple with bunches of sea lavender.

Through the diamond-paned side window we looked on to the pond. Where once the smugglers sank their barrels Ivan created a unique little wildfowl sanctuary. Within smell of the sea, so near that in the early mornings you hear the creak and rattle of a smack getting up its anchor, he collected brent-geese, cripples saved from a punt-gunner's moonlight shot; widgeon, whose shrill whistle was answered by their wild brethren in the night; mallard and teal; garish shell-duck and lordly pintail; saucy little tufted duck which dived at a flash, and greylag geese sailing stately as galleons. There were odd, exotic eccentricities—Carolinas, mandarins, and wood ducks. In a pen at the back were golden pheasants, a host of parakeets, a tame magpie, a garrulous old carrion crow, and, triumph of triumphs, a tame nightingale who sang no less sweeter for being prisoned.

Alas, since that September afternoon, a ribald crew of Canadians broke down the wire one rowdy night, caught up or let out the ducks and geese, wrung their necks and made off across the fields with suppers for the pot, suppers which had cost poor Ivan about £60 to collect.

"We've never had such a night like it since the time when that old skipper from Mersea, the one with the ringles in his ears, walked into the pond one night up to his shoulders, as drunk as a lord. There he stood with on'y his head and arms above water, hollerin' out, 'I'm the Rock o' bloody Gibberaltar. All you ships what want to goo to Biscay keep hard a' starboard and all you b——s what want to goo to Italy keep hard a' port. Do ye don't, I'll sink the bloody lot on ye!'

"That took two men and a cart-rope to get the owd sod out."

If you were to draw a line north and south from the Peldon Rose to Burnham-on-Crouch the one way and Beaumont-cum-Moze the other way, you would, I dare say, have traversed in peace-time between twenty thousand and thirty thousand acres of once rich corn land which in the last forty years have gone down to grass, to thistles, and to dereliction.. We sat and talked in that bar, five or six of us who know the marsh country, of the farms and estates which we had seen robbed of their birthright of corn.

In the south there were the islands of Wallasea and Potton, 2200 and 1025 acres. Havengore and New England, both now under the sea at high tide, victims of broken sea-walls. Bridgemarsh Island, in the river Crouch, which used to grow fine crops, fatten beeves, and yield vast hauls of eels, is now a total loss. At high water the chimney of its derelict farm-house sticks out like a forlorn lighthouse, the broken line of its sea-walls shows barely above the waves. Hundreds of acres of Foulness Island were thick with thistles, riddled with charlock, poisoned by ragwort. In the Dengie Hundred, between the Crouch and Blackwater, farm after farm, some of the richest land in England, was either down to grass or scarcely farmed at all. On Northey Island in the Blackwater the tide broke through the sea-walls and drowned three hundred acres of land which, within the memory of man, grew twelve to fourteen sacks of wheat to the acre. The same happened at Fambridge Ferry, up Brandy Hole Creek, just across the Strood on Mersea itself, on the Fingringhoe fresh marsh within spyglass sight of the Peldon Rose.

In the twenties Guisnes Court and its sixteen hundred acres, Abbots Hall, Wigborough, with six hundred and ninety acres, Langenhoe Hall with nearly one thousand four hundred acres, and most of Horsey Island and Hedge End in the Walton Backwaters, near enough a thousand acres, were all either derelict or merely thistle-grown, rabbit-infested grazing runs for half-wild cattle and herds of unbridled horses. I shot over them all, eeled in their fleets, sailed up their creeks in my gunning punt, and coursed their hares year after year in the twenties and thirties when you might walk all day, load a man and a boy with ducks and game, and never see another human being except a shepherd or a marshman on the prowl.

We recollected these things, compared old days and nights with guns and nets, with boats and dogs. And we told each other of the wholesale ploughings up, the clearing of acres of bushes, the dredging of dykes, repairing of sea-walls—all the miracles which the bitter needs of war had forced within a twelvemonth upon an England whose town-bred, Stock Exchange fattened politicians had bartered their people's birthright of corn and cattle for a mess of foreign exchanges, a poisoned pottage of false riches. The bomb and the torpedo, the tank and the Hun, have changed all that. We are back to the values of our grandfathers, the true values which made the Elizabethans great.

As we sat and talked we heard the hum and clank of a 30-h.p. caterpillar Diesel tractor ripping up grass marshes half a mile down the road.

"Time I were a little owd boy them mushes growed fifteen sacks o' wheat to the acre. Time owd Pertwee farmed Langenhoe and Lord Carlingford hed the place, that was one of the headest farms in Essex for wheat. Growed nigh as tall as a man. They used to send ut away by barge.

"Owd Squire Binney over at Guisnes Court runned a thousand sheep on Owd Hall Marshes and them big graziers from up North used to send the cattle down to him by road to fatten 'em up for Smithfield. Abbots Hall was all under wheat. Then that was under rabbits! 'Tain't above a few years agoo when I recollect you and yar party, Mr Day, killin' six thousand rabbits on that place in a year. That was like an owd battle to hear you and them Colchester orficers a-shutin' there on a Saturday."

"Ah! Blarst! That ain't ne yit all o' the head an' tail on it," chimed in another. "Look at some o' they farms on Marsea. Time I was a young 'un, owd Jimmy Round, the Squire o' Birch, growed wunnerful crops there. This last twenty years they've smuddered the place wi' bungalows an' beach huts, till that ain't no more than the tag-end o' bloody London. A lot o' good land starved and stifled under bricks and mortar. I knowed that when that growed forever of corn and good roots. That's a nice way to use the land what God gie ye. Why don't they put they places on the sandy lands what 'on't grow nawthen?"

"Har! They've ketched up wi' common sense now, I reckon," chimed in a red-faced farm hand, "but, Lawd a' mussy, that'll cost the country a pretty penny. I reckon us and our kids'll hev to pay for it in beer and baccer, and the owd wimmen'll hev to goo short o' their tea for the next fifty year. I reckon they ought to hang that owd Baldwin, time owd Ramsay MacDonald's a-turnin' in his grave."

A moment of silence and tobacco to ponder this momentous vision.

"Har! Guv'mint's a rum 'un. Yu niver know what capers they'll git up tu. They lets us chaps on the land down in peace, makes an almighty fuss on us in war, an' then I don't doubt they'll kick us up the backside when peace cum agin. I count we want more farmin' chaps like Stanley Ratcliff, an' more o' the gentry like Charlie Round and Ruggles-Brise and their kidney in Parlymint—chaps what knows the land. There ain't enough on 'em up there in Guv'mint. That's cludded up wi' lawyers and men what make their fortunes from fetchin' in foreign food to cut us out. I'd hang owd Hitler if I ketched him, but, damn! I reckon I'd gie 'im half a pint aforehand jist for larnin' these fellers in Guv'mint where they b'long."

A farmer, who entered, dog at heel, chimed in with that perennial plaint of war-time agriculture: "As for these War Agricultural Committee officers, half of 'em couldn't farm well in peace-time, but they get paid for telling us how to do it in war—that's a rum game! They're like these agricultural professors that write in the papers and yap at us at meetings—know everything about farmin' except *how* to farm!"

Thus the Peldon Rose parliament. Take any hedgerow inn in any English county which you love, and you would hear the same talk, with local variations, any night this last twenty years. It is the essential common sense of England. If we disregard the lesson again our children's blood will be on our own heads.

CHAPTER III

> Who soweth too lateward, hath seldom good seed;
> Who soweth too soon, little better shall speed.
> Apt time and season, so diverse to hit;
> Let air and layer help practice and wit.
>
> THOMAS TUSSER,
> *One Hundred Points of Good Husbandrie* (1557)

Two Essex Characters—Ted Allen, Adder-catcher and Bull-tamer—His Battle with 'the City Gent'—When the Devil mowed a Field of Hay—How to tame a Bull—Wick Farm and Langenhoe Marsh—The Roman Temple of Fingringhoe and the Mystery of Arch Hall—Follies of 'Committee Farming'

WE LEFT THE ROSE IN A HALO OF GOOD FELLOWSHIP AND RODE off down the hard road to Langenhoe—"For if you don't look up owd Ted, Marster, he'll be the death on ye. He 'on't never forgie ye. An' if you start a-scribblin' in the papers d'ye mind an' put owd Ted in. He's the headest owd gunner an' a double cunnin' man wi' a bull."

Ted Allen, market gunner, marsh keeper, bull-tamer, adder-catcher, naturalist, and great character, whom B.B.C. listeners may remember as "the Essex marshman," is spiritual king of that windy, sea-bitter tongue of Langenhoe Marshes which goes nosing into the salt water, four and a half miles long by a mile wide at its landward end. A long ridge-back of Essex corn land, where stand great elms in stark symmetry, shelving into a thousand acres of cattle marsh. Slim fleets, reed-bordered, cut it like crooked swords. Dykes gleam blue in summer, steel-grey in winter. An ocean of bleached, blent grasses rolls between the sea-walls of the Pyefleet, home of noble oysters, and the sea-wall to the west where the Geeton Creeks and the drowned marshes of Fingringhoe stretch their snaky fingers into uplands that melt into the tall woods of Donyland.

There is no road on the marsh, no house save the old shepherd's black cottage. It is a lost, wild prairie of cattle and curlew, of springing hares and shell-duck that swim proud among gulls. Teal whistle in the great reed-beds, and foxes come down from the upland to a sanctuary where no man may gallop on a horse and where fat mallard doze in the sun. There are snipe, probing in the oozy rills, redshank wading delicately, more than once a glimpse of an avocet, lovely as porcelain—they nested two years running, but we kept that quiet—and away back in 1931 I saw a pair of white-tailed eagles swinging in lordly arcs. More than once a bittern has lumbered out of the orange reed-beds. The short-eared owl breeds in spring, and if you sit on a winter eve in a duck-hole by the edge of the Horse-shoe Pond, the Snipe Pond, the Pea Fleet, or the Star Fleet you will have mallard, widgeon, pochard, teal, shoveller, mergansers, tufted duck and snipe buzzing about your ears like flies. There was one unforgettable night when we killed forty-four fowl at flight, and parcelled them out on the cottage floor into eleven different varieties.

It has always been a noble marsh, known to the elect. Lord Carlingford owned it once. James Round waded its fleets and garnered its crops. Rimington-Wilson, one of the greatest shots that ever lived, swore that it gave him more pleasure than the best pheasant shoot in all England. "Crawley" de Crespigny loved it; Lord Gough, that gallant soldier, astounded the Essex natives when he shot with me by knocking down flighting teal with his one arm and a twenty-bore. One by one, princes and peers, great shots and unknown shots, they have come and gone on this marsh whose wildness has not changed since the Dutch built its sea-walls three hundred years ago.

The genius of the marsh is Ted Allen. Ted has lived on Langenhoe since he was a year old, carried a gun since he was six, rowed a punt since his seventh year, and he learned how to catch adders and tame bulls when he was ten. He knows the run of every fox, the way of the eels, in spring, the flight lines of the fowl, the rabbit buries and the otter slides, the bar-ways where the peregrines perch, the mud-banks where the black geese sit out in the creeks, the beat of the Dutch owls as they cover the marsh like setters, the line of the curlew when the tide lifts them from the mud in thousands, and the tree where the carrion crow will croak the note of death.

He is wily as the fox, silent as the otter, hardy as the wild goose, with the ears of an owl, the sight of a falcon, and the primitive spirit of a Leatherstocking. I believe that if you took him from the marshes and the crawling creeks, the smell of the sea and the whistle of curlew, he would shrivel and die.

Brown-skinned, with bleached brown hair, a wiry, waving moustache, a Viking face, and strange, lambent eyes that can twinkle with humour or flame with sudden passion, he looks what he is, a primitive man with all the arts and wisdom of half-forgotten worlds.

You will sometimes meet a woodman whose soul and spirit are

part of the very growth and scent of his own wide woods, secret as their dimmest, owl-haunted dell, unchangeable as their oaks. You may meet a stalker whose eyes are lifted to his tall Scottish hills, whose spirit is bred of the heather, whose mind is unchanging as the deepest loch, whose soul moves as the deer move, from the glittering sea-loch shore to the dark corries of the raven, the high white tops of the snowline.

Even so, Ted Allen is a creature of the wild marsh, of the wide and deadly mud flats, a stalker of the creeks, a son of the salt tides and the shifting cloud-scapes, one with the rough cattle and the swift duck. He sees ghosts and believes in spirits that walk by night.

In that part of Essex if they have a marsh infested with adders, a field where no man dare walk or stock may be put, they send for Ted. He catches the adders alive, stuffs them in jam-jars, takes them out at will, and sells them to hospitals at half a crown apiece to make anti-snakebite serum. He has been bitten dozens of times. The backs of his hands are criss-crossed with tiny blue marks where the fangs have entered. Each time he nicks the bite with the blade of his knife, sucks out the poison, rubs in tobacco, and gets on with the next one. He reckons he is "so full of snake poison that a little more can't hurt anyway."

If they have a bull which is the terror of the parish they send for Allen. For half a sovereign he will round up the bull and pen him in a yard. For a sovereign he will get him into the bull-cart.

Once, ten years ago, when I first held that enchanted marsh, a bull came suddenly over the sea-wall, trotting towards me. He was heavy in the shoulders, fleet in the legs, with an eye like a balefire. He came across the marsh, head up, tail straight as a poker, with the kink in it which means mischief. I cocked my gun.

"Hold you tight," said Ted quietly beside me. "Take my bag and me owd gun. I'll give him a taste of my cosh. Stand you still."

He took an ash cudgel out of his great, blood-stained, feather-littered canvas-side bag. He walked towards the bull. The bull stopped, stared. Allen walked steadily on. Down went the bull on his knees, horning the earth, tossing tussocks of grass into the air. He moaned and he groaned, that blood-curdling rumble which is the warning of a charge.

Down flopped Allen on hands and knees. He too bellowed and grumbled. He grabbed handfuls of earth and grass, flung them high into the air, and, still muttering, waddled on hands and knees like a fantastic guinea-pig towards the bull.

The bull, unaccustomed to such unwonted acrobatics, rose from his knees, stared uncertainly at the advancing human quadruped, lashed a nonplussed tail. Allen still advanced. He crawled to within two yards of that puzzled bull. Then, springing to his feet he fetched it a mighty clout on its snout with his ash cosh and, as it wheeled about, seized it by the tail and galloped after it, belabouring its buttocks.

"I larnt that little owd trick when I was a titty-totty owd boy no more'n ten. I was on this here marsh with me catapult, stalkin' a lot of larks on me hands and knees when a herd o' cattle cum latherin' round me. I worn't no bigger'n tuppence, so I makes a run at 'em on me hands and knees, and off they goes. All 'cept one. He was an owd bull. He stood and moaned. So, thinks I, if I can make the cows run I can make the master run too. I hulls up a lot of grass and lets out a horrible row and makes a run at the guv'nor on my hands and knees. Blast! he went off like a train! You can allus scare a bull if you do something he can't make out.

"I've rounded up many a bull that no man dare touch. Only had to shoot one in me life. That was when we were gettin' it into the bull-cart up at the Hall. Some silly fule let go the rope through the ringle and round come his lordship straight for me. I was penned in the angle of the wall. I shot him no more'n two gun-barrels off, and he dropped with his snout on my boot."

He catches adders either with a forked stick or by putting his boot on them and picking them up. He stuffs them into jam-jars, sometimes two or three in a jar, ties a cloth-top over the jar, and goes home with a bag full of squirming reptiles. But he is frightened of a horse. When I rode my old hunter into his garden he backed into the brew-house like a scared cat.

"Take that damned thing away. I'll handle an owd bull, but you can have the hosses. They bite at one end, kick at t'other, and they ain't safe in the middle."

Ted is no respecter of persons. When a prince of commerce mortally offended him on the marsh Ted went by hedgerow and field-path to the lodge gates, wired them up with barbed wire, and waited grimly until the pillar of finance arrived pompously in his Rolls.

"Cum out of that b—— motor-car," Ted demanded. "You're my master down on the marsh, but you're man to man on the high road. Cum out of that! I'll take off my jacket to you and see who's the better man. I've always served gentlemen in my time, not b——

tow-rags that ha'n't neither the eye to shoot nor the good manners to behave."

For quarter of an hour the petrified magnate was held in pawn until friends arrived and persuaded the irate Ted to withdraw. But I shall never forget the scorn in his voice when I took him round to see London after one of his first broadcasts to the world. Ted's eyes lit on the portly façade of a great commercial house of which his enemy is chairman.

"So that owd b—— has got one of his damned shops up here, has he," said he witheringly, gazing at the seven-storey building. "I've a damned good mind to go and haul him out from behind the counter and rub his nose where the sparrers feed." I led him gently away.

Ted, like many marshmen, believes in ghosts. He has seen queer things down on the marsh when the snow mists come over the sea-walls. One night, lying up on a spit in the saltings, he saw a giant man, eight or ten feet tall, come down the peat-way from the sea-wall, stride over creek and rill, and go walking over the face of the waters into the wall of mist where the bar-geese were laughing in ghastly merriment. He believes that vision. He told it on the wireless and defied the scorn.

There is a field by his house called Hoppin' Tom's Piece. In that field is a pond called the Devil's Drink Bowl.

"Same as that were forty years ago," said Ted, "they was hay harvesting, twelve men a-swingin' scythes. The master up at the Hall know'd every one on 'em. But when that cum arternoon time there was a thirteenth man slipped in among 'em, a reg'lar mowin' master. He swung a better scythe nor any on 'em. When the rest knocked off work this owd chap went on a-mowin'. He mowed all night by the moon. Cum mornin' time the hay crop was half cut. Some on 'em said he was the Davvle. Next night time they dropped a lot o' iron bars in the hay what still stood. But this chap cum and mowed in the moon again. He sliced through them iron bars like cheese. Cum mornin' the crop was cut.

"The men goes up to the Hall to draw their pay, this owd chap among 'em. The master looks down at his feet and sees he's got the cloven hoof. So he says, 'I 'on't pay you no money. You're old Hoppin' Tom.'

"With that the Davvle lets out a shrik an' flew off in a sheet o' flame. He hulled his drink bowl into the middle of the field, drownded the whole hay crop, and that's where the pond lays to-day.

"No, I ain't never seen the Davvle, but we call that owd shepherd's hut where you used to sleep the Found Out, 'cause I reckon that when God made the world that was the last place He found out—and the Davvle's been about this owd marsh ever since. Happen he'll catch that owd City man one day and shove him in the mud! If he don't I will, if I only get me clappers on him. Bulls'll be nothin' to it."

I left Ted with his mirage of vengeance to ride down to the marsh. There was a time, twenty years ago, when a fine, old, red-brick farmhouse with a Queen Anne doorway and wide windows stood on the farthest point of the upland ridge-back. Its shingled roof, red, yellow, and grey with lichens, was shaded by oak and walnut, its garden gay with flowers, its orchard full of apples and plums, pears and bullaces. It looked east to Mersea. The sun on salt water winked back from its windows. Its dairy was busy with the clink of pails, the drone of milk churns. Its passages were lively with children's feet. It reared a strong brood. Harold Proctor, the best amateur punt-gunner in Mersea, was born there. Strong as a horse, ruddy-faced, he is now, as I write, mine-sweeping in the North Sea.

Ten years ago his old home was empty and windowless. Doors hung drunkenly on their hinges, owls roosted in the bedrooms. Cows and young colts blundered into sitting-room and kitchen, the shingles slid and fell—an empty, forlorn home. Its fields were rough and unkempt, half drowned with water in winter, alive with adders and rabbits in summer, wildernesses of rank grass, sour herbage, blowing thistles, docks, and poppies. Fourteen hundred acres of good land lay idle, not worth a pound an acre. The lower marsh, indeed, was under salt water, four hundred acres or more, for a whole winter when the sea broke in. For years afterwards it was too sour for sheep or cattle. Sheep simply scoured and died. Cattle refused to eat the rotten stuff.

To-day, as I rode along the old lane, between hedges full of blackberries, rich in the sun, alive with finches and blackbirds, a magpie dipping and chacking ahead, rabbits scuttling into the ditch, the upland fields on either side, fields which I remembered as rough grass, were harvested, golden-brown with stubble. Long rows of sheaves stood dozing in the sun. The waters of the Pyefleet glittered bluely.

Ahead, at the gate where the marsh begins, a crowd of peewits rose wheeling and screaming from a shallow fleet. They looped and stalled, black and white against the sky. The cottages on the right which had been derelict, mere shelters for calves in wet weather, were newly roofed, their gardens fenced about, children squealing.

Farther on, the great barns and cart-sheds of the Wick Farm still stood as of yore. But the old farmhouse which was built when Anne was Queen had disappeared. Not one brick stood upon another. The garden had gone back to wilderness. The apple-trees and walnuts were forlorn. A heron rose with leisurely protest from the pond. A carrion crow slid stealthily out of a tall elm and drooped to the marsh in a half-mile, sinister glide. War's rebirth of farming, although it has reclaimed the fields and saved the cottages, had come too late to save the house which had mellowed in two hundred years of summer suns and nursed two centuries of sturdy yeomen.

The sea-walls on the lower marsh were patched and strong. No longer was there fear of the tide overmastering them on some winter's night, blowing a great breach in the dark hours, and springing in, spume-crested, like a hairy monster pouncing from the sea.

We turned and rode across the marsh by the snipe pond through a hole in a fence, over South House Farm, where soldiers eyed me askance but asked no question, and so by winding lanes to that lonely, red-brick cottage which sits on the high point of Fingringhoe Wick, looking out to the estuary of the Colne and far beyond to the glittering loneliness of the sea.

This peninsula of land, farmed largely by Colonel Claude Furneaux, of Fingringhoe Hall, and old Mr Daniel Green, of East Donyland Hall—a fine old-time Essex yeoman living in a fine old square Elizabethan house—contains at its farthest, seaward end some of the best deposits of sand and gravel on the East Coast. The Freshwater Sand and Ballast Company work the pits, and their fleet of barges takes thousands of tons of ballast round the coast each year. Since the war began many an Essex coastal barge has been lost by enemy action, not including the five which I remember being blown out to sea one wild day when war was a half-realized threat. They cast upon the coasts of Holland, Belgium, and France, but, by some miracle of the god who looks after sailors and little ships, not a man was lost.

You would agree that this Fingringhoe farm land and these ballast pits are worth much good gold. But cast your eye from the upland sandy lane down on to those creek-riddled saltings, purple with sea lavender, cut up by rills and gullies, clamorous with gulls and curlew. As the tide creeps in they will go under water, until from the sea-wall at field foot to the far wall on Mersea Island the whole wide expanse will be a young sea, glittering in the sun, with an odd hummock standing up where maybe an old dog fox, artful as any sailor in his knowledge of tides, will sleep out the afternoon in safety, curled up in bent grass and sea lavender.

Those saltings, totally valueless except as occasional grazing for sheep and as a paradise for the shore gunner, were bought by the War Office for £4 10s. an acre. Four pounds ten an acre for hundreds of acres of drowned mud and slimy creeks, 'land' which, twice in twenty-four hours, disappears beneath the sea! Four pounds ten an acre was paid for these saltings just before the war, when, less than half a mile away across the creek, the neglected farm lands of Langenhoe, which in a decently run farming country should have been worth twenty or thirty pounds an acre, would not have fetched four pounds an acre in the open market. If ever there is a grand inquisition—which I doubt—into the squandering of national finances by the War Office this case of the Fingringhoe saltings should come high on the list.

I drew the attention of Sir Victor Warrender,[1] then Parliamentary Secretary to the War Office, to the matter at the time, but, as was usual in those locust-ridden days of the Munich era, got no satisfaction.

As we sat in our saddles in the hot sun gazing on these purple wastes, the tide crept in slowly. Slowly it flooded the marsh, crawled like silver snakes in widening channels towards the land. The saltings and the sea lavender went under. Herds of curlew rose and came skirling overhead for the upland stubbles. A gay white-and-chestnut company of bar-geese flickered out to sea on swift-cutting wings. Redshank trilled their million bells. Herons—three, four, six, seven of them—rose solemnly and drifted, blown grey rags, over the Colne to the dusky-gold woods of Alresford Hall. The tide swelled in until it covered all the land beneath a shield of beaten silver.

"Tidy-lookin' place to put a plough into—cheap at four pound ten an acre if you want to sail a boat though!" said a voice at my elbow.

Bob Brown, manager of the ballast pits, is one of those quiet, faraway-eyed men with burnt skins and bleached white hair whom you find in deserts and on marshes by the sea. Bob lived twenty years of his roving life in the deserts of Arabia, in the red, scarred hills of Persia, alone with the stars at night, burned by the sun by day, before he picked on this lonely, almost houseless peninsula for a home. His nearest railway station is seven miles by winding lanes.

[1] Now Lord Bruntisfield.

So is his nearest big shop. He bicycles four miles for his evening pint of beer. His hobbies are shooting, solitude, and digging for Roman remains. Apart from the bargemen, the gravel workers, and an odd wildfowler, he sees no human face from Saturday to Saturday, when he joins the jolly company at the Langenhoe Lion to talk rabbiting and foxhunting with Bert Amos, the landlord, whose old father, for forty years Whip to the East Essex and the Essex and Suffolk Hounds, is still fit to sling his leg over a horse at seventy-eight.

"When I was a boy," said Bob, his eye on a broken line of sea-wall half a mile across the saltings through which the tide was pouring like a mill-race, "all that Fingringhoe Fresh Marsh, that the tide's flooding now, was walled and safe. They ran scores of cattle on it. Now look at it—good land gone to salt water. And if I go into Colchester to buy a joint of beef it's ten to one that it's come from South America in a ship that's manned by some of our East Coast chaps at the risk of their lives. Funny world, isn't it?"

He told me of the Roman temple he had found—now in Colchester Castle in bits—of the skeleton in the gravel and the ruins of Arch Hall, that vanished house of mystery which once stood strong and tall on the point, an avenue leading to its front door. We agreed that it was probably the ruins of the temple used by some Elizabethan as a house or barn and christened from its standing arch. Now it is a mere antique name on the old maps—a mystery unsolved.

We had a drop of Bob's Scotch, admired the turkeys, congratulated his boy on ferreting thirty-six rabbits in a morning, and rode slowly back across the fields, following a rutted lane from Westhouse Farm which skirts the shallow marshy valley, rough with reeds and bushes, splashed with sudden pools, lively with lapwings and rabbits, dotted with humped cattle—the valley where runs the Roman River. That little river, a mile or so lower, piles itself in a muddy basin of reed-fringed waters against the tall, old tide-mill at Fingringhoe, one of the last tide-mills in England still to grind corn by the force of salt and fresh water mixed. Below the mill the saltings open out. The river, there a muddy creek where great, red-sailed barges twist and turn, crawls through sea-asters and sea-lavender, quick with dipping terns, to the tidal Colne.

As we rode, watching the changing tapestry of colour in the tall woods which straggle raggedly up the far side of the valley, a woman passed us driving a Canterbury, with a neat little blood horse in the shafts. I had not seen one on the road for years. She raised her whip in the driving salute, bowed, and smiled as she passed. She was a stranger, but we were horsemen and therefore freemasons.

It is sometimes amusing, always interesting, and occasionally pathetic to see the horsed vehicles which war has brought out on the roads again. They creep forth from cobwebbed stables, from dusty coach-houses, from owl-haunted cart-sheds, from dusky barns, sibilant with pattering rats, to take the air again, dressed in new imperial coats of glossy paint. Some are a hundred years old. Some were on the roads before tarmac was known, when the great Duke of Wellington was still a potent, living figure. Like sailing-ships and other good things made of wood, they go on for ever. They never die. They simply creak and fade away.

The last few months I had seen curricles and even a cabriolet, phaetons and Pelhams, a Lawton gig and a high spider-wheeled dog-cart which should properly have had an auburn-haired woman with a pink complexion, a motor veil, and leg-of-mutton sleeves sitting in it Edwardianly. Traps, spring carts, and wagonettes are back again on all the roads that knew them in their dusty hey-day.

When I talked of these things with Jim, this renaissance of forgotten vehicles, whose prices have suddenly sprung to bubble-heights, he cocked a sly wink at me and said, "There's a nice bang-up new road coach by Shanks tucked away in Bonner's Barn down on the marsh. I got it off a young gentleman in the Army. The officers used to run it on the road before the war. I reckon we can do a deal with him when the war's over and keep it down here. If you get one of your coaching gentlemen friends to come down and give me a lesson or two with the ribbons Maurice and I will find the horses, and there you are—a road coach to run about East Essex. What a time we'll have!"

"We'll run it from the Officers' Club in Colchester to Mrs Hone's at Mersea," I said. "Charge 'em a couple of guineas for the day with a bang-up lunch, and we'll fill it. It'll pay for the horses' nose-bags, anyway."

We rode on, dreaming of the distant sunshine of peace, imagining the tantivy notes of the yard of tin challenging 'down the road,' the jingle of harness, the rattle of bars, the shuffle and clatter of hooves, and the brave sight of that most English of all things, a road coach with four-in-hand, horn blowing, swinging and jingling through the English lanes in the sweet pageantry of May hedges and hawthorn billows tossed against the green.

A farmer joined us out of a by-road on a bicycle. He complained bitterly of the contradictory orders given him a week before by War

Agricultural Committee officials, whom he described as "titty little bits on motor-bikes—never got their feet wet yet—clerks dodging the Army—trying to teach me my job when I've been farming forty years."

It is a grievance which you meet bitterly in some counties, and scarcely at all in others.

Whatever may be the expensive benefits of War Agricultural Committee methods in war we must, as soon as possible, rid ourselves of their petty bureaucratic tyranny when peace comes. They are the thin end of the wedge of land nationalization—the death-knell of good farming.

It was a hard road back on to Mersea Island, near enough six miles on slippery tarmac. The harvest sun sank in a magnificent balefire. Crimson and ochre in the furnace of the west lit mackerel clouds with an unearthly pinkness. Gulls, winnowing out to sea, took on a sudden ethereal sheen. In the fields on either side reapers and combine harvesters were still hard at it.

Over the Strood into Mersea, by the headlands of a bean-field where a hare cantered prick-eared, and so down the old City Lane between tiny, toylike cottages, framed in pill-box gardens, full of pinks and lupins. The lane opened suddenly on a vista of foreshore, opal mud, smacks tipped sideways, yachts snugged down in mud berths, gun-punts lying like grey cigars on the tide edge, dinghies swinging at anchor. This is "the Old City" of Mersea, a huddle of barge-boarded cottages with here a cream-plastered wall, and there a flash of pink or that sudden blue which fisher people splash on boats and farmers use brilliantly on ploughs and carts. A colony of red roofs, tiny alleys, back-yards where boats, nets, and dogs lurk. You step over oars; find a punt-gun, nine feet long, leaning against a boat-shed; come suddenly on girl sail-makers stitching in windows; riggers working minutely; blue-jerseyed men stumping along in red rubber thigh boots.

The black bank of clouds in the west above which the sun flared red broke suddenly as though a mountain range had split asunder. Full level rays lit foreshore and cottages, boat-sheds and smacks, masts and rigging, in a sudden, Cuyp-like splendour. It was a picture straight from the Dutch masters, an illuminated page from eighteenth-century England, a lost, lovely echo tossed by the hand of war from a gentler past.

For in peace-time you would find that foreshore road pestilent with motor-cars, staccato with motor-cycle engines, the creek noisy with outboards, the Hard garish with blondes in trousers.

CHAPTER IV

Come home, lord singing,
Come home, corn bringing,
'Tis merry inhall,
Where beards wag all.

THOMAS TUSSER,
One Hundred Points of Good Husbandrie (1557)

Bill Wyatt, 'Admiral' of West Mersea—An Elizabethan Philosopher—How he lassoed a Porpoise—"The Little Owd Boy up Street" who was bombed—On London, "that Wicked Owd Hole"—On Women—At Mrs Hone's—On Drink—"Eighteen Thousand Barrels o' Beer in Me Life"—Duck-driving in the Blitz—The Harbour-master of Pin Mill and his Little Way with Germans—On Towns and how they make Monkeys of Men

BILL WYATT SETS OVER THERE. I KNOW HE'D LIKE A WORD with you," said a bright female voice behind me. The brown face and cheerful grin of Mrs Sydney Stoker peeped over the tiny laurel hedge of the Old Victory. "Soon as I heard them horses come down the lane I said to meself, 'That's Mr Wentworth for sure. If he don't want Albert Greenleaf he'll want Old Bill.' And there he sets.

"We ain't seen you since the war started, but Bill don't alter. He's had bombs all round him—back o' his shed and back o' his house. But he's like the rest of us Mersea folk—that'll take more than Old Hitler to move us. But we've had some rare good fights overhead—better'n a regatta. Hundreds of bombs on the island! Several housen down but, thank the good Lord, nobody killed. One old lady, ninety-three she was, said when they pulled her out of her cottage that was all down about her, 'I ain't dead yit! I'm gooin' to git to me hundred, Hitler or no Hitler.' But there, Old Bill's a-waitin' for you."

He sat on the stern of a dinghy, tipped sideways, his blue eyes humorously quizzing us. The peak of his yachting cap cut a sharp shadow across his brown face, finely seamed. The beard that has warmed his throat against forty winters of North Sea gales swept the salt-stained reefer jacket as he bent to the basket at his feet and scooped out an oyster. Out came his shut-knife, and he opened it with one quick scoop. He held the oyster out, grinning.

"Hev one! Fust o' the season. But git orf o' that hoss an' set aside me. Yew'd look better in yar owd duck punt what I built than yew du on that damned great thing. . 'Sides, he've splattered me wi' mud already."

Behind him, bright as twin swords, the Ray and Thorn Fleet glittered broadly far into the salt marshes, dreaming in the evening sun. The tide ebbed slowly. The muds, opalescent, were lively with redshank, musical with curlew. Peewits wept and tumbled. A party of oxbirds flashed by over the water, turned suddenly like falling shillings. A mile ahead a carrion crow croaked deathlike in the twisted thorn-trees of Ray Island, the haunted place. On that bleak sea island no man dare build a house for fear of the ghost of the Roman centurion who walks at night in the full moon, his footsteps ringing. But you see no body, human or astral. There is only the terrifying ring of soldierly feet across the marsh and round you in a narrowing circle. Ivan Pullen has heard it on a full-moon night in August.

Behind us, the red roofs, the spars and masts, the grey church tower, and the tall trees of Mersea Island cut a tumbled skyline against the North Sea blue.

Captain Bill Wyatt, seventy-six-year-old boat-builder, descendant of Elizabethan shipwrights, is 'Admiral' of West Mersea. Long, long ago, generations of villagers now old men, of fishermen lost at sea, of Edwardian yachtsmen who sailed these waters when the gaff-topsail was the last word in rig, promoted him to that nebulous office.

His quarter-deck is his own boat-yard. His ships are the sixty or seventy small yachts, converted smacks, dinghies, one-designs, duck punts, and odd off-casts from other yacht yards and forgotten designs, which clutter up his mud berths. His crew are seventy-year-old Brother Frank, who has seen the world, since he was once in John Brown's yard and then in a mine-sweeper; two nephews who are riggers; an odd, shifting pay-roll of sail-makers, carpenters, and the like. In peace-time the 'Admiral' paid out to twenty hands per week.

His ships have sailed half the seven seas—"Right across to Halifax, Nova Scotia, up the Dutch canals and down the French waterways to the Mediterranean. Bill Wyatt is knowed in most waters where yachtsmen sail.

"My grandfather had a thirty-six-ton cutter-rigged fish carrier named the *Nancy*, close on sixty foot over all. He used to go up north to Scotland in her, takin' his wife, an' a goat for milk, fish them waters for a month, packin' the fish in ice, and then bring 'em south to Billin'sgate. He used to go to Jersey in old Boney's time and drudge their oysters up right under the Frenchies' noses and bring 'em back to Marsea. But they ain't so good as ourn.

"He married a Miss Witty, daughter of a ship- and smack-builder here. But we Wyatts really came from Buckler's Hard, down on the Beaulieu river in Hampshire, where we was shipwrights tew hunderd and fifty years afore that. Right back in owd Queen Lizzie's day when they built the big 'uns that hammered they Spaniards. He built a smack called the *Saucy Jack* when he took over the Witty's business here and another called the *Thomas*. Buth on 'em lasted a hunderd years. A good smack will. So will a barge.

"I've sailed in the old *Unity*, built by Bob Aldous, of Brightlingsea, in every Marsea Regatta for fifty years. We won a lot of prizes—and she's seventy-seven year owd.

"Ha! But the best little boat I ever built was the *Mersea Hard*, sixteen-foot, sloop-rigged, handy as a kitten.

"I used her in the last war for cartin' canvas from here to Tollesbury. A ton at a time, tew hunderd pounds' wuth. That blew suffin' tempesty times, but we never lorst a reel o' cotton.

"Work? We'll dew anythin' from a new mast to a new keel. I've repaired duck boats, French 'uns and once a big Norwegian named *Ezda*. B'longed to some people that sold water. Yis, water! Stuff the toffs take when they've hed too much to drink the night afore.

"But I like buildin' duck punts best. I built dozens o' they. Charlie Stoker, the gunner, has a punt what I built him tharty year agoo, an' he's gittin' his owd gun down to hev a goo in her agin this season.

"Puntin', smackin', yachtin'—us chaps can handle 'em all. Why, owd Bob South, my rigger—he's sixty-six, yit he's bin' acrost the Pond three times arter the America's Cup. He was seventeen summers with Sycamore[1] in different yachts. When the last war bruk out Bob an' they wuz half-way acrost the Pond. But they dodged they owd Jarmans so they de'n't git copped.

"Jim Mussett was with me too arter he'd been in the *Endeavour*, paintin' and riggin'. They had a rare tew-dew comin' acrost the Pond when the tow-rope broke. But that warn't half so bad as the papers made out. Yew paper chaps don't harf spin a yarn. But yew ain't so bad. I allus reckin' you're more of a gunner than a writer!

[1] The famous Captain Sycamore, of Brightlingsea, one of the greatest yacht skippers of all time.

"My pore clerk what kept the accounts, he's jist been blowed up in a mine-sweeper in the Thames, pore chap. We lorst another Marsea man, an' a Tollesbury chap, an' a D'Arcy boy, an' a man from Wigborough, all at one go, only last week off on the Main [North Sea]."

A grey mullet jumped noisily up Thorn Fleet. The 'Admiral' turned his head slowly, gazed up the shining waterway where a heron stood, grey and delicate, on the mud.

"Tharty-six year agoo I hed the biggest thrill o' my life up there. A shoal o' porpoises come up one mornin', 'bout ten o' the clock, half-flood. They goo right up Thorn Fleet, forty or fifty on 'em, pitchin' and divin', fat as pigs, throshin' the water like young whales.

"Away goo the landlord of the Owd Victory, named Trim, an' a man named Jennin's, in a boat with a double-barrelled gun. They frightened them porpoises by shuttin' at 'em so as they kept 'em up there. 'Cum on, boy, we're a' goin' arter them porpoises,' I says to my nevvy. Away we goo in my punt, rowin' like one o'clock.

"We gits up the hid o' the crick, an' there they wuz, fifty o' the davils, rollin' about like pigs in five foot o' water, bleatin' out like rabbits. One big owd feller keeps whiskin' his tail up out o' the water. So overboard I goes, up to me showders, and took two half-hitches round his tail, quick as light. T'other end o' the rope was fast to the bows of my punt.

"Blarst, boy! Round flew that owd porpoise quick as light. He towed us down the crick at a good four knots. I thought we should swamp. Suddenly, up the crick comes four more porpoises from the sea, roarin' up like a lot o' davils. They wuz jumpin' a good ten foot in the air—hit the water like a barn a-fallin' down.. Great God! I thought they wuz gooin' to jump on me an' flatten us out.

"As soon as Wyatt's porpoise seed these four he whipped round and roared up the crick at a good eight knots. My nevvy was that scared I hed to cut the tow, put him ashore, and thin I rowed orf arter my porpoise agin.

"I got all in among 'em, seed his owd tail flick up wi' yards o' my tow-line on it. So oover I jumps and made it fast agin.

"Whitey Mussett hed rowed up by this time, and he hitches his punt on as well. 'Tween us we got that owd porpoise down tew the Hard, we got a drag-rope on it, wi' twenty or tharty fishin' chaps haulin' on it and pulled him out on the mud. Fourteen foot long. Weighed a ton. People all down for days garpin' at him. Like a Regatta.

"My nevvy said to me only the other day, 'How about another porpoise, Uncle Bill?'

"'I'm ready, boy,' I says. 'Let's goo.'"

"Well, you've had livelier times than that on the island lately, Bill," I suggested.

"Lively! Damn! We've had more'n a hunderd bombs. You'd think we was the Rock o' Gibraltar. Some o' them damned owd bombs weighed nigh on a ton. They knocked several housen down, but they never killed nobody. I doubt we Marsea folk are too tough. Don't, that's the good Gawd what looks arter us. They allus say He hev a soft spot for fishin' chaps and sailors.

"But there, deary, deary me, did you hear about that little owd boy up street? No?

"Well, they Jarmans dropped a bomb right on his dad's cottage. Down that come. They found the little owd boy—he warn't no more'n nine year owd—under the kitchen table. He crawled out as spry as a tarrier dog. He lifted his little owd fists and shuk 'em at the sky and says, 'Yew b——rs! Yew wait till I get my dad's gun. I'd shut ye like an owd rabbit if yew come down in that field.'

"What do you think o' that, sir, for a little'n? That's the right colour on 'em, ain't it? He 'on't jine no League o' Nations when he grow up to be a man. He 'on't trust no foreigners arter this lot.

"I reckon he'll say what my owd dad hammered into me when I was a young'n. 'Boy Bill,' he'd say, 'what we want in this here country is a rare gret owd Navy, plenty o' ships an' guns, every man to hev his bit o' land so that he can grow his own grub, and bring 'em all up to put their trust in the good Gawd.'

"I reckon we ain't had enough o' none o' them three things this last twenty year'n more." Bill gazed at me, solemn trouble in his old blue eyes.

"Not near enough o' none on 'em, sir. We cut the Navy down an' done worse by the flyin' chaps. We fetched the food in from foreign till that got so bad that if you wanted to buy fresh veg'ables you hed to goo to a shop in the town if you hadn't got a garden o' your own and buy 'em straight from London. Like as not they hadn't bin growed not more'n a mile from where you lived, afore they were sent up to London to come back to you down in the country. A cruel waste o' time an' money, an' half the freshness gone out o' the veg'ables. There was a rare crop o' plums 'bout here year or tew agoo. If you growed 'em you couldn't get more'n a ha'penny a pound for 'em. But if you bought 'em in the shops they was fourpence. Some of the yachtin' gentlemen towd me they was a tanner a pound in London. I don't like that owd place. Thass a wicked owd hole.

"Every time I goo up there I lose suffin'. Went up one day with a bag full o' veg'ables an' a pair o' nice young rabbits for a ship's captain what I know'd. Put 'em down in the bar o' a public outside Liverpool Street an' hed me half-pint. Time I'd swallered that an' looked round, me taters an' me tew nice young rabbits hed gone. There's a wicked caper for ye!

"I count there was more people gooin' into them cinnymas than ever went to church to thank the good Gawd for what he'd put in their bellies an' hung on their backs. You'd think them film-actin' girls was little owd goddesses the way they fussed 'em up in the papers. Sluts—the half on 'em! Strumpets, I reckon. Allus a-choppin' an' changin' their husbands till half the world copied 'em, an' people didn't seem to git married afore they was gittin' unspliced agin.

"A good woman, sir, is like what the Bible says—'a pearl without price.' Yew can't buy 'em. They jist happen. Treat 'em right an' you're the better man for it. I've hed tew good wives in me time, an' I don't know but what I shouldn't hev me eye on a third if my dear owd lady went orf up aloft. But there, sir, d'yew come up to Mrs Hone's wi' me, an' we'll hev a pint. I've talked me owd throat parched."

So to Mrs Hone's we went. If you know Mersea you will know that sprawling, picturesque collection of wooden huts which is Mrs Hone's. It is a club for fishermen and wildfowlers, for oystermen and yachtsmen, for soldiers on leave and sailors from the sea, and lovers of good food. For Mrs Hone, a descendant of John Evelyn, the diarist, is a wise woman with a great heart, the best cook in all Essex. Indeed, it is no high secret to tell you that when the Prime Minister, Mr Churchill, was in our marsh country inspecting defences, his hosts sent for Mrs Hone to plan and cook the meal.

Bill Wyatt is the commodore of this unique club. Mrs Hone and her two Junoesque daughters run it. Mr Hone, in his day a good wildfowler, now, alas, almost blind, sits by the iron stove in the bar and smokes the pipe of wisdom. In that little wooden, raftered bar there are pictures of great ships, winking brass, bottles, and bowls of flowers, the glint of gun-barrels in the corner, echoes and talk of shooting days and sailing days, of yachts and ducks, of farming and foxhunting, the war and memories of peace.

In the cosy dining-room with its red-brick fireplace, its water-colours of the sea by Charles Pears, you may swallow oysters in their season, eat widgeon and wild goose, hares from the marshes, grey mullet from the tide, and watch the slick dexterity of Ted Milgate, long-bodied, blue-jerseyed, rubber-booted oysterman and gunner. Ted can open oysters at the rate of sixty a minute. He is, in his way, a champion. So, too, is William.

Settling himself comfortably on his high stool the commodore expatiated:

"Thank you, sir. A pint to be agooin' on with. Beer's my hobby time I'm indoors. Gimme a gun when I'm in Gawd's fresh air, an' me owd pint pot time I set here. Beer and rum—the buth on 'em 'll niver harm yer. I've drunk a masterful gret owd lot o' beer in me time. That ain't niver hut me yet. That 'on't, time you keep in the open air a-workin' hard. I started when I was a little owd nipper ne more'n five. Now I'm seventy-seven an' can still make a hole in the barrel.

"There was a gentleman here one day with an arithmetitical mind. He questioned me about me beer-drinkin'. An' how d'ye think he worked it out, sir?

"Eighteen thousand barrels o' beer I've drunk in me lifetime. Eighteen thousand barrels! There's a master drink for yew. That'd float a tidy-sized owd smack."

There entered Arthur Hempstead, oysterman, sail-maker, and sailor. Arthur is one of the hundred thousand who have their bomb story to tell on that adventurous coast. William winked:

"I reckon they Jarmans was arter owd Arthur. He set on the after-deck of his houseboat one sunny evenin' smokin' his owd pipe, time his missus was down below gittin' the grub ready. He heerd an owd aeroplane a-comin' close an' low. That come right over the village, no higher'n the tree-tops. A gret black owd thing with that ugly cross on it.

"Arthur's missus poked her nose outer the companion-way an' hollers out, 'Look up, Arthur, he've a-dropped suffin'.'

"Damn, he dropped a gret owd bomb, straight as if he'd aimed that at Arthur where he sat. That hit the mud not more'n a few yards from Arthur, skidded along, went straight threw owd Sir Claude de Crespigny's yacht, split that in half, smashed a couple o' dinghies, and then that bruk in half. One half skipped across the crick a hunderd yard or more. That went up like the crack o' doom, sunk two smacks at anchor, an' hulled up the mud an' water fifty yard in the air."

TED ALLEN

"A genius of the wild marsh."

"ADMIRAL" BILL WYATT, ELIZABETHAN PHILOSOPHER OF MERSEA ISLAND

Photos Douglas Went, Brightlingsea

Walter Linnett, the Fowler of Bradwell-juxta-Mare, in his Gun Punt with the Nine-foot Punt-gun

Photo Douglas Went, Brightlingsea

Arthur Hempstead solemnly nodded approval.

"What did you do, Arthur?" I asked.

"Do? Blarst! I fell backwards!"

I heard tales of dog-fights fought over the creeks and the village, of aeroplanes which fell out of the sky like wounded ducks, of how Ted Allen, the gunner, and his boy Bill lay in a creek in the saltings where they were shooting duck while machine-gun bullets thudded into the mud all round them. And of how when Bill suggested a move Ted grunted, "Lay you still, boy. There's hunderds o' duck set out in the big reservoy. One of our chaps'll shoot one o' them Jerries down right in among 'em, and all them ducks'll come over here. We'll git the flight of our lives."

And, lo and behold, a German bomber was shot down into the great reservoir which floods that shallow valley beyond the mainland marshes. All the duck came over Ted and Bill. They got nine in ten minutes. As Ted later remarked, "That was the finest bit o' duck-drivin' as ever I seed."

The utter coolness of these East Coast folk when England trembled on the brink of an invasion worse than Napoleon threatened brought to my mind an incident in that momentous week-end preceding Munich. It exemplifies perfectly the reactions to war of the simple sailor of the eastern seaboard.

I was on my way to the Orkneys and Shetlands in the seven-hundred-ton motor yacht *Evadne*, owned by my friend Mr C. R. (now Sir Richard) Fairey, the aircraft manufacturer. Dick Fairey, like many men of great character, was the son of a yeoman farmer. His forbears owned their land and farmed it near us in Huntingdonshire and Cambridgeshire for centuries. They are of the straight Saxon stock, men big in mind and body.

He began life by earning ten shillings a week at the age of fourteen and was a millionaire, a pioneer of aircraft design, by the time he was twenty-six. For years before this war began he warned Cabinet Ministers and M.P.'s alike of the rising aerial might of Germany. He employed his own trade spies to ferret out secrets of German aircraft production and design. He hammered at official doors in Whitehall until his patience was worn thin. His warnings fell on deaf ears.

That Sunday morning before Munich four of us were aboard *Evadne*, ploughing the summer seas northward on a shooting and fishing holiday. There was Dick, our host; Norman Holbrook, who won the V.C. in the last war when he dived the submarine E 11 under four successive mine-fields at the Dardanelles and torpedoed the Turkish battleship *Messudiyeh* at anchor; Gerald Penney, brother of Lord Marchwood; and myself.

Early on a perfect morning the yacht hove to off Harwich, and a launch went ashore to collect the Sunday papers. Their front pages were strident with screaming black type. War was imminent. Invasion might come within twenty-four hours. Mr Chamberlain had not then taken his umbrella to Munich to gain us a year's respite before the storm broke.

Norman Holbrook and I were the only two up. We read the papers and paced the deck. *Evadne* slid smoothly through satin seas. We drew abeam of the lighthouse on Orford Ness. I was admiring its black-and-white loveliness through the morning prism of mists, the yellow beach of Shingle Street, the white trouble of the waters on the bar. Suddenly bells rang in the ship. She shuddered like a spurred horse, turned almost in her own length, bells clanging.

"Good God, Norman," I exclaimed, "what's up? Have we missed an old wreck or a mine left over from the last war?"

"No! Old Dick's just read the papers!"

Along the deck came the white-coated, grey-haired figure of Parrott, the steward, treading precisely.

"Gentlemen, Mr Fairey would like to see you in the saloon."

We went below. Dick sat at the head of the breakfast-table, majestic in a purple silk dressing-gown. His voice boomed, "Boys, I'm sorry to spoil your holiday, but I've put the ship about. We're going home."

"Why?" I asked foolishly.

"Why? Because there'll be bloody war before we get there. Haven't you read the papers?" He rose to his full impressive six feet, seven inches. His voice took on a vibrant note. "If Goering's got the sense I think he has he'll bomb half London flat within twenty-four hours. He'll catch us on the hop. He's got the machines. You'll see. They've got a Blitz technique up their sleeves which will make a shambles of London and half the cities of this country. They've worked it all out.

"I've warned the Government for years, as you boys know, and now it's on us. We'll all get ashore at Harwich. I advise you to ring up your wives and families and tell 'em to get out of London right away. I'm going to put my works on double time, night and day, right away. I've got the dugouts and the air-raid shelters all ready—but would they let me have a gun! Not on your life."

We went ashore. In the Royal Harwich Yacht Club we rang up our wives and families to give them urgent warning of that horror of flame and bombs, of death and destruction, which was to overtake London just two years later. Most of the women were unbelieving. Men in the Yacht Club politely thought we had gone mad.

Then, because of the turn of the tide, we had to wait in Harwich until after lunch rather than punch the tide all the way back to the Thames. So I borrowed a launch, a long, white, graceful thing with gleaming brass rails and yacht hands in white tops, to go up the river to Pin Mill and collect a friend from my tiny 'fowling cottage for lunch.

Now Pin Mill is an Elysian hamlet of whitewashed cottages. It has gardens warm with flowers, and an old inn, the Butt and Oyster, which stands with its feet in the tide. Its windows peer through the masts and cordage of stranded barges and anchored yachts. Behind Pin Mill the Suffolk cornlands swell to the sky. Across the river, in the massed oaks and green shade of Orwell Park, Mr Pretyman's new mansion, built in the Georgian style, gazes down the estuary to Butterman's Bay where coasters lie at anchor.

To Pin Mill, then, I came in unaccustomed style and pomp.

Down the hard to greet us came the long rakish figure of George Burrows, ginger-haired, near enough sixty, deaf and loquacious. He is harbour-master of that hamlet-port. George, who had never seen me in anything grander than my little duck punt, in no more impressive garnishing than water boots, jersey, and mud, stared in wonder. The white launch, the smart yacht hands, the brass rails, took his eye.

"Why, blarst, if that ain't Mister Wentworth. Where did ye get that damned great larnch, bor?" in a voice like half a gale.

"'Tisn't mine, George. It belongs to Mr Fairey."

"Ho! So you're aboard *Evadne*, are yer. Up among the nobs, eh! Where are ye bound?"

"Well, we were going to the Shetlands for a bit of shooting and fishing, but Mr Fairey's put the ship about, and we're off back to the Hamble."

"What do ye want to do that for? You've got a month's good weather ahead on ye."

"It looks as though we shall have a war on us before that month's out," I said.

"Yis, yis. I count there's a piece in the paper about that 'smornin'. My missus read it to me time I was a-hevvin' me breakfast. I count that owd Kayser's gettin' up to his tricks again. We shall hev them owd Zeppelins over here one night a-droppin' bombs. You mark my words." He wagged a minatory forefinger and grinned cheerfully.

"I don't doubt it, George," I answered. "What are you going to do about it?"

"Du! I'll tell you what I *hev* done. Soon as my missus read that piece I swallowed me bait, went down to the boat-shed, and got me owd punt-gun out. I ain't used the owd bitch fer three years since she bruk her breechin' one Jann-wary night an' knocked me bloody front teeth out. She onsensed me! I was floatin' about on the tide fer half an hour, smuddered o' blood, like a dead hog, till a chap off a smack picked me up.

"Well, I loaded that owd gun 'smornin' with a pound o' swan-shot as big as doctor's pills. She's nine foot long—an' if them owd Jarmans come up *our* river I 'on't half warm their backsides! She'll tiddle 'em up!"

There, I think, is a perfect example of the unshakable native courage of these East Coast folk. No matter how much they have been bombed, machine-gunned, and lived in nightly fear of invasion, they have flinched not from their farms nor left their cottages. They have trawled in waters full of hidden mines, been machine-gunned at sea and on shore, and have carried on as they did when Napoleon threatened.

I do not doubt that had the invader landed one foggy night he would have been met, not by swarms of panic-stricken refugees, but by a country people who shot at him from hedges and ditches, who blew up sea-walls and drowned his infantry, who used scythe, billhook, and pitchfork as their forbears used pike and dag. They might have been mown down by the score, but they would not have given in. There was never a thought of it.

To-day, when the rural Home Guard is trained in guerrilla warfare, armed with bomb, rifle, and machine-gun, it would be a different story. There would be no question of pathetic heroism, of machine-gun murders in cottage gardens, and of a countryside overwhelmed by a remorseless tide of steel. The invader would meet a stubborn defender, cunning in attack, wise in the ways of hedge and ditch, knowing his marshes and woodlands, able to fight for every field and bridge, every cross-roads and ford.

If the war has done nothing better it has at least taught the English people to value every acre of their land, every mile of their coast, as they never valued it before. It has brought home the hard facts and true values of national patriotism. It has skilled its young men in the use of arms, taught its thinkers and writers the brittle illusion of leagues of nations and wordy internationalism. Peace, like charity, begins at home. It can only be maintained in future if Britain, her Empire, and the English-speaking peoples remain armed to keep safe the seaways and airways of the world.

I told old William my tale of the harbour-master of Pin Mill as we sat in that little wooden club in the boat-builder's yard at West Mersea. We talked of the future, of world peace and the Navy, of fishing and farming, and of what may be in store for those who live by those twin arts.

William put his finger on the essential truth. "We gotter keep our young chaps in good work, fishin' and farmin'," he said, solemn purpose in his apostolic old eyes. "We bin a-lettin' the fishin' folk and the farmin' folk down too long. They're the salt o' the sea an' the salt o' the good earth, sir. They're a wunnerful wise lot o' men. Take a chap what's fishin' or in a merchantman. He knows the way o' the sea an' the wind. He can read by the tide an' the stars. If he's a ship's engineer he's a witch with an engine. He ain't only clever, but he's self-reliant—*self-reliant*. That's what we want.

"They're the chaps when you want ready-made men with good stummicks an' hard heads for the Navy in war. You can't make a sailor out of a clerk overnight. That's what we've tried to do with some on 'em this war!

"We gotter keep up the fishin' industry after the war, so as we keep the young chaps at sea.

"An' if you've got plenty of folks farmin' an' livin' on the land you've got young fellers that ain't only able to feed you, but are fit ter fight—not like some o' these pore, herrin'-gutted, holler-chested little fellers what the towns breed. We can raise men on our soil as big as them Australians and New Zealanders. I count if they hadn't bin so ready to come forrard with some o' their big six-footers we might ha' copped it worse'n we have. The towns o' this country is too big. They swaller up the men an' make monkeys on 'em."

CHAPTER V

I leave my neighbours to their thought;
  My choice it is, and pride,
On my own lands to find my sport,
  In my own fields to ride.

WILFRED SCAWEN BLUNT, "The Old Squire"

Linnett, the Saxon Fowler of Bradwell-juxta-Mare—Vigil by the Roman Fort—Gossip at the Victory on Mersea Island—Poaching on Old Hall Marshes—When Bill Wyatt blacked his Face—The Shooting of Swan Mussett—"He's Still Full o' Shot"—"A Head Place for Rum 'uns"—Salvaging an Uncle from the Mast-head with an Eel-pick—The Gunner who looked like a Hot Cross Bun

WE STABLED THE HORSES THAT NIGHT IN A BARN BY WEST MERSEA Hall. That Elizabethan manor farmhouse crouches by the Saxon church, its face looking across the estuary to the lonely chapel of St Peter's-on-the-Wall on the south shore. That old chapel, built of narrow Roman bricks from the vanished fort of Othona, a garrison of the Count of the Saxon Shore, is the oldest 'cathedral' in Britain. Once a year in June they hold a service in the tiny chapel on the sea-wall. Lonely amid sea lavender and corn-fields, it holds barely two dozen people, but it marks the site and has some of the stones of the original cathedral of Bishop Cedd, Bishop of the Eastern Saxons in A.D. 650.

Through the fields, knee-deep in wheat, walks the parson, white and black canonicals blowing in the wind. The choir follows and behind them fishermen, rubber-booted, the ploughmen from the plough, the farmer from the stock-yard, and villagers from Bradwell-juxta-Mare. Their sweet singing rouses the curlew from the marsh, the dove from the elm, and the finch from the dog-rose. There, betwixt sea and land, on the verge of the hazy flats, they praise God.

In Stuart times the chapel was a beacon tower for seamen. Georgian smugglers hid their barrels within its walls. In the war of 1914–18 it was an orderly-room for a lonely outpost of troops. In the years between cattle wandered in and out, horses sheltered in it from the easterly gale, the peregrine paused in his lordly quartering to gaze upon sea and corn-field from its roof-tree. The jackdaw nested in its walls, and the white owl snored beneath its rafters.

To-day, thanks to the generosity of the late Mr Parker, of Down Hall, it is restored to the worship of God.

I thought of these things, of the pageant of thirteen hundred years of ships and men and history which that humble little church has seen, as I unsaddled Robert under the pear-trees of West Mersea Hall.

I thought, too, of Walter Linnett, that leather-faced, blue-eyed Saxon with the fair hair of far-off northern blood. Linnett lives in a three-roomed cottage, founded on Roman brick, built of ships' timbers and barge-boarding, on the seaward side of the sea-wall at the foot of the old chapel. Slow-spoken, soft-voiced, he is of the last of the true fisherman-fowlers. His tiny house, crouching beneath the sea-wall, shadowed by wind-swept blackthorns and apple-trees, is one of the loneliest dwellings in all southern England. To north and east of his door stretch saltings and the sea. His duck punts swing at his garden fence. A big tide and a high wind blow the salt water into the garden and spume into the kitchen. The village is two and a half miles across the fields by footpath. His neighbours are the brown marsh hares, the redshank piping and curlew ghostly in the mist of dawn. In winter black geese in thousands come clanging up the coast. In summer the terns dip and scream, hover like white butterflies, and plunge like plummets into the tide. Eels work in the mud, and crabs scuttle in the shining rills.

Linnett has shot more wild geese than any man I know. In peace-time he supplied the London markets with brent-geese at a shilling a head, mallard and widgeon at ninepence each, teal at sevenpence, and all the plover, oxbirds, godwits, and redshank you could desire at a few pennies apiece. It is a poor reward for the hazards of gunning in those bitter tideways, lying on his belly in a cranky, home-made punt with not more than six inches of freeboard above water, a death-trap in ice or stormy weather. When the fogs shut down there are no fog bells to guide him home across the treacherous flats. He lives by instinct. A wise man, a natural man.

In summer and autumn he works at fishing and eeling, or winkling on the mud with, chance times, a week or two at the plough or in the harvest field. He sees no company and desires none. Wise in winds and tides, he knows the way of a bird and the going of a ship. He is near to God, far from man, and the better man for it. London he has never seen, and I doubt if he has ever been in a train or a cinema.

He and his shrewd, humorous wife have raised a family of fine, strong young men, fair-haired giants with the true East Coast Saxon blood in them. From that tiny cottage which, with a fine dignity, has put itself *outside* the sea-wall, within the jurisdiction of sea and not of land, they have gone forth in big ships to the four quarters of the earth.

When the bombers droned over in the bitter stars, when land-mines fell and bombs uprooted great elms, when the whole coast shook and shuddered with the fierce thunder of the Battle of Britain, when on any night the grey German hordes might have come stealing up the estuary as came the invading Dane, Linnett stayed on. His duck guns were loaded, his heart high in a fine faith in himself.

The sophisticated may call it a pathetic and ridiculous picture. But to Walter Linnett, the last human outpost on that bleak point of the marshes where the Romans set their great fort, it was very real. The simple 'fowler, sitting at night in his lamp-lit, tiny kitchen, his wife sewing by the fire, his cases of stuffed wildfowl gleaming in the fire-light, was the ultimate sentinel. He stood in the ghostly shoes of the centurions. He walked the dark sea-fields where once the Roman eagles flew. He slept, when day dawned, beneath a humble roof whose proud foundations were the bricks of Imperial Rome.

When at last, in those early days of war, troops, guns, and search-lights came down to the marshes, when barbed wire went up and concrete was put down, I doubt if a man or an officer among them knew that they were merely taking over from the old Saxon 'fowler.

Thinking of Walter Linnett and his sons, now fighting in destroyers and merchant convoys, I walked with Jim from the Hall barn to that comfortable inn, the White Hart. It faces the church and the great walnut-tree. It keeps an eye on the smugglers' look-out, that odd, black, dovecot-like erection on the roof of the barn in the bend of the road. Built when Charles I was king, its cellars have known many a smuggled keg of brandy and of rum.

Here, indeed, is a pretty thought, that, within a square hundred yards of this village, capital of a highly independent island whose creeks and saltings cut it off from the rest of England, you have the church and the manor house, the smugglers' look-out and the Carolean inn with the great walnut-tree and the flowering chestnut round whose base sit the elders on sunny evenings, the Witan of the village.

There is a road which they call Captains' Road, because of the sea captains who live therein, and in the garden of a house, called in the Roman way Casa Pontis—for this Blackwater was to them the river Pont—you will see, dug plainly in the grass, the wheel-like foundations, yards wide, of the Roman pharos, the lighthouse whose leaping beacon guided the galleys up-river when Hadrian was Emperor.

Now Mr Fahy, who is landlord of the White Hart, is in the pattern of Mersea. He has soldiered in India and the East, fought in his fair share of wars, earned his medals, and never yet lost the grip of his hand or the twinkle in his eye. He has a fine taste in old glass and gleaming mahogany, a nice eye for Georgian silver and old brass, a sentimental hankering for that Victorian sort of oil painting which shows you *The Harvest Wain*, or *A Windmill in Suffolk*, or, better still, *Stormy Day at Sea off Great Yarmouth* with a herring buss beating in, reefed down, spray flying, gulls wheeling in the trough of the waves.

Those simple, grandmotherly daubs in oil are out of date, laughed at by the slick, lazy poseurs of the last twenty years. They find it easier to slap gobbets of paint on a blank canvas, to draw childish crudities, mix screaming colours, to outrage sense and form in order to win the magpie attention of the half-baked. But, like Mr Fahy, I like the soft colours, the grace of form, the truth of detail, the presentation of real things.

I like his Victorian oils, his grandmother's mahogany, his winking brass, his stuffed ducks in glass cases, his fat spaniels and scrubbed kitchen, his bar full of salty men in peaked caps and blue guernseys. I like his hand-grip, which would hold a mule. I like his shrewd, dark, Irish eye, his sense of fun, his fine contempt for little minds and little values. Which is why we slept that night in his great four-posters after we had eaten a leash of early widgeon and drunk a bottle of his port.

But first there was a walk down the road to the Victory. Now do not think that all life on Mersea Island centres in its inns, although to be sure it has a fine showing—the Dog and Pheasant, lonely in the fields by East Mersea, where the Royalist gunners fired on Cromwell's ships as they sailed up the Colne to besiege Colchester; the Fox, which lies artfully at the cross-roads to catch the unwary; the White Hart, hand in glove with the church; and the Victory, standing bold on a little bluff on the coast road, with a shiplike balcony, a tall mast to fly its flag, its face to a fleet of anchored boats, its windows winking in the western sun.

West Mersea Victory is a password wherever yachtsmen sail. If the owner has not slipped ashore one time for a chop or steak be sure that his skipper or a hand has smoked a pipe and drunk a pint within its walls. It has a bar, long and many-windowed, bright with coloured prints of wildfowl; a snug parlour which is a picture-gallery of foxhunting and shooting, pig-sticking and deer-stalking, tiger hunting and coursing, a gallery of Cecil Aldin, Lionel Edwardes, "Snaffle," and G. D. Armour. A few years back its dining-room carried a fine show of heads—tiger, buck, antelope, pig, red deer, fox, and otter. They, alas, have gone.

In the Victory the talk is always of the sea, of 'fowling and yachting, fishing and oysters, eels and raids on Old Hall. Old Hall is that wonderful peninsula of marsh which you may see from the windows. To the south it is bounded by the salt water of Tollesbury Fleet, where the smacks lie, and to the north by Salcott creek, where scarce a boat sails. It has nine hundred acres of grazing marsh cut by innumerable creeks and fleets. There are more than a hundred acres of fresh water on this paradise of duck. You can run a thousand sheep on it or graze four hundred cattle and a hundred wild horses. When "Crawley" de Crespigny had the shooting he and his party bagged 1340 duck in a year. When my old friend, Dr Salter, of D'Arcy House, had it, forty years ago, he saw or shot anything you like to think of from a golden eagle to an avocet and an osprey—both now at Layer Marney Towers—from a great white heron and a spoonbill to a quail and a Temminck's stint. Most of his collection is in the Chelmsford Museum to-day.

Ever since Old Hall was embanked it has been the natural raiding ground of the Mersea men. No matter who was squire at Guisnes Court, that odd house built out of the stones of Old London Bridge, whether it was Thomas Godfrey Binney, who first invited me there in 1914; the Belgian adventurer Loewenstein, who bought it after 1918 and left it derelict for years, or the late Hurlstone Hortin, Old Hall has always been a battle-ground. Mersea men have raided it by night and day. To poach its duck or hares is their honourable adventure, like a Zulu boy's first spear in a lion.

"Time I get me owd porchin' cap on I'm fit to goo anywheres," said William, who, by some curious telepathy, walked in at one door of the Victory as Jim and I entered by the other. "There's forever o' ducks jist gone into Pennyhole Bottom on Owd Hall. I've half a mind to git me gun out and goo up an' sing 'em a song. Charm 'em, yer know!" with a wink.

"Do, ye'll het to black ye face, Willum," sang out Old Zeb Milgate, from the corner. . . . Zebedee is old, very old, small and shrunken, with quick eyes, a Captain Kettle beard, and an uncomfortably clear memory. William guffawed.

"Thass forty year agoo," he explained. "Time I hed ter black me face. I was on Owd Hall gittin' me dinner. I peeked over the wall, with me face well hid in the grass an' me owd hat jammed down. . . . There set an owd hare, jist t'other side of a bullick what was a-grazin'. I cud see that owd hare right through the bullick's legs. So I shoves the snout o' me gun through the grass, squinted down the barrel, an' says, 'Now, Miss Sally, you'll hev to jump quick if you don't want to line my belly!'

"Bang goes the gun. Oover pops the hare. Dead as a stone. Up goes the bullick on all four legs, a yard an' a half in the air. Sprung up like a jumpin' jack, he did. Across the marsh he goes like steam-o. Down the wall I runs, quick as light, jumps a dyke, collars me owd hare, an' legs it back up the wall.

"'Howd you on!' hollers out some one. Damn! There was owd Fell, the keeper, an' his mate a-comin' fer me like a couple o' long-dogs. I warn't a-goin' to howd on fer them. I hops in me dinghy, shoves orf, an' owd Sam Jennings an' me rowed orf like one o'clock. Over the wall comes they two keepers. They hops in a little owd skiff what lay in a rill. I ha'n't seen it—du, I'd ha' stove the b——r in! They rows arter us, oars a-goin' like windmills, hollerin' out they'd shute us.

"'I know yer! I knows the names o' both on yer. I'll hev the law on yer!' hollers out owd Felly. I know'd he didn't. He were too fur orf. But I tips up me owd powder-flask, gits a half-handful o' that black powder, spits a great gob in it, an' I rubs that all over me face, an' me mate's. We looked like a couple o' blackaboys.

"'Now row for the b——r,' I says to Sam. 'Head on, boy, hard as ye goo. Ram 'em and sink 'em. We'll make the b——s swim!'

"Away we goo, rowin' like one o'clock. Straight for 'em. They seed what was up. They was only in a cranky owd skiff, easy upset. Tide a-flowin' an' sixteen foot o' water under 'em!

"Damn, they turned and rowed for the shore like one o'clock. We never catched 'em, more's the pity. But we shot by within six foot on 'em, an' as we passed I hit the water wi' me owd oar sich a crack. Chucked a bucket o' water over both on 'em. That christened 'em!

"'Keep you on land, ye b——s!' I sings out. 'That's your right place. You're safer there. This here creek's ourn. We don't want no trespassers.'"

There was a guffaw from a knot of fishermen. 'Duck' Mussett [1] advanced the opinion that William was still "as fit and fierce as a fleet of lions." An ancient mariner in the corner with a long white beard, a fine, statesmanlike face, and a thoughtful brow nodded wisely. William was "allus a young tarmagant."

Jim, accustomed to grooms and huntsmen, whips and men who travel on the back of a horse by way of woods and fields, was glancing curiously at these sons of longshore and foreshore. For there is a great gulf fixed between your uplander, even though he comes from only two or three miles inland, and the fisher and 'fowler. They are worlds apart. Two different races of men, different in thought, outlook, manner, and speech. He nudged me quietly, pointed to the bearded ancient in the corner, and said through the hubbub of talk:

"Who's the fine old gennelman, sir? He's got a face on him like a regular old wiseacre."

I explained that he was 'Swan' Mussett, "well into his eighty," great-grandfather and head of the Mussett clan. They are a fine, centuries-old family of fishermen and sailors. They have produced great gunners and notable yacht skippers, descendants of a Huguenot family who settled on the Essex coast after the Revocation of the Edict of Nantes. They own their own smacks, oyster-beds, houses, acres, and boats. A free, fearless, independent race of yeomen of the sea. They and the D'Wits, who came over from France and the Low Countries when a religious terror, forerunner of the pagan tyranny of Hitler, stalked Europe and hounded free men to English shores. Even so, with the Poles, the Dutch, the Czechs, and the Free French, history repeats itself to-day.

I explained that he was christened Swan because, winters before, he had been shot in the face by a punt-gunner who mistook his white beard in the moonlight for a wild swan and gave him a pound of swan shot to be getting on with. Pointing out of the window, I added, "He was shot up Samson's Creek, just over there."

"No, no, Mister Wentworth, no, no. That he warn't. He were shot up Mell, a moile away. I know 'cos I shot the owd b——r. Damn, he's me uncle. I oughter know."

A long, beaky-nosed, young fisherman regarded me reprovingly.

"That was like this here. That was one cowd Jannywary night, tide a-flowin', bright moon, sharp as a knife. There was several owd wild swans about. That young Captain Campbell what live at

[1] Since blown up and killed in a Tollesbury smack.

Layer Marney Towers had told me that he'd gie me a half a quid if I'd git him a swan. So me missus says, 'Goo on, boy, git yer gun. There's several owd swans a-singin' out up the crick.'

"Orf I goos in me punt. I got round Shingle Head, up the river past the pier an' into Mell Crick afore I seed anythin' like a swan. But there, under the cant [the high lip of the saltings] I seed suffin' shine white in the moon. That looked jist like an owd wild swan. Damn, that was me owd uncle's white beard where the moon catched it! He was a-squattin' on a board on the mud.

"How was I to know the owd fule wud be out on a cowd night like that? He was well on into his seventy, an' he oughter bin happed up in bed, 'long of a nice young woman to keep him warm."

A shocked wink and a shamefaced grin from Swan, who was listening unobtrusively.

"I lays down in me punt, sets her nose right, an' sprits along head on for this owd swan. There that set all comf'able. I gits within a hunderd yards, creeps up to eighty, squints down me barrel, an' sez to meself, 'Now, me beauty, I'll git yer. There sets me half quid.' I sprits along another yard or two an', thinks I, 'I 'on't spoil his plumage. I'll let him hev it now.'

"I pulls the lanyard. Orf goes the big gun with a boomp an' a holler like a row o' housen fallin' down. That ketched me owd uncle slap in the face an' the belly. Got the owd b——r right in the middle o' the charge."

"What did he do?" asked Jim, awed.

"Du! He shot up like a bloody monkey! He blared like a bull. He jounced up and down in the mud like a jumpin' jack. Damn, he did holler! He'd ha' done fine in parson's choir.

"I runs me punt ashore, jumps out, and ketches hold o' the seat o' his trousers. He was a-clawin' away at his owd face, bleedin' like an owd pig on pig-killin' day. He kep' all on a-hollerin'.

"'Howd your owd clapper, uncle,' I says. 'Thass yer nevvy what shot yer. Blarst, yew goo a-settin' out on the mud this time o' night, an' you might know suffin' 'ud happen to ye. Come on, git in my punt, an' I'll row ye home. We'll draw them shot out on yer.'

"Damn. He wouldn't listen nohow. He kep' all on a-shrikkin' like an owd barn owl. An' a-jouncin' about. So I fetches the silly owd fule a clip on the jaw. That onsensed him! Then I drug him across the mud an' got him in me punt."

"Good lord," I said. "First of all you shoot your uncle, and then you knock him out."

"Ah! I hed to. Couldn't git no sense out on 'im no other way. I reckon he'd upset the punt if I hedn't." A chorus of professional approval. Even Uncle Swan nodded judicially, muttered softly, "That he did, the young hound."

"I rowed him home," went on the young hound; "got him on me showders, carried him up the Hard an' into the house-place. Me daughter went orf on a bike an' fetches the doctor. He come with a bag full o' tools, gits out his twizzers, an' starts a-workin' on owd uncle. I reckon he drawed half a pound o' shot out on him. But he's all right now. Fit as a fleet o' lions. Look at him settin' there with his owd quart pot, likin' hisself!

"But there," he added seriously, "he's still full o' shot. D'yu goo acrost, Master Wentworth, an' run your hand over his owd chops. They're full o' shot. They run about under the skin like a lot o' bloody lice!"

Uncle Swan nodded. Jim looked troubled. He swallowed his beer with an odd, apprehensive, far-away look. I suddenly remembered that I had promised to take him punt-gunning that winter.

"That'll gie ye somethin' ter scribble about, Master Wentworth," put in William. "Marsea's the head place for rum 'uns. Time I wor a little owd boy there warn't a place in all England cud come nigh it. Telly fer why. We had a dancin' doctor, a fightin' parson, an' a whorin' magistrite. I count there ain't another place in England kin show ye the head o' that."

There was a moment's silence. Native pride, justified to the hilt, modestly forbore self-commendation. Albert Lovechild Greenleaf, that excellent man who once tended my ferrets, mended my roof, looked after my punt, and was ready for sport by day or night, broke in.

"What about the time some o' you chaps salvaged owd Swan?" he asked. Delighted chuckles savoured the memory. Swan looked mildly embarrassed.

"Ah! That was a rum 'un. Owd Swan bought hisself a smack. Now when us Marsea men buy a smack we reckon ter keep that in the family. But owd Swan kept it to hisself. He hed a little owd titty-totty boy from Tollesbury as a hand—a furriner! Fust day he was out in this smack that blew a gile. Big tide a-runnin' an' wind easterly. 'Bout midday my missus comes ter me an' says, 'Git yer spyglass. Goo yu into the garden an' hev a spy. There's a smack gorn agroun' on the Naas End. I du believe thass owd Uncle Swan.'

"I has a spy. That was—hard and fast! Waves a-breakin' oover the deck, Uncle Swan up the mast. There warn't no boy nowhere.

"Orf I goes in me dinghy with another chap, rowin' hard. That took us half an hour agin' wind an' tide. Time we gits there the decks was under, an' thar warn't no more'n ten foot o' mast stickin' outer the water.

"Owd Uncle Swan sets atop o' that mast like an owd cormorant. His beard was a-blowin' out in the wind like a pennant. He looked reg'lar sour.

"We rows round an' round, within a yard or two on him, niver once lookin' up. Thinks I, we'll hev a game. We'll pretend we ain't seen him. Then I looks up.

"'Lord, Uncle Swan,' I sings out, 'what on airth are ye a-doin' settin' up there? Pole-squattin' or larnin' navigation?' Damn, he did swear! Langwidge! That was a head masterpiece. He must 'a' bin bargin' up London River when he was a nipper ter pick up them words.

"'Come on,' I sings out. 'Shut your blaspheemious owd clapper. Git in the boat, and we'll row ye home. Ye carn't stop there all night. We'll git the smack orf in the mornin'.

"'Thass my smack, an' I'm a-stoppin' wi' her,' he hollers. 'I know what you're arter—salvige! You 'on't git no salvige outer me.'

"'I don't want no salvige—I'm yer nevvy, ain't I?'

"'Nevvy! I knows yer! You're arter money. Salvige is thicker'n blood wi' you.'

"Well, that reg'lar riled me. 'Are ye a-comin' down or not?' I says. 'No,' he hollers, 'I ain't. I'm a-stoppin' here.'

"Wi' that I picks up me owd eel shear, five damn' great prongs on it big as yer fingers, an' I gives him a shove up the backside! Damn, he let out a squawk like an owd cormorant, an' he cum down in me boat with a run like a sack o' wheat. We salviged he orl right!"

I suddenly remembered a story which had reached me by letter when I was lying ill that second winter of the war. It had borne the authentic Mersea touch. Here was the time and place for the baptism of truth.

"What was that about an amateur gunner that some one peppered last winter?" I asked.

"Har! So we did. That was a rum 'un. Some young London feller cum down here. New punt, new gun. Know'd everythin', high an' mighty. Reg'lar liked hisself.

"Out he goos one night in his punt. Half a moon an' a lot o' cloud. He gits well out in the river where the tide runs a good four knots. Lucky that warn't a-blowin'. Seems as though he couldn't handle his punt right.

"Anyway, along comes young Harold, sprittin' along. He sees this punt broadside on ahead on him. That looked jist like a pack o' ducks swimmin' close together. Yu know how they look.

"So young Harold no more'n has a goo at him with the big gun. He give him half a pound o' B.B. Reg'lar riddled the punt."

"Did he hit the man?" Jim inquired, with more than professional interest.

"Hit 'im! Har! He couldn't ha' know'd how ter work a punt properly, 'cos his backside was a-stickin' up in the air. There was one pellet ketched him fair across the cheeks on it. That cut a reg'lar furrow. I reckon that chap looked like a hot cross bun for a month arterwards!"

On that happy note we retired under the moon to the comparative security of the mahogany four-posters at the White Hart.

HARVEST HEAT-HAZE OVER CORNFIELDS BY ALRESFORD CREEK

Photo Douglas Went, Brightlingsea

HOLKHAM HALL

Photo Harvey Barton and Son, Ltd., Bristol

ON WALLASEA ISLAND

Will Goodchild (*centre*), of East Horndon Hall, with (*left*) Jack Rebell, whose great-great-grandfather worked for Will's great-great-grandfather.

Photo Douglas Went, Brightlingsea

CHAPTER VI

> Far away and far away the distant Horn is blowing;
> The chasing, chiming beauties are a cloud against the cloud.
> Waves of white and scarlet down the open field are flowing,
> And through the heart of England the Horn is blowing loud.
>
> WILL H. OGILVIE

The Little Ways of Foxes—The Fox in the Owl's Nest—Reynard on a Roof—When Sir Claude de Crespigny swam for a Fox—"A Rum Old Day"—Charles James and the Ploughman—On boxing Horses—The Start by Road—To the Heckford Angel and Maldon

A MOTHER-OF-PEARL MORNING. SUN GLINTING THROUGH CHESTNUT leaves. Jackdaws chacking about the church tower. Curlew calling down on the opal muds, their voices clear in the crisp air. The church clock stood at a solemn, golden-fingered six. I rolled out of an enormous mahogany bed and looked from the diamond-paned windows. A high, blue, September morning. White clouds spread like lambs across the sky. The early sun was drawing up the mist from the mud flats. It glistened on the dewy grass by the roadside, glowed in geraniums and hollyhocks. From over by the barn came the cheerful whistle of Jim at horse-work. That man always surprises the sun.

I got up. A cold bath to straighten the back, and out into the early sunlight. Down by the Queen's Hard there was the usual stir of oystermen and longshoremen, rubber-booted, rowing off in dinghies, baling out punts, or busy in oyster-pits. A smack was cranking up its anchor. Gulls wheeled and mewed. A heron stood delicately in the mud on Packing House Island.

"I count thass better'n mucky owd London, ain't it?" said a voice behind me. "I reckon ye like yesself time you're down here."

"I do."

"Ah! London's a rum owd hole. Yew may make a bit o' gowd up there, but that owd London, that'll rob yer in the end, sure as harvest."

We discussed oysters. The winter's bitter cold and grinding masses of ice had destroyed millions of spat. Icebergs, formed by great slabs of ice which the swirl of the tides had up-ended and knitted in frozen pinnacles, had scraped thousands of oysters from every 'lay' in the creeks. But the harvest, now beginning, was not so bad as they had expected. There were still enough oysters to make dredging worth while, still a few to spare for an early morning crack with a friend. He scooped up half a dozen, opened them with his shut-knife. We swallowed three apiece, fresh with the tang of salt water. Earth nor sea can offer no finer morning eye-opener.

"Same as you wuz sick an' had a dozen Marsea oysters fer yer breakfast, another dozen fer your dinner, an' another goo on 'em afore yew went to bed, an' tuk a swim in this here salt water an' a roll in that owd black mud, a man'd be as strong as a bull. Telly fer why. That owd mud's full of phorsphorus. Har! I reckon rajium tew. Watch a man walk on that owd mud at night. That pick up all in fire. That fare to reg'lar glitter same as if that wuz alight. Hev a roll in that. That can't do yer northin' but good. I count that'd liven up a dead 'un!"

There is truth in this longshore philosophy. East Coast mud is undoubtedly radio-active, charged with phosphorus. I have a theory that it holds the ozone much more effectively than a sandy shore, and that this accounts for the strong air, the most bracing in all England, the air that blows between the North Foreland and the Wash.

Breakfast over, we rode by the top of the sea-wall to the Strood. A shaggy, cattle-dotted marsh lay on the right, and beyond, stubbles and yellow mustard ran to the skyline. The creek and the saltings lay on the left, salt water brimming to the foot of the wall. Islands of sea lavender glowed purple. It was a narrow path to ride, barely two feet in width, a drop into salt water on the left, a sheer fall of ten or twelve feet to the right. The horses trod it like cats.

Beyond the Strood, back on the mainland of England, with the little independent land of Mersea dreaming behind in the harvest sun, we took to the fields and set a course by the north end of the great Abberton Reservoirs, that chain of new Essex lakes, to Abberton Manor and Friday Wood. The horse-box was waiting at Brickwall Farm beyond Bottle End. The plan of the day was to cover the ten miles from Mersea to Brickwall across country, box the horses over thirteen miles of hard road to Maldon, stay the night, look up a few fishing and farming friends, visit the Fordson Estate farms at Boreham House the next day, box on to Canewdon, see more farms, and travel thence by road to Hatfield in Hertfordshire, where Jack Olding had promised to stage a demonstration of the most modern farming machinery, before we set out on the greater adventure of Suffolk, Norfolk, the Fens, and Lincolnshire.

It was as we came by Abberton Manor, where once lived that cock-angel of all great shots, the late R. H. Rimington-Wilson, that we fell to talking of fox-hunting and the little ways of foxes. What is more natural when you are on the back of a horse, on a grand cubbing morning, September crisp in the air, the trees full-leaved as galleons?

There is a boggy field below Abberton Manor, where peewits wheel white-waistcoated. At the bottom runs the Layer Brook, sweet-bordered by cuckoo-flowers in summer, quick with springing teal in winter.

Of a sudden my mind went harking back to that hunting morning, four long, unbelievable winters ago, when the horn went twanging on the wind, hound music raised echoes in the valley that the Saxons loved, and the fox set his mask for Wigborough and the safe harbourage of the marshes beyond. Jim Rodd, that wiry, whip-cord, dapper little man with the quick legs and twinkling eye who is half-fox and half-farmer, remembered it also. For three-quarters of their lives Jim and his brother Maurice have farmed their land and hunted the fox in that triangle of country which you will find marked on your hunting map as the territories of the East Essex, the Essex Farmers', the Essex Union, and the Essex and Suffolk Hunts. It is a dukedom of foxes whose borders range from Burnham-on-Crouch in the south to Manningtree in the north, from Bradwell-juxta-Mare in the east to the barley stubbles and Elizabethan manors of Gosfield and Finchingfield, Leez Priory and Moyns Hall to the west.

Have you never taken a stretch of country which you love, enshrined it in memory when it is far from you, and recaptured, in the nostalgia of absence, the high days and bright days of sport, of singing birds, of shining waters, and the smell of June roses which made it the enchanted land? So, on this September morning we recaptured as we rode the memories of foxes and their little ways.

There is no limit set by man and little by God to the way of a fox when he is pressed. I remember as a boy puzzling to myself over that story of the fox, infested by fleas, who rid himself of them by backing gradually into a pond until the fleas were driven from the tip of his brush along the highway of his back to the tip of his nose—

which he ducked suddenly, leaving them swimming. It is a pity Mr Churchill cannot perform this aqueous feat with some of his yapping critics.

I told Jim this nursery tale. He had never seen its like happen. But he remembered the fox who, when they hunted him from Oliver's, pointed his mask for Abberton Manor, dashed in the front door of that dignified Queen Anne house, scuttled, muddied, up the stairway, scattering shrill maids, and went to ground in the bath. There, in an immaculate setting of tiles and marble, he was killed in a welter of mud and blood.

From below Abberton Manor, as we rode, you can just see sometimes, under a cloud of gulls, a glimpse of the chimneys of Berechurch Hall. In the park of that derelict mansion stands an old oak. In that tree, six times running, a dog fox, wise to the last grey hair in his brush, took refuge. Many a fox takes to a tree, but this one evidently had a plot with a barn-owl. For he scrambled up the hollow inside the trunk, dislodged the owl, and went to roost in its eyrie of feathers, bones, and small white skulls.

There was a fox, Jim recalled, over at the village of Elmsett, in the Essex and Suffolk country, who regularly climbed up *two* houses at once when hard-pressed. I recollected Sir Alfred Pease telling me of a Yorkshire fox in his native dales who had a recognized pre-emption on the roof of a brewhouse belonging to one of those lonely dale farms which grow and brew all they need for the master and his men. Time after time it got to the brewhouse roof in a quick scramble up the ivy and there lay safe, nose between paws, grinning wickedly at the baying hounds beneath him. And Sir Alfred would doff his cap to the shrewd old varmint and whip them off.

But this Suffolk fox had discovered in that sweet village of thatched roofs and bee-murmurous elms two tiny cottages which clung so closely together that a man could not edge himself through the gap between them. They were indeed like two elderly spinsters who, having suffered the guileful wickedness of man, were sworn to an everlasting close defensiveness.

The fox would make straight for these twin cottages, spring a yard in the air, and, using hind legs and forepaws on either wall, scramble up, like a sailor on a rope ladder, until he reached the roof-tree where, said Jim, "Our old Master Reynard would sit and giggle at us. But he was too good an old boy to have him off it."

I told him that pretty story of a day with the Quorn when the fox, hard put to it, in a last ironic desperation, shot like a rusty streak into a chicken-house in the middle of a field. The fox went in at one end, and a cackling cascade of hens flew out at the other. And there, amid the discarded feathers of his would-be victims, Charles James was killed in their bedroom. A sardonic story.

We topped the hill and saw, miles to the south-east, the broad estuary of the Blackwater gleaming like a red-gold sword in the sun. Memory went back to that day, twenty or more years ago, when the East Essex found a fox hard by Champion Lodge, hunted him through the Tothams, pressed him close by the medieval walls and pepperpot turrets of Beckingham Hall, down on to the marshes at Goldhanger, past the old decoy pond of which Folkard writes that the 'coyman once took a cart-load of dun-birds at one fall of the hinge-over net, and on to the saltings where a bitter January tide was brimming against the sea-wall.

The wind blew easterly. Widgeon rose in their thousands. Curlew went screaming down the creek. The fox, bold as a North Sea marshman, took to salt water. He swam fifty yards out to a patch of saltings, no bigger than a dining-room floor. There, safe and dripping, he stood and grinned at his pursuers. Master and whips, huntsmen and hounds, followers and marshmen, stood shivering in the wind.

Down the old green barge road came galloping that latter-day Corinthian, the hero of my boyhood, the late Sir Claude Champion de Crespigny. That fine, fighting old man—boxer, duellist, balloonist, soldier, fox-hunter, and squire—must then have been "near on his seventy."

He took one look at the fox, threw off his pink, called a man to lug off his boots, plunged into the bitter salt water, and swam out to the patch of saltings. Then, as Charlie Stoker, the marshman of Goldhanger, tells you, "Our owd Sir Claude he runned that there fox round the salts, ketched him, bruk his neck, give a holler, and swam back with the b—— between his teeth." On the sea-wall, dripping from head to foot, freezing in the bitter wind, the inextinguishable old baronet raised Reynard in both hands and with a "Who—whoop! tear 'im and eat 'im!" flung him to the baying hounds. That, I think, epitomizes the East Coast spirit.

There will be those who say why not leave a gallant fox to run another day. But if you have ever owned or tenanted a sea marsh, cut up by rills and gullies, riddled with rabbit-holes, a death-trap to man and horse, you will need no telling that these salty wildernesses are perfect sanctuaries for renegade foxes. They prey on the duck, kill the lambs, and lie out on the saltings, basking in the sun in a purple bed of sea lavender, safe from hound or gun. You must catch them where you find them.

For the other side of the picture there is the true tale of the fox at Colne Engaine who, four years ago, was hunted hard on a bitter, wet day. "I took a toss in a brook and came up with my mouth full of mud, moorhens, and eels," said Jim reminiscently. "When I jumped the next brook I saw a top hat floating about in the water under me. There was a gentleman in the Cavalry underneath it. That was a rum old day."

Well, this fox on that rum old day dragged himself wearily across a heavy plough. He came to two men ditching in a wide, wet ditch. Beyond them a ploughman rested on his plough handle, watching the chase.

The fox jumped deliberately into the ditch. It waded up it for twenty yards, scrambled painfully up the opposite bank, crawled across the furrows to the stationary plough.

And there, calmly and of set purpose, he crawled under the breast of the ploughshare and lay hidden—within a yard and a half of the ploughman's feet.

Hounds paused, baffled, at the ditch. The ploughman neither moved nor spoke. The ditchers stood and grinned. The Master saw—and turned a blind eye.

"Good-day, gentlemen," he said, raising his cap, "good-day to you, and to a great old gentleman who deserves another day to live."

And, so talking, we came to Brickwall Farm with its yellow walls and three-gabled red roof, a paddock full of ponies, and the tall pear-tree laden in the sun behind the long brick wall which gives its name.

There in the yard stood a great cream and black double horse-box, the object of solemn admiration by Mr and Mrs Robertson and Sheila the goat. Now a word about this horse-box. When peace reigned Derby winners trundled in it from Epsom to Doncaster. It is sprung, padded, painted, and chromium-plated fit for a king. It will take two horses, three men on the driving-seat, two in arm-chairs in the back, and two or three trusses of hay on the roof. There is electric light inside and a bell to tell the driver to stop if trouble starts in the back. You could not wish for a finer horse-box. I hired it from Mr Marsh, of Daimler's, for at that stage of the war there was little use for such vehicles for racing and not much good they could do in war. There it stood, shining, beckoning almost with a smug complacency as if to say that even the Department of Petroleum had sanctioned its appearance on the road. It is now an ambulance.

Now there is an art in boxing and unboxing horses. You must coax them in and coax them out. You must, to use a lovely old English phrase, "charm them to it." It is not much use hauling, pushing, or pulling. For if you do they may kick half the box to bits, yourself down the ramp, and lame themselves for a week.

Robert had travelled in many a horse-box. You do not grow to the philosophic age of nine without having learned a thing or two about horse-boxes. They teach you to expect strange unstablelike sounds, sudden jerks, starts and stops, and a new country each time the great side doors are opened. You travel with your tail pointing to the front and your head looking over a sort of half-door into the back cabin where sit, if you are a Derby winner, a couple of stable-lads to minister to your wants.

There is a zinc manger right under your nose, and under and beyond the mangers on either side of the cabin are drawers and lockers for such human and equine essentials as pads, brushes, rubbers, oils, embrocations, bottles of whisky, loaves of bread, a bit of cheese, a bag of apples, and anything the road may yield.

There are saddle-trees on either side of the back door, screwed firmly to the wall. Hooks whence swing bridles and curbs, jingling musically. Crops are hung up, their lashes tickling the floor. Stirrup-irons swing and jangle. There is hay in the mangers, beans in the bag, a pleasant, warm, companionable smell of horse and man. And from the back windows, if you lift your nose, snuffling from the manger, you will see the rolling roads of England unwinding between the hedges. It is no bad life for a horse.

"Lumme, I could live and sleep in here," said Jim, opening the back door, and sniffing. He looked exactly like a terrier who had found a new rabbit-bury. "Don't you worry about any bedrooms for me on the road. I'll curl up in here in me blankets on a truss of hay."

We loaded up. The typewriter, that soulless emblem of a mechanical age, was thrust, oil-cloth shrouded, into a cupboard. I hate machines. Boxes of paper, notebooks, and carbons, clips, envelopes, and rubber bands followed. "Huh! Looks like a damned office on the go," grunted Jim.

"Now, don't you swear—and keep out of my way." Mrs Friedberg, my four-foot-nine secretary, martyred to me for seventeen years, thrust him on one side. For a moment the two midgets glared. Here was something undreamt of in Jim's philosophy. She was fresh from London. He had never seen her before. She had never seen untouched rural England. Hitherto he had handled nothing more horrifying than an unbroken buck-jumper or a bag of ferrets.

His Waterloo had dawned. He gazed at her with the half-mournful surprise of a terrier which has suddenly had its nose bitten by a rat. From a distance I had the quiet laugh of a lifetime. It was better than cock-fighting.

A primus stove, saucepans, a frying-pan; tea, sugar, lard, pepper, salt; tins of cocoa, condensed milk, cups and saucers, knives and forks; a couple of jars of pickled onions, a bottle of port, apples, and plums; Spot, the terrier; a rabbiting spade; my great double-barrelled 8-bore, two 12-bores, boxes of cartridges, some wire snares; a couple of rods and tackle—all were loaded and stowed.

Two trusses of hay were hoisted on to the roof, a sack of oats shoved inside, and then the ramp was let down, and first Browny Boy, followed by Robert, was loaded and secured with head-stalls. Browny Boy, a six-year-old bay, standing fifteen two, neat and active, had never been in a box in his life. He gave the minimum of trouble. Five or six minutes of coaxing, having first allowed him to see Robert enter, and he mounted the ramp, stepping delicately as a cat. We were ready for the road.

Jim mounted the box, Mrs Friedberg clambered up—we had to lift her on to the first high step—and I got up on the nearside. Jim was driving.

And here let me pay a tribute to that remarkable little man's motor sense. Like me, he hates machines. Unlike me, he is sufficiently broad-minded to have learned to drive one. I have a vivid memory of his first essay with a motor-car. He had suddenly decided to pay his court to a young woman in Bournemouth some years before. So he hired a tiny car in Colchester, took a lesson in driving up and down back roads for an hour, got the hang of the thing, and started off for Bournemouth. He arrived—safely.

Since then he has driven cars, lorries, tractors, and motor-cycles, but never a horse-box. He started that day with a horse-box weighing, empty, just under four tons, fully loaded with two horses, three human beings, a load of hay, and a jumble of odds and ends. In the next few weeks he drove 1355 miles, always over un-signposted roads, through country new to him, often in total blackout after a hard day's riding over fields and farms.

We frequently cast up in villages after nightfall, several times at midnight, travelling down rutted farm roads and by-lanes in imminent peril of capsizing in dykes and ditches in the darkness.

He was up at five each morning, grooming his horses, rubbing and polishing. He cleaned boots, fed and watered, rode all day and drove half the night. He did not miss the road once. We had no accidents, neither horse went lame, and both returned as fresh and fit as when they set out. No man could earn a higher tribute.

We went by way of Heckford Bridge where the brook prattles under the road through an ancient red-brick bridge. A score of cottages sit sunning in the shallow valley. I have a great love for Heckford Bridge. I like Gold Grove, that long, hanging covert which straggles along the side of the hill above the brook, full of tall elms and silver birches, with a great oak here and there, primroses in the spring, foxes and pheasants in the autumn.

There are badgers in a sett in the hillside within a mile of Heckford Bridge. It is my secret joy to sit in a pollard oak and watch them snuffling and grunting among the leaves on a quiet night when the moon rides high and the hamlet is asleep. But wild horses would not drag from me the whereabouts of that citadel of Brock, the largest and cleanest wild animal in Britain. The badger is far too pleasant, too brave and too harmless a fellow to be shot, trapped, or hunted. We can spare him a few young rabbits for his breakfast, bless him for the rats he kills and the wasps' nests he destroys.

We can envy him his labyrinthine sett, deep in the hill, which contains sleeping-chambers, eating-chamber, closet, and storehouse. A great heap of hay or straw makes the beds in a badger's sett. If you sit up in an oak-tree, early in the flush of dawn, you will see Mrs Brock bring it all out to sweeten in the sun.

There is an old forge in Heckford Bridge, a farrier's shop with a pretty brass of a saddle-horse on the door, hard by the Angel. And when I dream a dream of inns, often my fortunate nightmare, you may be sure the Heckford Angel is among them. Cream-fronted, bow-windowed, and Georgian, it sits by the roadside in the sun, hard by the brook. There are six great iron rings in the wall for farmers to tie their nags thereat, a yard full of chickens and ducks, a red-roofed, rambling row of stables and hen-houses, and in the yard, a thing you will not find at one inn in a hundred—a watercress pond. It is perhaps twenty feet long by about six feet broad at the top end and two feet wide at the bottom. A pear-shaped little pond, red-walled, holding six inches of crystal-cold water. The spring gushes out under a stone, and tinkles under the floor of the cellar and dairy of the Angel. Do you wonder that the beer is always cool, the butter fresh, and the eggs new? There are even men who go to the Heckford Angel to drink, first, its water before they sample its beer, for they say that it is a medicine which the Romans knew. That was before the Elizabethans made the watercress pond.

The back door of the Angel is of grey, old, oak timbers, nail-studded, iron-bound. The bar is stone-flagged and raftered. Jones, the innkeeper, is shrewd and humorous and loves a horse. Mrs Jones is plump and merry and cracks a joke. So, of course, we stopped at the Angel for a glass of cold beer, a bite of bread and cheese, and watercress. Then on by the winding road past Birch Hall park gates. Past Layer Wood, where that grand old sportsman, Dr J. H. Salter, once commandeered a travelling German band and put them all into the wood, blowing cornets, clarionets, and trombones and beating the big drum to flush the pheasants. Past Pods Wood and Tiptree Heath, where the smugglers in the old days hid their barrels from the Blackwater in pits among the gorse. Through Great Totham, where Williams, who sailed in the great gaff topsail cutters of Lord Dunraven's day, keeps the Cricketers; by Captains Wood and Champion Lodge, where old Claude de Crespigny lived as the uncrowned king of Essex, to Maldon.

CHAPTER VII

He rises early and he late takes rest
And sails intrepid o'er the wat'ry waste,
Waits the return of shot-seal [flight time] on the lake
And listens to the wild-fowls' distant quack;
At dusk steers homeward with a plenteous freight.

Life of a Fenman (1771)

Maldon, the Town of Plough and Sail—Mother of English Poetry—Northey, Isle of Ghosts and Birds—Vikings and Wild Geese—At the Blue Boar, a Medieval Inn—The Seaman and the Bomb—Company at the Jolly Sailor—Old Fowling Days in the "Joseph and Mary"—The Three Claydons—Liquor Smugglers of Osea Island—"'Git up, hoss'," he say

MALDON IS AN ANCIENT, LOVABLE TOWN. A TOWN OF PLOUGH and sail. It huddles, red-roofed and many-gabled, upon its little hill, its eyes to the sea and its hands to the land. It has lived for a thousand years by ships and the sea, by nets and the plough. It is among the most ancient towns in all England, a blend of Saxon, Danish, and Norman, of Tudor chimneys and Georgian doorways. It builds ships and sells corn and cattle. It knew the long-ships of the Dane and saw the bloody carnage of the three-day battle of Maeldune, whose tale is told in the *Anglo-Saxon Chronicle*, the first epic fight to be set down in English poetry. Yet for twenty years it has seen men leave the plough for the garage, the fishing-smack for the smell of an oily rag. It has mourned them with the wise eye of history.

The salt water glints at its feet. Gulls mew against its tall trees. The rich, elm-guarded cornlands of Essex roll poppy-reddened to its walls.

As we rumbled into the gravelled yard of the Blue Boar, lovely among Elizabethan inns, with its half-timbered walls, its wooden mounting-block cut from the full bole of an oak, I thought of Cobbett on his "Rural Rides" in 1820 and of Defoe's tour through England and Wales a hundred years before that. Both visited this broad, bright land of moated farmhouses, of tall elms and salty winds. Arthur Young came here. He wrote of "the tall Essex wheat" which came up to his knees against the saddle. There is such tall Essex wheat growing again to-day on farms dotted throughout the Maldon marsh lands which for twenty years had been down to grass. That evening I rode by lanes to Northey Island, by headlands where the tall wheat brushed the stirrups and dusted the knees, as they hugged the saddle-flaps. We trod in the hoof-marks of Cobbett and Defoe. The shadow of Arthur Young beckoned across the harvest fields.

Northey is a whale-backed, almost derelict island farm in the head waters of the Blackwater estuary. There are old men in Maldon who remember when all its land was under wheat. Great harvest wains rumbled over the slippery stones and gravel of the sea-road at low water. Harvesters went then by boat to their work in the morning, and hundreds of tons of corn were thrashed by flail in the island barn. That is all a dead memory.

To-day what were once the shining corn-fields of Northey are saltings, drowned by the rush of the sea at high tide. You can row a gunning punt over two hundred acres where once beans and clover grew, where scythes swung and the sheep fed. Northey to-day is a place of ruin and desolation. Ploughs and harrows lie rusting under the broken sea-wall. The farmhouse where Victor de Crespigny lived in wildfowling solitude and Sir Norman Angell wrote *The Great Illusion—Now* is partly unroofed, blasted, and knocked sideways. Barns and cowsheds are bent and twisted as though struck by a giant fist. That is what happened when a German raider dropped a bomb on Northey, because he thought that its farmhouse, with the strange look-out tower where Angell philosophized, was a fort.

The agricultural depression let in the tide. The sea-walls went. Two-thirds of the fields were drowned. It was never worth while to reclaim them. I doubt if it would pay to do so to-day. Germany has crowned the final destruction.

The island which once grew enough corn to feed a hundred families is to-day a place of shining waters, of salty levels, of bent grass, and sea lavender. Redshank spring and pipe. Curlew rise in grey herds. Herons fish its creeks. The red-breasted merganser fishes among its stranded hulks, and the sandpiper flits along its beaches. It is alone with its ghosts and its birds. Perhaps, when this war is done and Sir Norman Angell returns, it will see the birth of another philosophic "Great Illusion"—a tale of the illusion of the last twenty years of false values in England.

An old barge lay derelict on the foreshore as we rode over the slippery stones of the sea-road. A few horses and cattle wandered in windy fields above high-water mark, fields whose hedgerow elms held the nests of almost the last ravens in Essex at the end of the last century. There are no ravens on Northey to-day, but I have seen a peregrine strike down a pigeon above its fields, a marsh harrier beat its saltings, and the brent geese rise in hundreds from its creeks.

In the shallow stony ford between island and mainland there was fought in the bright sunlight of August the eleventh, A.D. 991, a battle which settled the fate of all Essex and half Saxon England for a century. Nights before, under the moon, Danish longships had come up the river, between the wide and glittering marshes. They came from Sandwich where they had raided and burned. Osea saw them pass in the moon, the banked oars rising and thrashing, the ravens at the mast-head.

Off Northey they dropped anchor, and the Vikings, helmed and golden-haired, waded ashore under Anlaf, the Dane. They made camp on the isle, threw up a stockade, and laid plans to burn and pillage Maeldune, the Saxon town.

To them came Brithnoth, Earldorman of Essex, a descendant of Mercian kings, with his Saxon warriors.

The three champions of England, Wulfstan, Aelfhere, and Maccus, stood three deep in the salt water, targes and swords in hand. The Vikings stormed on them through the shallows, shouting berserk war-cries, swords flashing. Wulfstan killed the first and for a space he kept the ford heroically, hewing them down, as Horatius kept the bridge. It was a fine and epic fight in the blood-reddened waters of Northey, steel clanging on steel, hoarse cries in the sunlight, men floating reddened and slashed on the tide, the ravens croaking, and the Saxons fighting the last stand of their England against the Dane.

Somewhere by Garland's Farm the battle surged back until it reached the ford by Maldon itself—a three-day mêlée of hand-to-hand hacking and fighting. Brithnoth was killed and his head cut off and taken to Denmark for the jarls to drink from his skull. The English were broken, and "The Song of Maeldune" was born. Florence of Worcester and Simeon of Durham wrote the tale, and Brithnoth's wife told it in a tapestry which hung at Ely.

I sat thinking of these things for a moment in the saddle under tall elms which once knew the gusty beat of ravens' wings. I sat and looked down the estuary towards the sea whence came the Danes. A still, golden evening, the sky in the west apple green, overhead a deep indigo blue. Light and sea and air seemed to stand still in the hush. A mile across the water Osea Island stood up, tree-crowned, its tall elms etched against the upland stubbles of Goldhanger. Plum-coloured ploughlands, far off, ran down to Tollesbury. It was almost Egyptian, that frieze of high-topped trees against the clear water, the yellow stubbles, in that clear light. Memory went back to a palm-covered island in Lake Karoun, the flamingoes drifting in pink clouds against the sky, the red desert hills stepping steeply into waters which cover the lost city of the Pharaohs.

I thought in that poised moment between earth and sea and sky of the hundreds of years of human endeavour which have gone to make fertile these broad Essex lands, these immemorial farms, these old yeoman families who are ancient as their elms, lasting as their oaks.

Away there, lonely in his little island kingdom on Osea, sat old Jack Bunting. I could picture him smoking by the barn door while the hens chuckled up to roost, and the partridges called in the fields. I could see him stroll, in mind's eye, down to his little pier where the crabs scuttle on the sand, and his yacht, salty from North Sea and Baltic days, lies at her anchor, every spar and runner mirrored in the water. There were Buntings on this old Blackwater river, farming their land two hundred years ago, just as for centuries there were Eves in Maldon, Seabrooks and Speakmans, Spittys and Pewters, Cants and Claydons, Pitts and Woodcrafts, Handleys and Cottises. They lived, some in moated farmhouses, those gracious yellow-walled sturdy homes which call themselves halls, some in cottages, and some hardly by the sea. They are of the land as surely as the land is of them. They and the land are jointly body and soul. They are of the life-blood of England, the fluent stream which makes our essential manhood.

Far down the estuary to the right the thin neck of land whereon stand a few grey ruins of Stansgate Abbey ran blackly into the shining tide. The farmhouse stood limned beneath its trees. Barn eaves and stack-tops showed stark as toy buildings cut from card-board. An oyster-smack slept upon the water. On the upland beyond, under the rising moon, red-gold as a guinea above the water . . .

. . . a lonely hound
Telling his loneliness all round
To the dark woods, dark hills, and darker sea.

And, answering, the sound
Of that yet lonelier sea-hound
Telling his loneliness to the solitary stars.

The hoarse bark of a great cob gull, wheeling beneath the first stars above Stansgate, dominated that silent scene. Beyond, beyond the low uplands of Steeple and Latchingdon-cum-Snoreham, that sweet village, lay old and lonely farms, scattered on marsh and upland, bearing names of ancient, ironic testimony to their worth. There is Starveall and Smallgains, Badknocks and Bitchhunters, Twizlefoot and Chinklefoot, Merks and Packards, Old Shrill and New Shrill. Up behind Goldhanger, where a heron drifted like a lorn wisp, there is a white and lovely little Georgian manor with the Georgian and lovely name of Folly Faunts. At Tollesbury, where that tall line of elms steps down to the glittering sea, stands Bohuns Hall, echo of the Middle Ages, farmed by that stout yeoman, Arthur French, who might have stepped straight out of the reign of Stephen. And, for finality of all earthly desire, there is a nest of cottages named King's and World's End.

The green in the west died. Coral-red crept along the edge of earth and sky, blazed suddenly upward in unearthly flame. A fine day to-morrow. Shepherd's Delight was alight on the fields. The moon, changing from guinea-red to gold, climbed higher. The great cob gull barked to the stars.

Robert picked his way through the thin hedge, down the lane, stepped delicately on the shining gravel and slimy stones of the sea-road, and we left Northey for the land. We rode by headlands and field gates, across stubbles where jugging partridges sprang like sudden bombs. The night was warm with the smell of corn-fields, the confiding heady scent of meadow-sweet, chequered by the flickering wings of bats. High in the dusk the bombers droned.

We stabled the horses at the Blue Boar in loose boxes which had not known the snuffle and scent of a horse for a score of years. They had turned out bicycles, biscuit-tins, a lawn-mower, empty bottles, and a pile of crates to make welcoming room for the friendliness of a horse. Arthur White, the landlord, leaned shirt-sleeved, broad-shouldered, over the half-door while we hissed and rubbed. He smoked contentedly in the dusk while bats wheeled.

"Just like old times," he grunted. "Makes a man feel young again. I love the smell of 'em."

It is the same anywhere in England, in any country town or village where you take a horse to-day. Man and maid welcome them. Something deep in the English being holds out its heart to a horse. Not all the smell nor glitter of a motor-car can touch that emotion which is part of the English blood.

In the raftered bar, whose black beams were adzed and built when a Tudor was on the throne, the talk was of the town's miracle of escape from heavy bombs. In two nights eight fell round it in the fields. A bomb squad had been dealing with bombs in the neighbourhood for weeks before. But this sudden descent of evil midnight manna called for outside help. So a second bomb disposal squad arrived in the town. The result, in the bar parlour of the Blue Boar, was uplifting.

Two enormous sappers, lordly as grenadiers, were leaning against the bar, gazing with stolid good-humour into their pewter pots when the door flew open. In burst a minute, indignant Cockney of No. 1 B.D. Squad. Red-headed, blue-eyed, and freckled, he stood a bare five feet six. A holy flame of indignation blazed in those blue eyes, ripped from that Cockney tongue. Prodding the nearest six-footer in mid-battle dress, he rasped:

"What the b—— 'ell d'you bleeders mean by pokin' yer dirty noses in 'ere? Do yer fink we chaps carn't get on wiv' the job wivaht you bleedin' amachewers nosin' in?

"I'm perfeshional, see! You ain't. See! Arf you blokes wos in civvies six munfs ago. Leave us ter git on wiv the job, and you go back ter yer civvies."

The grenadier gods stirred sleepily from their pewters, hitched their belts. Their good-humour wilted. Battle was in the air. Mr White, benign, firmly interposed.

"Now, now, Snipey. You leave 'em alone. They're only here to help you and your mates out with this packet that Jerry's dropped on us."

"'Elp! We don't want their bleedin' 'elp." He rose to a shrill crescendo of indignation. "Anyways, 'oo's bombs are they? We got 'ere fust. Fer two 'apence I'd chuck these two dogs'-breakfasts aht!"

"Never mind whose bombs they are," soothed Mr White. "You're welcome to all your bombs and the V.C. into the bargain. You can have all the danger you like—but no fighting in this bar."

"Danger! 'Oo said danger? There's no danger"—spitting scornfully into the fire. "We likes playin' wiv 'em. If you wants danger, guv'nor, go up ter London. I 'ad me leave an', Cor, strike me trahsers pink, there was plenty o' danger—bits of old iron, ruddy nosecaps, and 'arf 'ouses flyin' rahnd like coconuts on 'Ampstead 'Eath. I lit aht quick back 'ere. Give me a nice quiet job dahn in the country 'ere, an' I'll git on wiv it. There's no *danger* in it—not fer us perfeshionals!"

On that querulous note of bizarre rivalries and new values of war, the scene ended.

Dinner was good that night. Hare soup, steak and onions, and spotted dog with treacle, a pint of local beer, and a glass of port as big as a tea-cup. What more could mortal desire? It is a pleasant panelled dining-room, and most of the panelling is true from Elizabeth's reign. They have some pleasant silver, Sheffield plate, and brass in the Blue Boar. There is good walnut and mahogany to set it on, a post-boy's red jacket and black velvet cap hanging up in the hall, his yard of tin slung from two nails.

Perhaps it was the port, perhaps the sirens which suddenly shrieked and wailed to the stars, waking the town echoes with their banshee dirge, but Jim, with a sly twinkle, said, "I wonder if I'm too little to blow that horn. It would make five of any I've ever heard out hunting." So blow it he did, while the searchlights patterned the sky, and the inhuman dragons of Germany droned over.

I walked down the street. Down the hill which dips by the Saxon church, headlong to the tide where the barges lie and the estuary opens all before you. There is a little Georgian inn on the right at the foot of that hill. It stands with its bland face to the salt water, a sea captain's look-out perched on its roof. It calls itself the Jolly Sailor, and it is high in the company of all the jolly inns I have ever known.

It has cherished two centuries of barge skippers and smacksmen, of yacht hands and wildfowlers, of horny-handed winklers who ply their bitter trade on the freezing muds, and oystermen and shrimpers whose life is lived with wind and tide. It is small, warm, and cosy, and its roof rang that night with gusty songs and rolling choruses while the guns thudded and searchlights splayed the skies.

"Hap owd Jerry'll hear us a-singin' out, master," grinned Ernie Pitt, the fowler. "He'll goo back to owd Hitler an' tell him that the Maldon chaps don't care nawthin' for him. We should have pore hearts if we was to cower down, shouldn't us?"

They were all there, the Pitts and Handleys and Woodcrafts, whose names are as famous in wildfowling annals to-day as they were when Colonel Hawker wrote his classic and Payne-Gallwey punted with their fathers; the three Claydons, Alf and Cliff, long, lean, and keen as hawks, with Brother Bill, rotund and rosy, who sailed in the Pagets' yacht and has seen the seven seas, from Guam to Suez, from Amboyna, the scented isle, to the icy waters and unearthly lights of the Norway fiords.

I thought, in that smoky, noisy, jolly little bar with its whistling birds in cages and its prints of Queen Victoria, of the merry nights in peace-time winters when the three Claydons and a few good 'fowling friends sailed and fished, netted and shot from their sturdy little smack, the nine-ton *Joseph and Mary*. Alas, that company is scattered by the gust of war. Tony Heckstall-Smith won the D.S.C. for "great gallantry" in the evacuation from Crete; Jimmy Gordon-Dickson was colonel of a battalion somewhere in the steaming, murderous forests of Burma; David Wolfe Murray, that delicate artist of birds who conceals himself as "Fish-Hawk," was that night in action with a heavy battery of A.A. guns in the night battle for London; and Yurka Galitzine was in Ulster. We who had slept in our clothes, two in a canvas bunk, three on an oil-cloth floor, with our heads in the salty fo'castle among the nets, our feet in the ashes from the stove, we who had punted under the winter moon at the shouting geese, trawled in the deeps when other men were at breakfast, netted the creeks, swum the cold tides on icy mornings for fun, and cooked and lived in the close comradeship of that tiny cabin where you could neither sit upright nor lie down straight, were scattered like chaff. I counted myself fortunate that an accident of illness had brought me back to the company of these men of the smacks who are the salt of the sea.

We talked of the old days of sailing and fishing, of the far-off days after the last war when Osea Island for a brief, fantastic period was a home for wealthy drunks. Charrington, the brewer, built there a large house which he filled with dipsomaniacs who could afford to pay. It was a pretty paradox.

Prettier still were the tricks of the Maldon men. They did a roaring bootleg trade in whisky, brandy, gin, and rum. Night after night smacks would drop anchor off the island. A punt loaded with bottles would steal ashore and the bottles were planted carefully in corn-sheaves, in stacks, in whin-bushes, in rabbit-holes, pre-arranged. When morning came the drunks, in quest of air, would be seen roaming the fields, ostensibly searching the hedges for the beauties of botany, the charm of a nesting bird.

But every now and then a hijacker reared his ugly head. Evil men from other smacks crept ashore. They combed the hedges, plunged questing arms down innocent rabbit-holes. There was much revelry, afloat as well as ashore. And the Maldon waterside pubs did a roaring trade in strong waters.

On occasion the gentlemanly drunks of Osea would find them a boat and, most decorously, go for a row. They rowed up the river on the tide. They poured into the Queen's Head from whose windows you can spit into the creek, the inn where "Jumping Jack" Clarke, the midget waterside Napoleon, is king. They invaded the Jolly Sailor, the Anchor, and a host of inns great and small. They stayed till the top of the tide. When the tide turned the boat-load would return, borne on the bosom of a motherly stream which cast them, happy, singing, but un-nautical, upon the brewer's beaches. It was too good to last. The home stands empty. Osea has gone back to farming.

"Time I laid in me smack off Steeple Crick t'other night," said Bill, as the distant thunder of a bomb rattled the windows, "one o' them owd Jerries come over right low. If I'd had your gret owd eight-bore I reckon I could 'a' winged him. He warn't no higher'n a duck 'ud fly. I set in me cabin and thinks I, 'He'll see the sparks from the chimney.' The stove was a-goin' like one o'clock, so I sez to the boy, 'Hop you up on deck and clap my owd hat on the chimney.'

"Up goos the boy, sees the sparks a-flyin' like fireworks, an' rams my owd hat on the chimney. Damn, that scorched the crown off. Round comes owd Jerry lookin' for us agin'. But there warn't no sparks ter guide him. So he dropped a rare gret owd bomb lower down the river. That blowed all the tiles off the King's Head at Bradwell. I reckon that spoilt the beer for some on 'em."

"Did you hear of owd Jake goin' a-roonin' [mushrooming] t'other mornin'?" asked another. "He went down on Iltney marsh ter seek a hoss. That was half light, 'bout fower o'clock. He seed suffin' big an' black layin' in a low in the high grass, an' he thinks that's his owd Dobbin. 'Git up, hoss,' he say, an' he give that a stub with his foot.

"Har! that wore a suck-in fer him. That wore no hoss. That wore a gret owd bomb. Jake took one look, an' he shruk out, an' he lit off fer the farm like a hare. I reckon he 'ouldn't do in the Navy." A tide of laughter. Jake, in the corner, grinned sheepishly.

"Har! Happen I'd know'd that were an owd bomb I'd ha' tuk me halter to it an' hulled that in the Crick," he challenged.

"Time, gentlemen," cried Mr Robinson, rattling the pots. A shuffle of feet, an eddy of blue smoke as the door opened. A chorus of good-nights, and the salt wind struck sharp as we stumbled down the steps in the bright cold light of a full moon. The tide gurgled in. Wind sang in spars and rigging. The burgee of a barge flapped at the mast-head. Great sails, brailed up, strained and creaked. Curlew were calling on the mud. Far off an early widgeon mewed like a cat. Overhead the bombers droned, searchlights patterned the sky with the fantastic geometry of war.

CHAPTER VIII

On every moonlit roadway, down every starry lane,
Forgotten hoofs make music, lost wagons creak and strain;
The mantling mist of moonlight half hides and half reveals
The glitter of pale harness, the curve of shadowy wheels.

Will H. Ogilvie

The Mechanical Miracle of Fordson Estates—A Visit to Boreham House Farms—Mr Ford's Agricultural Shop Window—Lessons in Practical Farming—The Maxims of Lord Perry—Follies of Bureaucracy—Farm Wages and Income Tax—Loss of the Smack "Teaser"—A Morning's Fishing—Cousin Luke and his Rifle

A SMELL OF FRYING BACON. COFFEE SCENTING THE CORRIDORS, cheerful with mahogany and old silver. Swallows circling the church spire against a bird's-egg blue sky. The sun and the birds were up. The sharp smell of the sea came in at the open window. Down in the yard under whose beamed arch the London coaches once rumbled the twang-twang of the post-boy's horn woke sudden leaping echoes. Jim, up an hour already, had got at the yard of tin again.

I went downstairs, ordered breakfast to be ready in three-quarters of an hour, and, to christen the day, walked out at the back, up Coach Lane, by tiny, eaved and gabled houses, so small and twisted amid their hollyhocks that they might have come straight out of Hans Andersen. There is a pleasant early morning walk above the river at the back of Maldon. It is a gentle scarp of corn-fields and green, with great hedgerow oaks, and it falls to the reedy edge and tide-bared muds of the river Blackwater, which is here a true tidal stream and not the vast estuary which opens below the town.

A broad, pleasant valley, well farmed and well grazed. Great fields of roots glistened in the sun, mangolds as big as a man's head, and turnips white and firm. Wheat was shocked in red-gold lines whence rose the clap of pigeons' wings.

I saw as I walked a sight I have not seen on any English stream—thirty-seven swans sailing solemnly, three and four abreast, like lovely cutters taking the light air on the Solent. You will see more, hundreds more, at Abbotsbury, in Dorset, and I once saw seventy-two, set out like a scattered armada on the flats below the Cat House in Woolverstone Park, on the Orwell. But I have never seen thirty-seven sailing in line of battle on any other narrow stream.

I turned about at Beeleigh Abbey, surely one of the loveliest small monastic houses in England, part Elizabethan, part Ecclesiastical, set in its garden of roses and peonies, of apple walks and hollyhocks, hard by the falls. There, if you are clever and lucky, you may sometimes see a rare salmon splash or a sea trout jump. It was one of those precious half-hours in the fresh of the early morning which make the day a memory, the rest of the week worth while.

After breakfast we went by car through sweet-scented lanes by Ulting and Langford, by old farms and humming threshing-machines to Boreham House, where Lord Perry, the partner of Mr Henry Ford, has achieved a miracle in mechanized farming. At Boreham the genius of Mr Henry Ford, operating through the individual brain of his partner, has created out of an ancient English estate the most efficient—and I must confess, to me, the most forbidding—agricultural unit I have yet seen. Indeed, I should say that Lord Perry is both to blame and to praise. To blame for disparking the ancient deer park of Lord Kenyon and the Jolliffe Tufnells. To blame for cutting down old elms and ancient oaks. To blame, if you call it blame, for turning an eclectic Adam house into an agricultural school for boys to learn the most ancient craft.

But he is to be praised for having put three thousand acres of indifferently farmed Essex land into the highest cultivation I have yet seen outside individual enterprise. Mark those words well. I said "outside individual enterprise." For let it be noted that Fordson Estates, Limited, of Boreham House, near Chelmsford, is a limited company operating under the Friendly Societies Act. It is a shop window for Mr Ford's agricultural machinery. That is by the way. It is entirely justifiable.

From the practical farming point of view there is a lot to be learned at the Fordson Estates.

I am not sure that, as a sentimental countryman, I admire it. As a practical man who wants to see the most food produced with the greatest efficiency I was astonished. But I should not like to see a lot of Boreham Houses spread over England.

On its own it is an admirable object-lesson. I could not learn its capital. The area is a little over three thousand acres. It included four hundred and fifty acres of wheat, two hundred and fifty acres of orchards, two hundred acres of barley, one hundred and fifty acres of oats, one hundred and fifty acres of sugar-beet, one hundred and fifty acres of potatoes, two hundred and fifty acres of sprouts, two hundred and fifty acres of peas, one hundred and fifty acres of clover seeds, forty acres of flax, twelve acres of Bedford Champion onions, twenty acres of cauliflowers, twenty acres of runner beans, and about two hundred acres of grassland.

There are about eighty acres of old woodlands, and by a little stream they have planted more than one thousand cricket-bat willows. There are about three hundred breeding ewes, sixty head of shorthorn steers, about thirty head of dairy cattle, several hundred pigs, Essex saddlebacks.

About four and a half acres are under glass—tomatoes, cucumbers, lettuces, and radishes. I could multiply the convincing details.

This factory farming does not impress me. It is magnificent but unlovable. It succeeds, by virtue of its particular constitution, in paying its workers a bonus which has varied from rather over £100 a year—and that to a boy who normally earned about 26*s.* per week—up to more than £380 paid to a skilled farm worker whose average weekly earnings were £4 10*s.* a week. Is this practical farming sense?

I need not go into the scheme of bonus distribution, (*a*) because it has been minutely described before, (*b*) because I do not see that it is applicable to either the average English country estate or the average large farm, and (*c*) because it operates under the Friendly Societies Act.

What Fordson Estates have proved is that intensive farming on a mechanized system can produce great results. No doubt we shall see that principle extended. But it cannot be taken as typical of the bulk of English farming. Nor will it ever be.

Lord Perry is a practical, human man. He made his name and fortune from the bottom rung of the ladder. Therefore he should know what he is talking about.

When, therefore, he tells me (*a*) that sugar-beet pulp as a pig food is almost equal to oats in nutritive value, (*b*) that the reduction in feeding-stuffs has resulted in the fact that, whereas in peace-time one pound of pork could be produced for three and a half pounds of food, to-day at least five pounds of food are needed to produce the same weight of pork, (*c*) that the much-boosted town swill and dried town waste is useless as pig food, and (*d*) that owing to hold-ups of foodstuffs in ports much has been lost and damaged, I take notice.

One of the great secrets of Fordson Estates is that they have a central office through which their farm managers buy their requirements and sell their products. It establishes a central buying and selling market for the estate as a whole. Such a central organization is economically useful on an estate of two thousand or more acres—not less. Lord Perry believes that the ideal size for a farm is four hundred acres. Each of his is managed by a working foreman who is paid £5 per week. Would such a man earn more as the tenant of a four-hundred-acre farm, operating it with reasonable capital and a reasonable hope of decent prices? That is the question for the young farmer to ask himself. It is the question that he must ask his M.P. in the future. Are our English farms to become factory-managed or to remain individual units?

One answer is that this is one type of farming. It is excellent in its way. It produces the best sort of results in food production. It wastes not an acre nor a rood. It offers salaried jobs and bonuses. In normal years these bonuses ranged from 30 to 50 per cent. of a man's wages. But I doubt very much whether that level will be reached again when peace comes.

One object of the co-operative scheme is to prevent the growth of absenteeism. No man earns money unless he works. No man can draw his share of the profits as a bonus unless he works. Even should a man leave the firm owning a reserved deposit he cannot draw more than 4 per cent. on it, and it will certainly not be enough for him to retire on. There is therefore no question of vested interests growing up among the workers. It is a practical scheme, based on the principle of no work, no pay, and I doubt if even a member of the Fabian Society or one of those curious English people who see so much good in Russia and so little in England could find fault with it.

It is, in plain fact, based on the principle of compulsory saving out of income—a principle conceived and put into practice by Lord Perry long before Lord Keynes suggested that the Government in 1941 should take a part of every man's income and put it into National Savings Certificates. The wiseheads of the Treasury might follow this simple common-sense plan. Surely if Fordson Estates can afford to pay 4 per cent. to their wage-earners and guarantee them a cash bonus in years of depression the British Governments of the future should be able to do the same, or something like it, on a grander scale, for its people.

Another good aspect of the Fordson principle is that in peacetime it sells much of its produce to the consumer, cutting out the middleman. I am no lover of the Covent Garden nonsense, which means that if you live in a country town you probably cannot buy local fruit and vegetables on the spot because they have all gone up to London. There they pass through two or three different hands, add two or three profits to their original price, and return to the country shopkeeper, enhanced in price and diminished in freshness.

Anyone who has ever eaten a new potato a couple of hours after it has been dug out of the earth knows the incredible difference between its taste and that of the 'new' potato which has spent half its young life travelling up to Covent Garden and back again.

The system of direct marketing from producer to consumer has a long way to go. It is only stumbling in its infancy. But it will mean an immense saving in transport charges, railway running costs, lorry charges, and other overheads, as well as a direct gain in health to the individual consumer when it is more widely adopted.

That good squire and practical farmer, the late Christopher Turnor, of Stoke Rochford, near Grantham, was one of the pioneers of the scheme twenty years ago. He set up a roadhouse in a corner of his park on the Great North Road, to sell fresh fruit, vegetables, and other produce direct to travellers. He told me at the time that his principal customers, even for such expensive things as peaches, were lorry drivers and vanmen. Regularly, week by week, they bought baskets full of stuff, fresh from the earth or the tree, which they took to their families in London and the great cities of the North.

Lord Eltisley copied the scheme on the Cambridge-Huntingdon road. I believe Lord Bledisloe has marketed produce direct from his home farm for many years..

Our grandfathers did it. We should return to it. I should like to see every country town and city, big or little, with an open market where the local producer could sell direct to the local buyer.

To return to Fordson Estates. Boreham, like a good home farm in the days when a squire could afford to spend money, is valuable as a research and breeding station. It acquires knowledge which is at the disposal of the many. It is businesslike to the hilt. You realize that the moment you step into the white-walled, green-tiled, parquet-floored estate office on the main road between Chelmsford and Colchester. From a distance it looks like a Hollywood villa, gay and bright. You realize this businesslike angle even more when you go to, say, Duke's Farm, where there are nearly three hundred acres of fruit orchards. Here are super-modern steel and galvanized iron packing-sheds, capable of storing 180 tons of food, but designed to pack three times that quantity.

The walls are of thin sheets of galvanized iron inside, wooden outside. Interior walls, floors, and ceilings are thoroughly greased to prevent rust. A central temperature pipe runs from floor to ceiling. These sheds will store fruit in good condition for five to six months. Before the war about half the fruit produced at Boreham went to the consumer direct by mail order.

To-day bureaucratic control means that everything has to go through a licence-holder. This causes delay and adds to the expense of transport, packing material, and labour. It throws extra burdens on the railways and destroys the goodwill of the producer. Multiply that instance a thousandfold throughout England, and you may well cease to wonder why Lord Woolton, that super-bureaucrat with the Cheshire-cat smile, requires the nation to maintain a staff of hired publicists to trumpet his good deeds.

It is an odd paradox of bureaucracy that Ministerial mediocrities to-day invariably require hired apologists. The Churchills, Napoleons, Pitts, Chathams, and Disraelis of this world achieved their fame by merit, not by methods of the circus barker.

But let us walk in the pleasant apple glades of Duke's Farm. Each thirty-five-acre orchard contains eighty-eight thousand apple-trees. There are six acres of Morella cherries which, so Mr Boswell, the farm manager, told me, produced £200 gross per acre. An apiary is run on the edge of a wood next to the orchard in order to ensure the proper pollination of the trees.

I asked Lord Perry what he thought of inter-cropping between the trees.

"It doesn't pay in orchards," he said. "We've tried it with tomatoes, currants, and soft fruits, but we merely find that it exhausts the fertility of the soil and retards the growth of the trees. You lose on both crops."

He was indignant about the price-control order as it affected tomatoes.

"But for this fool order we could sell greenhouse tomatoes to the consumer at eightpence a pound instead of one and twopence. When the outdoor tomatoes come on we could sell them at fourpence a pound retail."

He added that, whereas last year outdoor tomatoes cost £100 an acre to grow, pack, and market, and showed a profit of £300 an acre, selling at an average price of fivepence-halfpenny a pound, they would cost eightpence a pound under price control that year, which puts up the profits to the grower and the price to the consumer. Merely another instance of Whitehall interference raising prices to the buyer.

We went on to the pigs. There are several herds, widely separated to avoid swine-fever.

Years ago Lord Perry, like most wise pig farmers, realized the advantages of the Danish principle of sties. He called in Mr Olsen, the Danish Government pig expert, who advised on the lay-out of the pig farms about 1935. The pigs, Essex saddlebacks, are kept under beautifully clean conditions. The sties, cement-floored with a runnel and drains to carry away liquid manure, are built under one great roof in buildings bigger than the average large barn. There is a free current of air and, as the sties are regularly washed down, a minimum of muck. Each sty has its feeding-trough, and the walls are just high enough for a pig to stand up and look over at its neighbours. The old idea that pigs like to lie belly-deep in filth should surely by now be exploded in even the remotest districts, but the fact remains that on many farms, both great and small, as well as in cottage back gardens and on allotments, you will find the wretched pig condemned to a life of squalor, stench, and filth.

The Boreham pigs have big grass runs, but I forgot to ask whether they are allowed out in herds to shack—to use a good old Essex word —on the corn stubbles and bean-fields in the autumn. Let your pigs out through September and October on stubble and orchard, on the remains of the uncarted potatoes, or in oak and beech woods with a good boy in charge, and they will be the better for it.

The modern farmer cannot, however, claim clean pigsties as original any more than some of the agricultural professors of to-day can claim their much boosted 'discoveries' as new. Half the 'new' ideas and theories which are produced with grandiose names or terrifying Latin labels are merely old principles dressed up in new language. Vitamins are what our grandmothers called 'goodness.' Equally, if you examine an old Essex "pigs' court" built a hundred years ago you will find that it was floored with bricks or stone and had a gentle slope to a trench.

Sugar-beet pulp is used extensively for pig feeding at Boreham. Mr Boswell told me that the pigs take about 20 per cent. of it, and he believes it is almost equal to oats in feeding value. I have already quoted Lord Perry's views on the uselessness of the much boosted town swill and dried waste as a pig food. He and Mr Boswell conducted the most careful experiments with both and came to the conclusion that this muck has not the slightest possible feeding value.

"Another example of the folly of the bureaucrats trying to run farming on a factory plus red-tape principle," concluded Lord Perry, with that disarming smile which hides his invincible contempt for the Whitehall Rabbit.

Town swill, of course, which is merely dustbin refuse, must not be confused for a moment with the swill from a cottage or farmhouse where bread, vegetables, fruit, and potato peelings are thrown into a bucket and constitute very high food value.

At Boreham they aim at two farrowings a year, but are satisfied with three in two years. They reckon an economical sow is one which produces not less than two hundred pounds of live pig at the end of eight weeks after the second farrowing. In normal times pigs were weaned at six weeks, but under war conditions they find it impossible to wean them under eight or nine weeks.

To sum up, Boreham is a fascinating example of up-to-the-minute farming. Perhaps, I guess, a little unsympathetic, a little de-humanized. It is not typical of English farming, certainly not of English land-ownership. But it has many good points. It will, in due course of time, educate within the classic walls of Boreham House, that classic Adam mansion, which looks down its long canal between the double avenue of tall trees, a highly efficient and essentially practical race of young farmers. It is worth watching.

By way of contrast we went by lanes where the harvest straw, carted from the fields, was hanging in streamers from the hedges, lively with finches, tits, and sparrows, to Cressing Temple, that loveliest of old manorial farms. It sits back from the road, bland and mellow, squatting comfortably on land which the Knights Templars farmed. Its great barn, with an enormous roof full of the soft and glowing colours of lichens, mosses, and the sun, is one of the biggest and most beautiful in all England. Its outbuildings are of the same noble proportions, the same simple English beauty.

To look on such a farmhouse, gracious without, spacious and homely within, warm in its garden, set about by great buildings which would store enough grain and yard enough beasts to feed a regiment, is to realize the ample prosperity, the comfortable worth which sound farming and sounder politics brought to English farming for centuries before the cry of "Cheap food" and a flood of tinned imports ruined the countryside at the expense of the towns and sapped the national vitality until the very Empire itself was in danger of total loss. Have the trumpets of war caused those false walls of a political Jericho to fall for ever?

We had lunch at the Spread Eagle in Witham, an inn, long-fronted, many-eaved, beamed and raftered. It has held my heart since I first knew it a quarter-century ago. Built in 1549, it has kept its feet on the road, its face unchanged, and its hands wide in welcome to the traveller. If you like the odd, unconsidered trifles of history which make half the charm of such an old inn there is a shaft in the wall by the great fireplace where the smugglers hid their kegs. There are relics of Tudor and Roman days, a parrot in a cage, and a mighty hound to lick your hands.

We talked of the new proposal to raise farm labourers' wages to 60*s.* a week. Lord Perry had long before anticipated it by paying his men a minimum of £3 2*s.* 6*d.* for a fifty-hour week to skilled permanent workers, but not to the casual unskilled labour which has been drafted on to the land through the muddlesome machinery of Whitehall. It is a good wage when you remember that cottage rents on the estate range from 3*s.* to 10*s.* a week.

The farm labourer does not do badly under such circumstances. In many ways he lives better than the town worker. His home is on top of his work. He pays no train fare and seldom even a bus fare. He grows his own vegetables and fruit. He keeps chickens. He usually has a pig. Some have a cow or a goat for milk. Their children breed rabbits. Pleasures are simple and close at hand. Their life is uncomplicated, healthy, and contented.

These are facts which city-bred trade union leaders, facile town critics of the countryside, and the brittle intelligentsia who constitute the readers of those weekly reviews which are the pillars of the Bloomsbury temple usually fail to appreciate. I do not think the farm labourer cares one way or the other what they think.

But it is an unfortunate fact that too many farm labourers, like many miners, object to paying income tax once they earn more than 60*s.* a week, which many do by working overtime or as skilled men —*i.e.*, carmen, horsemen, tractor-drivers, and in the orchards.

I have come across many examples, since the war began, of men refusing to work overtime because "they don't see why they should earn money to pay for the Government." Yet, like the miners and munition workers, they are only too anxious to ask for State aid. They accept free education, free roads, State doctoring and hospitals, housing schemes, and other benefits, without realizing that these things can only be provided by the State from the taxes.

This attitude of mind is not selfishness, but simply lack of understanding. Instead of wasting reams of paper on telling the farmer how to get on with his job the Government might try to explain in simple language to farm labourers the necessity for their contribution, not only in overtime, but in taxes on extra moneys earned.

Another aspect is that the Government, having first drained the land of its skilled workers in the past, has now drafted many thousands of unskilled town workers, formerly working on road construction, building schemes, in garages, or merely unemployables, on to the land through the labour exchanges. They do half as much work, but are paid as much money as skilled workers, men whose craft is a heritage of centuries. This is a cause of great discontent in the countryside and a waste of some millions of money a year.

I do not suggest that the raising of farm wages to 60s. a week is disliked by most farmers. They say, quite justly, that so long as a man works well and works the necessary hours he earns and deserves the money. But they rightly demand that the prices of farm produce shall meet the increased cost of wages.

We finished lunch when it was almost tea-time. It had been a long morning, and we had talked of farming; of the stranglehold of bureaucrats; of the need to safeguard the future of individualism if England is to be worth living in; of old memories of Herm, tiny and green in the Channel seas, where once Lord Perry lived in moments of philosophic solitude; of Sark, the feudal principality of Sybil Hathaway, who, like a good squire, stayed on with her people when the Germans came and is with them still; of Jersey and the fantastic days of Lady Houston, when I was first lieutenant to that amazing woman in her political battles against Baldwin and MacDonald. Who to-day remembers that we owe the Spitfire to her flamboyant generosity; that less than ten years before war broke out she offered the Government a quarter of a million pounds to start a territorial flying corps of Cockneys to guard London against aerial bombardment, an offer scorned by that arch-mediocrity, Ramsay MacDonald?

Witham High Street, long and wide and sunny, lay warm in the afternoon, a place of sleeping cats and strolling dogs, with its Queen Anne and Georgian houses, its placid shops and swinging inn signs, the White Hart couchant and the Spread Eagle rampant. With its half-timbered cottages and gravelled yards, a man might well expect to meet Mrs Gaskell on a corner, to spy Washington Irving quizzing up a by-lane, or see the coach and four of Squire Western spanking by in the sun, hot from London, bound for the Corinthian elegance of Felix Hall, a mile or two out of the town. But the Westerns have gone, dead and forgotten. Felix Hall is a shell, the park a mere pasture for cattle.

I thought, as I stood in the sun, of the fate which has overtaken some of the old estates which were once the pride of this rich centre of farming Essex. There is no longer a Du Cane at Braxted Park, and the present owner has, I believe, kept in hand no more than a thousand or so acres. Rivenhall Place still stands, mellow and musical with rooks above its little lake. "Crawley" de Crespigny is dead, but Champion Lodge is still in de Crespigny hands, though Lord Byron's mansion at Langford Grove is a school. There are Parkers still at Faulkbourne Hall, but I doubt if any deer roam the park at Marks Hall.

Lord Rayleigh, at Terling Place, enhances the great tradition of high farming which has made the name of Strutt honoured among generations of English farmers. I should say, at a guess, that he and the family firm of Strutt and Parker directly farm, on the best principles, between twelve thousand and sixteen thousand acres of Essex land. It is a remarkable achievement of continuity of tenure and principle, of enlightened practice and faith in the land. Boreham, despite its hewing down of ancient oaks and ploughing up of old park land, is a worthy neighbour to that great home of English agriculture.

It was time to be getting back to Maldon, for there was a plot on foot. A plot to go fishing on the first of the morning tide, so soon as sunrise should give us leave to up anchor. For it is a rule of war on this coast that if you move afloat between the hours of sunset and dawn you may be shot at. More than one Maldon smack has had a ripping stream of bullets across its bows because it moved in the moon. So I planned to go aboard after dark, roll up in blankets in one of the two bunks, and be on the spot.

In the first winter of the war, before sentries were about but when an odd bomb was not unexpected, there was an evening when I arranged to sleep aboard and be joined by Alf at six in the morning. I scrambled aboard in pitch dark, groped into the cabin, lit a match, but could find no lamp. I stuffed the stove full of paper and sticks—and then the match went out. It was bitterly cold. I groped for the coal in the dark, stuck my fingers in the frying-pan, upset the kettle, poked them into a panful of fat. But no coal. So I scrambled on deck, where I fell over a wet sack of hard knobbly lumps. Here, surely, was the coal. I lugged it below, groped for the stove in the dark, tipped a double handful on to the paraffin-soaked wood, and struck a match. Up blazed the stove, flaming furiously, fed with a bagful of winkles! That night I slept an uneasy slumber in an atmosphere heavy with the smell of roast winkles.

Alf had agreed that this time he would be aboard to welcome me: "For we can't hev you a-pisonin' yerself along o' they winkles no more."

So, after dinner and a glass of that memorable port, I picked my way catlike between spars and anchors, dinghies tipped sideways and cables spread like man-traps. Ten o'clock, the moon as bright as day, and time to turn in aboard the dark little ship.

"Halt! Who goes there?" From the black shadow of a shed three forms loomed. A rifle was poked in my stomach. Identity card and naval pass were scrutinized.

"They dropped a heavy one last night, sir," said the sentry. "Eight foot long, they say—up back of the town. There's another by Summerfleet Farm and two more over at Cold Norton. All delayed action, too."

I went aboard. The tiny cabin was warmly alight. Alf, blue-jerseyed, brown-faced, was making tea in the kettle, black and strong. The little stove glowed. It lit with the warmth of a Flemish interior the pile of nets by the fish-hold hatch, the canvas bunks, the long grey barrel of the spare punt gun on the floor.

"Owd Charlie Smith was blowed up in the *Teaser* by a mine 'smornin'," Alf remarked calmly, stirring the kettleful with a fork.

"Killed?" I asked.

"No! Only scairt. He got a wet jacket an' a bellyful o' salt water, but he's none the wuss for that. Smack's gone, though."

"Where did this happen?"

"Off o' Thurslet Spit. Runnin' wi' the wind, they was, goin' a-fishin' on the Main, when all of a sudden up she blew. Blowed the stem clean off. Charlie say the bowsprit come right back double on itself an' very nigh swiped him off the starn.

"Him and his boy tuk a lep into the dinghy, but the painter fouled the main sheet an' down she went an' dragged the dinghy under with the both on 'em in fourteen foot o' water.

"But lor! You wun't drown they tew. Take more'n an owd Jerry to do that. They clumb up the leach o' the sail an' got atop the mast. An' there they set like a pair o' owd cormorants from half after four in the mornin' till half-past six when we tuk 'em orf. Laugh? I very nigh bust! They're orf agin to-morrow mornin' in another boat. Lost the trawl, peter nets, punt gun, two hand guns, an' all their clothes."[1]

There is an everyday plain tale of the typical East Coast smacksmen, unarmed, who trawl from dawn each day, six miles out amid the perils of the sea, and back again at dusk. We made tea, warmed it up with a drop of whisky, pulled off our boots, and turned in.

Next morning at 6 A.M. we weighed anchor and stood off down the estuary in the pale light of new-born day. The drone of engines filled the sky like bees. They were coming back from a raid somewhere in the south Midlands. Suddenly in the cold, clear light there came the scream, like tearing silk, of a falling bomb. A shattering explosion, a mountain of water which tossed the smack like a cork, a terrific blast of wind shuddering through the rigging.

The sky was alive with screaming gulls and whistling wings. Curlew yelled like banshees. Dogs barked at distant farms. Far overhead the bomber, lightened of the last of his load, droned out to sea, to Germany. I should not like to guess how many bombs have been jettisoned in the waters and on the marshes of that estuary since war began.

"Come on arter they fish! He'll ha' killed a cart-load."

Over went the anchor, away went the dinghy, rowed hard downstream. The bomb had fallen two hundred yards away.

On the tide drifted fish of all sorts, belly upward, silver in the clear light. Bass, those brilliant fighters of salt water; plaice, sole, flounders; garfish, with their long bony beaks; roker (skate) and bull-routs, those nightmare fish with the goggle eyes and horrific mouths—all floating, dead or stunned. Swiftly they were scooped in with long-handled nets. In half an hour the big dinghy was knee-deep. Hundreds floated away.

The wind blew round to the nor'ard and a big sailing-barge, manned by one man and a boy, her great red sail full with the wind, came down the river. A sight for heroic eyes.

[1] Within six months of this total loss Charlie Smith, rising sixty, had worked and saved enough to buy another smack and gear—six months of stern self-denial and hard work. He neither drank nor smoked till he had a new boat.

"What's the betting they get machine-gunned before they make London River?" I asked.

"Har! I dessay. That's cousin Luke's barge. Let 'em try it. They got a gun."

"What is it—Lewis, Hotchkiss, or what?"

"No, no. That ain't no machine-gun. That's a rifle. Luke can use it, too. I don't doubt he'd tiddle up any German once he get his eye on him."

I thought, as we got under way again, forged in the wake of the barge, the main sheet tautening, the breeze fresh off the land, of the cool calm of that man and a boy taking a slow sailing-ship through shoal water and fairway, liable at any moment to be machine-gunned, yet supremely confident in themselves and their armament—one rifle. Of such stuff is the spirit of that gallant coast.

We trawled below Osea, took a few fish and plugged up, on long boards, in time to get ashore as the breakfast chimneys were smoking, and the dogs were chasing the late cats off the street. Another day of this farming adventure had begun.

CHAPTER IX

A nation that neglects its land and its peasants—which are its root-stock—will perish. . . . Napoleon said that toil produced a hard and virile race while trade produced a soft and crafty people; and that is true.

HENRY WILLIAMSON, in *English Farming*,
by Sir John Russell

Of Mr Lawrence Washington of Maldon—Woodham Mortimer and its Squiresses—The Windy Lands of Dengie—Will Goodchild's Prairie Farm—Marshes down to Corn—When the Devil threw a Man out of his Bed at Midnight on Wallasea Island—Old Mother Redcap on a Hurdle—Witches of the Islands—The Viking Ghost of Canvey Point—Cattle, Wild Horses, and Conscientious Objectors—A Short-sighted Horse Slaughter Policy—Wild Irish Gangs—"They lived like Hogs and fought like Dogs"—A Yeoman at Home

THE SUN WAS GILDING THE GOLDEN COCK HIGH ON THE SPIRE of All Saints' Church, opposite the Georgian porch of the front door, as we loaded the horses into the box. I thought, as their hooves clattered up the ramp, of the horsemen and carriages which were ridden and driven into this old yard on that January day in 1652 when they buried Mr Lawrence Washington in the churchyard opposite.

Now this Mr Lawrence Washington was an undistinguished country parson of Purleigh. He liked his drink, was a stout Royalist, and had his few good friends round about. But I doubt if the King in London or his Ministers had ever heard his name. When the King's head fell Mr Washington loudly proclaimed his horror. So the Cromwellians turned him out of his parsonage. They said that he was a drinker and frequenter of taverns, a wine-bibber and a loose talker.

None the less I do not suppose any thought of his funeral would have crossed my mind that morning were it not that Mr Lawrence Washington had a great-great-grandson named George, a gentleman of Virginia, who became the Father of the United States.

Thus Maldon, the lost, forgotten little Essex port, content with its own company, as remote from London as though it were five hundred miles away and not fifty, had its hand three centuries ago in the genesis of that union of the English-speaking peoples which, within our time, will set the seal of peace upon the world for a century to come.

The yard of the Blue Boar is no bad place on a sunny morning to muse upon history. History is all about you. That lovely, black and white, half-timbered wing of the old inn is pure fifteenth-century. Its red roof is supported by the most magnificent king-post I have seen anywhere. The broad sweep of its shingles is unbroken by any chimney. The whole inn is an amazing jumble of the centuries. It has taken six hundred years in the making, for parts were built in the fourteenth century when Crécy was the Waterloo of the day and the nave of Westminster Abbey was being built. De Vere, Earl of Oxford, whose heraldic badge was the blue boar, had this old house as his town residence in the port of Maldon, whence he rode half across Essex to his great Norman castle at Hedingham. The room in which I slept last night was once part of the Earl's ballroom. The wooden mounting-block which I used yesterday when we saddled up in the yard was here two hundred years ago when the coaches ran to London and there were highwaymen on Danbury Hill.

However, we are leaving this old house which stood much as it stands to-day, when the Wars of the Roses were changing all English history, for I have a mind to go down to "the islands," that lonely, unknown marsh country between the Crouch and the Maplins, to see what they are doing with the lands which the Dutch embanked from the sea when Mr Lawrence Washington was riding his horse over Essex stubble fields.

So we rumbled out of Maldon, with a fine view from the top of the hill by Maldon Hall, that sweet Georgian house, of the whole wide estuary of the Blackwater glittering in the sun, the islands of Northey and Osea standing hazy in the morning mist. For several square miles from here to Woodham Mortimer you will not see better-farmed land in all England. Hereabouts are the farms of Mr Stanley Ratcliff, of Brick House, one of the best and most clear-thinking farmers in the country. I do not know the full acreage of his farms, but they must run to between four and five thousand acres, clean good land, well farmed, carrying plenty of sheep and cattle, with broad fields of corn, acres of roots, peas, beans, and mustard. A good mixed farmer who believes in the hoof and plenty of natural muck. His stacks are big, and his stock-yards are full.

As you come up the little hill where stands Woodham Mortimer church there is, on the roadside hard by the church, a pleasant, yellow-walled, Flemish-looking old house with crow-stepped gables and tall chimneys. In this old house, Woodham Mortimer

Hall, once lived the chief surgeon to Charles II, and father of the modern methods of midwifery. When he died his secrets died with him, and it was not until some floor-boards were pulled up in a bedroom that a case was found containing a set of silver instruments on which the modern usages of midwifery are based. The original instruments from this old manor-house are now in the Museum of the Royal College of Surgeons, if they were not destroyed in one of the bombing raids.

Woodham Mortimer Place, that porticoed, grey-brick Georgian house which stands back like a little old lady in a small park on the left of the road half a mile on, is the manor-house of an estate of some sixteen hundred acres which, until a year or two ago, was entirely run by two charming old maiden sisters, the Misses Parker. They were good squires and practical farmers, loved by their people of the little village hidden at the back of the park, below that low range of toy hills, each crowned by a clump of trees or a farmhouse which might have come out of an eighteenth-century print.

All this country, from Maldon by Hazeleigh and Purleigh to Southminster and Tillingham, is yeoman farmers' country. It is farmed by men whose holdings run to anything from three hundred to three thousand acres and more. The local pack, the Essex Farmers' Foxhounds, is mastered and committeed by farmers—a full answer to the anti-sport cranks who like to pretend that farmers have no use for foxhunting. Alfred Stephens, the Master, lives, farms, and kennels the hounds over the hill at New Hall Farm, Purleigh.

There are few local landed gentry. Most of the land is owned by colleges, by the Dean and Chapter of St Paul's, or by landowners living at a distance. Many of these big farmers own their own land. Some have farmed for two hundred years in direct succession from father to son; some go farther than that.

There are no great mansions in this flat and windy country whose fields, in the Dengie hundred, dyke-bordered, run on to the wide horizon of the sea. But there are many big farmhouses, built in Tudor and Jacobean days, yellow-walled, moated and elm-guarded, with great thatched barns which stand open to the road. It is the country which Bensusan has made loved in his enchanting series of Essex country sketches from *Father William* to *Village Idylls* and *Comment from the Countryside*—a land broad and bold, dedicated to corn and cattle, bright under the high skies of summer, scourged by the sea winds of winter. It is no place for pretty villas or weakling people. It has kept its soul and wide spaces.

At Battlesbridge we crossed the head waters of the Crouch, where the barges lie up beside one of the last great tide-mills in England. From there to Canewdon the road runs on the scarp of a gentle upland with wide views of the river Crouch winding like a snake through green marshes dotted with cattle. Corn-fields were yellow in the sun, busy with the clack of reapers and binders, here and there a horse team straining lordly. I looked down from the road across the marshes to Brandy Hole Creek, Fambridge Ferry, and Bridgemarsh Island and thought of wildfowling winters when we shot mallard and teal, curlew and plover, on all those shining miles. You do not find many widgeon in the Crouch nor black geese, but there are always a few greylags in hard weather, and Mr Barrett's marsh at South Fambridge Hall is, for its size, one of the best in all East Anglia.

Canewdon, which got its name because Canute built there a don, or castle, showed me the first surprise in the reclamation of what I had known as wide and hairy cattle marshes, full of great thistles and bouncing hares, rank grasses and sour corners.

Charles Cottis, of Lambourne Hall, Canewdon, is a good example of a working farmer who has made his own way. Yet, with the utmost perseverance and hard work he could not have made a real living out of farming before the war. His father, born at Raypits down on the marsh under the sea-wall, began life as a rook-scaring boy at a shilling a week. He could neither read nor write. As soon as he could scrape a few pounds together he bought a horse and cart and started business as a carter and carrier. When he died fourteen years ago he and his sons were paying £500 a week in wages and had over a hundred horse wagons and lorries on the road.

To-day Herbert Charles Cottis, his son, farms a thousand acres of his own, five hundred acres for the Government, and four hundred for a firm. He starts his day at five-thirty in the morning and finishes at nine o'clock at night.

I went round these marsh farms which I remembered a dozen years before as desolate cattle-ranges. They had been ploughed up, put down to corn, and had shown a fair harvest.

"Mind you," said Charles Cottis, as we stood under a clump of elms looking down the stubbles to the salt water, "if I'd tried to live on farming alone for the last eight or nine years we should have lost a lot of money. It never could have paid. It was the haulage business, having one or two good contracts, that kept us going. The last twenty years has pretty near stamped out the breed of Essex yeomen. It's been a rough old path for people like Dad and me who started with nothing, to try and build up something."

We discussed wages and the proposal to put them up to sixty shillings a week.

"I don't care if they go up to fifty-five shillings or sixty shillings," he said, "but I do hate having to pay that money to men from the labour exchange who refuse, as one of 'em did lately, even to do harvest work at one and twopence an hour in fine weather. They only want to do jobs that suit 'em.

"Yet look at that old chap sitting under that stack over there having his 'levenses. He's fifty-eight years old. He can't read or write, and yet I can put him to any job on the farm and he can do it —break in the horses or colts, draw out land, draw furrowing, or do hedging and ditching. He can plough and harrow with anyone, and he can draw a furrow for five hundred acres and not be three inches out. I wonder how many Londoners could walk straight for that distance. Let 'em try in the snow and see."

In the lane outside Lambourne Hall, that lovely old Tudor farmhouse, I ran into a man driving a tractor. He was burned as brown as leather, bare-headed and with that horsy look about him which your true hunting man never loses even if you put him on a bicycle in a bathing-dress. We stared for a moment of mutual recognition.

The tractor driver was Jimmy Sexton, before the war a rare point-to-point rider who won races all over East Anglia. His family have farmed Essex land for six generations. When his father, who lived on one farm at Burnham-on-Crouch for fifty years, made money by selling building land near Romford and sent his son to Eton and Sandhurst, the change altered neither the blood nor the inclinations. "Back to the land I came," grinned Sexton, "and here I reckon I'll stop. I'm not farming a lot of land, but I'm happy, and it's the best way of living."

Beyond Canewdon you come by pleasant lanes and tall groves of farmyard elms to the sudden, wide horizon of Wallasea Island, the island which is no island at all except when the spring tides overbrim the hard road at the head of Lion Creek and flood into the salt water of Paglesham Pool. Then, perhaps, it may be an island for an hour or two.

Wallasea is a wild and windy land without roads or trees. Its horizon is the sea-wall. The passing sails of barges and the masts of smacks glide above the grassy walls. Its landmarks are the distant roofs of its five lonely farmhouses—Grass Farm, Old Pool, New Pool, Devil's House, and Lower Barn.

At Grass Farm, where we unboxed the horses for a ride round this trackless prairie, there waited the owner of Wallasea, an old friend of other years, William Goodchild. William is sixty-two. Six feet tall, straight as a ramrod, quick on his feet, and a master on a horse. There have been Goodchilds in East Anglia for five hundred years. They farmed at Great Yeldham, where a Goodchild lives to-day in the Hall, and at Hundon, on the Suffolk border.

When he was a boy he went to London. He spent twenty-two years in the meat markets and clothing business until, like a good country buccaneer, he controlled six different types of business. Then, having made money in London, he brought it back to the land. He bought two thousand eight hundred acres, just in time to meet the blizzard of farming depression which followed the last war. He was only saved from bankruptcy because he had the foresight to buy land near the main Southend Bypass and sell it for development. Thus, a man of brains and ability with centuries of farming tradition behind him was unable to weather the storm which Baldwin and Ramsay MacDonald unloosed on farming, without being obliged to find money outside agriculture.

He has eight sons and twelve daughters, a family of twenty in all.

"I believe in large families and putting them on the land—but they won't stay on the land in future if farming is let down again. We farmed in Essex and Suffolk since five hundred years. But if I hadn't sold land at a good price for the Bypass I should have been broke years ago. The same with my neighbours. They're men who farm from one thousand to five thousand acres, but not one could have kept going on farming alone. They had to sell road frontages, sand and gravel, building sites for ribbon development, and beach huts—yet we hate to see 'em spoiling the countryside. One man kept going by running a brickyard, another by selling marsh land for a dock site. We only sold so that we could hang on to the land.

"The last twenty years brought farming down to the level of a prostitute. Now we're cultivating every acre we can. But we look for a better deal after this war than we had after the last one." There speaks Will Goodchild.

Will has done a great work with Wallasea and its two thousand two hundred acres of flat grass marsh, rich alluvial soil. In the last war it grew bumper crops of wheat. It is bounded by crawling creeks where the widgeon mew in winter, by shining mud flats, curlew-musical.

Eight years ago I had the shooting—a wild, flat, wide land of blenched grasses and singing winds, peewit-haunted, dotted with cattle, alive with hares, empty of man, its five farmhouses in ruins, its broken-down barns crowded on bitter nights by woolly waves of baaing sheep. There were wild geese and peregrine falcons seen suddenly in bitter winter dawns. There were oysters in the creeks and great red-sailed topsail barges which glided silently above the land behind the grassy sea-walls.

So that day I rode over it again. It has neither roads, hedges, nor trees. Three families live on it. The tiny school has four pupils. The island has no church, post-office, shop, or public-house. Jack Rebell, Will Goodchild's foreman, is great-great-grandson of another Jack Rebell who worked for Will Goodchild's great-great-grandfather at Hundon. Since the war Will has reclaimed six hundred acres of this marsh land. It is down to wheat, barley, oats, beans, sugar-beet, mangolds, and mustard seed. Jack Rebell's two sons, John and George, and their young wives, work the tractor binders. Sixteen-year-old Kathleen Rebell drives a milk-float round the island which takes bread, meat, candles, paraffin, beer, tobacco, matches, and groceries to the farmhouses. In between she drives the horse rake.

This harvest on Wallasea would never have been got in but for the help of forty-five schoolboys from Brentwood Grammar School. I rode among them, watched them, sun-burned, cheerful, tossing hay, stacking wheat and barley, rounding up sheep and cattle on horseback, free of the wind and the sun. Nearly half of them said they wanted to stick to farming. Their average age is sixteen. Dr Bryce, their English and music master, works as a labourer on another Goodchild farm. Albert Victor Shelley, white-haired, with a white moustache as monstrous as that of Marshal Budienny, was driving a sailer reaper, built in the seventies. Here in Essex they call it a flacker. Shelley and the flacker are of the same age.

I reined in my horse by Devil's House and asked why it was so called.

"They say that a man saw the Devil on the marsh here," said Goodchild. "All I know is that some nights the cattle in the stock-yards seem to go mad. They rush about like devils. One night they had the gates down and were out all over the marsh."

The night before in the Jolly Sailor, on Maldon water-front, Alfred

Herbert Martin, who has worked as a farm labourer on these islands for forty years, had told me his story.

"Same as that owd Davvle's House. I know'd that well tharty year agoo. An owd thatched place with a rare gret owd barn—suffin' lonely, I tell yer. I bided a week there. One night my mate found hisself hulled out o' bed an' down the stairs. He never know'd what done it. That owd davvle wore strong as a hoss.

"Tew nights arterwards he rowed over to Foulness Island across the creek. He come back late in the moonlight, bright as day that wore.

"'Alf,' he say to me, 'what do you reckon I seed when I was a-rowin' acrost the crick? I seed that owd Mrs Smith and Mother Redcap, from Foulness, comin' across the water on a wooden hurdle in the moonlight. She dedn't hev no oars, but she travelled same as if she was in a boat. She's the headest witch about these parts. Yu look out, bor! She's on this island somewhere now.'

"An, yu believe me, sir, when we looked in the barn next mornin' there was that owd witch curled up in the straw like a cat. She come in the house, 'cause we had her son workin' along wi' us, an' I mind her well settin' by the fire, peelin' pertaters, nippin' her owd lips tergither, an' a-mumblin' 'Holly, Holly! Brolly, Brolly! Redcap! Bonny, Bonny!'

"Blast, boy, she scat me. There was several witches them days, but that owd Mother Redcap was the headest one o' the lot. I got out o' Davvle's House suffin' quick arter that."

And, believe it or not, as the evergreen Mr Ripley would say, I have known the Essex marshes well enough for more than a quarter of a century to know that this belief in witches still lives—within forty miles of London.

It is only a few years since that I was rowing one night down Paglesham Creek by Dead Man's Point with Fred Keeble, the marshman of East End, when he told me that he had seen the Devil swim across the creek from Potton Island in the moonlight and run up the mud, dripping with blue fire.

"Lor! I wopped on me knees on the bottom boards of the boat, an' I prayed to the good Gord when I seed that owd davvle. But, blarst! When that topped the sea-wall I see that warn't no more'n a gret owd hare, drippin' o' phorsphorus from the mud. So I ups wi' me gun an' knocked the b——r over!"

Poor Fred! He believed firmly in witches and a ghost who haunted the three hollow elms in the bend of the road to Church

End, where the smugglers used to hide their kegs. "The three owd widders," he called them. He died painfully, from cancer in the throat, gasping with a last flicker of his old fun, "I'm like that owd smack on the mud, master—tore-out! I reckon there 'on't be much to salvage."

Strangest of all first-hand Essex superstitions I have come across was the story told me by Charlie Stamp, the wildfowler and fisherman of Canvey Point, in 1925. Charlie lived right under the sea-wall in a shack he had built from the timbers of an old barge. A dyke divided his garden from the sea-wall. A plank spanned it. Beyond the wall the saltings and the mud flats ran out under the moon, misty and dim, shelving into the tide, into the wide waters of Thames-mouth. This is the island that Ptolemy called Connos. These are the saltings where the tide casts up Roman pottery and bits of Samian ware from Rutupiæ, the lost fort by the twin towers of the Reculvers, lonely on the tide edge of Kent.

The Danes came to Canvey when they had their camp in the hills of Hadleigh. De Ruyter's Dutch seamen chased its flying sheep when his fleet blockaded Thames and Medway. It is an isle blanketed in the mists of very ancient history.

"I laid in me truckle bed lookin' out o' the winder of a midnight," said Charlie. "Bright moon that was, bright as day. An' I reckon I had a dream. I dreamt there was an owd feller come up over the saltin's, over the wall an' across the plank into my garden. A rum owd feller. He stood six foot. He had a leather jerkin on wi' a belt an' a sword and cross-garters below his knees. He had a funny owd hat on his head—like a helm that was, with wings on. An' long moustaches an' a beard.

"'I've lost me ship, mate,' he say, 'I want to get a ship back to me own country. I'm a lost man.'

"'Goo you up to Grays or Tilbury,' I says. 'You'll get a ship there, mate, to carry you to any port in the world.'

"He wagged his owd head an' looked at me right sorrowful. 'I count I 'on't find no ship to take me to my port. I'm a lost man.'

"An' he walked over that sea-wall, marster, an' away out on the marsh, an' I never seed him no more."

I thought of Charlie Stamp, the marsh gunner who could neither read nor write, who had never seen a drawing of a Viking in his winged helmet and cross-gartered buskins. I thought of his strange dream and of the lost Viking ghost walking the misty moonlit marsh—one with the witches of Foulness and the devil who threw the man out of his bed one dark night on Wallasea. It is an odd world, a strange world, the coast marshes under the moon.

I went up on the stack-top at Devil's House to watch Dick Warner, the thatcher, at his eclectic craft, and look out over the six hundred acres of ploughed-up marsh. Ten women were at work among the schoolboys and three grown men, conscientious objectors.

"They won't fight, but they'll work, and they obey orders. This lot are really conscientious—some of 'em are only scroungers with no more conscience than this hay rake," said a voice from the bottom rungs of the ladder.

A month ago there were thirteen hundred sheep on the island, mostly Kents, about two hundred cattle, and sixty unbroken horses, most of them foaled on the marsh. They had never seen a hard road or a stable and knew no blanket but the stars.

William came up the ladder, bitterly to resent the fact that he had been obliged to slaughter eight horses since the horse slaughterers were offering £20 to £25 each. The horses of Britain are going into half the so-called breakfast rolls and meat rolls which an unsuspecting urban public, that professes to love its animals, is buying and eating at between sevenpence and a shilling a tin.

"I used to run fifteen hundred sheep and four hundred cattle on this island and about five hundred unbroken horses which slept under God's heaven at night," said Will, beside me on the stack. He waved his hand over the broad marsh. "One of the nicest pieces of corn land in all England—been robbed and left for hundreds of years. Now I haven't got as good a crop off it as I'd like. We shan't get more than two-thirds of the barley we ought to because of the heat. Too low to cut—over-ripe.

"Horses, I love 'em," he went on. "Used to please me no end to see a mob of wild young 'uns galloping all over this marsh with my boys trying to round 'em up on horseback like cowboys. This policy of slaughtering off cattle and horses is shortsighted. It'll react badly in a year or two. The horse slaughterers come down into these country districts and buy up any screw they can put their hands on.

"There are lots of little farmers who can't afford tractors. They rely, at this time of the year, on buying up more or less worn-out London horses at fifteen to twenty pounds a head. After they've been on the London streets for years with the railways, the breweries, and the haulage companies they react to country food and air like heroes. They'll help you get in the harvest sometimes for several years. They do a lot of useful work and die decently in a green old age. Nowadays the slaughterers snap them up at twenty to twenty-five pounds apiece before they can ever get to the country.

"I'll show you a sight to-morrow that'll make your heart bleed —sixty good horses down on Bulphan Fen, a dozen thoroughbred hunters among 'em, all waiting for the knacker's man to put the pistol to their heads. That's a fine sight for an Englishman, isn't it? Why don't some of these humanity societies stop *that* game instead of spending all their money on standing up for the fox who robs my hen roosts?"

Wallasea is not the only island which war has reclaimed from windy cattle-marsh and curlew-haunted loneliness. Potton Island, that pear-shaped pan of one thousand and twenty-five acres, when I had the shooting in 1925 was a sheep- and cattle-run full of great hares with widgeon on its fleets and a shepherd living in the old farmhouse which was built in Charles I's day. The shepherd had never seen the streets of London or ridden in a train. They brought the fresh water in a barrel from the mainland, and the only tree was a plum-tree in the garden. That island to-day is under the plough. It grows the tall wheat as it did half a century ago when H. J. Elwes, of Colesbourne Park in Gloucestershire, owned it, and the corn was thrashed and went by sailing-barge.

In those days Potton and Foulness, "the island of the birds," Rushley with its shining fleets, and Havengore and New England were as lonely and remote from the rest of England as Doughty's "Arabia Deserta." They were owned from afar and farmed by foremen who could neither read nor write. They got their harvest labour from gangs of wandering Irishmen, a troublesome, murderous crew who came over to England each year to lift potatoes and get in the corn harvest.

Old Squire Ruggles-Brise, of Spains Hall, Finchingfield, father of the late M.P. for Maldon,[1] used to tell me that when he was young and went partridge- and duck-shooting on these islands the Irish crew lived like hogs and fought like dogs. They slept all together in the great barn at each farm, and the only person they were afraid of was the foreman's wife, usually a sharp-tongued, hard-faced woman of the marshes, who drilled them like a sergeant-major. She cooked all their food by the simple means of throwing each man's contribution, whether a lump of meat, a rabbit, a piece of liver, a couple of eels or a duck, into a great net bag. This was filled

[1] The late Sir Edward Ruggles-Brise, Bart., of Spains Hall.

up with swedes, turnips, potatoes, and onions and then dumped into a vast iron pot which simmered on the whitewashed kitchen hearth for hours, until the whole gorgeous mess became an Irish stew in fact and being.

More than one murderer and wife-beater, more than one hedgerow robber, many a man of lesser crime, found sanctuary in the islands in those days at the end of the last century. The old Plough and Sail at Paglesham, that aptly-named inn whose sweep of roof nearly touches the ground, could tell many a story of these rough men, kin with the smugglers, who found safety on the lonely islands, cut off by the creeks from the rest of England. Even at the beginning of the last war, in 1914, there were men on Foulness who had never travelled in a train, and many who had never seen a soldier in uniform.

We trundled back that evening to East Horndon Hall, Will's old half-timbered manor farmhouse, whose site was first built upon by the monks of Waltham Abbey in 1188. They had killed a couple of ducks, so we dined well, topped up with claret and good port, talked horses and hunting, farming and shooting, and the future of the yeomanry.

I asked William his definition of an English yeoman. It came pat.

"A man who owns and farms several hundred acres of land or has it on a long lease under a good squire. Nearly all arable. Your real yeoman is always a corn grower. He doesn't go in for dairy herds. They stink, and they foul the land. He leaves them to Scotsmen, though he may keep a few cows for his own house. But beef cattle and sheep—he'll breed the best of them.

"He can afford to hunt or shoot once a week. He sees to it that his boys and girls get a jolly good grammar school education and no frills. He brings 'em up to go to church, fear God, and honour the King. As for himself he hunts in rat-catcher, has lunch with the squire every now and then, but doesn't expect to be asked to dinner and doesn't want to. I should say he generally votes Tory, but there's plenty of good Liberals among 'em.

"Whenever there's a war on, you'll find his sons first in the fighting—I've got one or two up in the air and one or two on the sea. Keep that breed alive, and the country'll never go wrong. They're like the Scots parsons' sons—they can turn out anything from a good farmer to a field-marshal or a Colonial governor. Help yourself and pass that port. My father put that down, and it'll never fetch a quack out of that old duck that you've just swallowed. Have a cigar, and we'll go to bed."

We slept that night in the oak-beamed dining-room, packed to its ceiling with trusses of straw. It is William's nearest concession to a dug-out. Bombs have fallen on both sides of his house. Splinters have ripped into his walls. In the next bay, on a little white bed between the straw trusses, William retired, wagging his beard over his evening chapter of the Bible before switching out the light.

I thought, as I lay there, with the light winking on horse pistols and armour hung on the ancient walls, with that straight-backed old man reading the Scriptures next door to me, that if England ever barters her yeomen for a mess of commercial pottage, for a slick programme of State ownership and factory-run farms she will throw away the best of her manhood, the promise of the future. There will be none left then of the old English stock but the New Zealanders and Australians, the Canadians and South Africans, to restore to us the old values, to keep alive the simple faiths, to breed the straight, independent type of Englishman. The Dominions have kept faiths and values which we are in danger of losing. Neither Committee farming nor Boreham Housedom will ever breed the yeomen of England.

CHAPTER X

Each soil hath no liking of every grain,
Nor barley and wheat is for every vein,
Yet know I no country, so barren of soil,
But some kind of corn may be gotten with toil.

THOMAS TUSSER,
One Hundred Points of Good Husbandrie (1557)

A Wayside Word with Charlie Brown, the King of Limehouse—The Mechanized Monsters of Hatfield—A Bit of Bread and Cheese with Jack Olding—Bulldozers which move Mountains—American Farming comes to England—What the Caterpillar Tractor can do—"The Indivisible Trinity: Landowner, Farmer, and Labourer"—Hannen Swaffer's Definition—Beak, V.C., of Malta—To Easton Lodge—A Vanished Herd of Noble Deer—Hedingham Castle and the Great Yeldham Gaol

WE LEFT EAST HORNDON HALL NEXT MORNING ON A LONG RUN to Hatfield in Hertfordshire. For there that good sportsman and pioneer of modern mechanized farming, Jack Olding, had not only promised to put on a full-scale demonstration of up-to-date farming machinery, but had invited me to bring a few friends for what he described as "a bit of bread and cheese in the canteen."

It was a queer change from one's memories of peace-time days, that almost uninterrupted run along the straight ribbon of the Southend Bypass, mile after mile without a sign of a private car. We saw no wheeled vehicle whatever save a few Army lorries, an odd Bren gun carrier, and once or twice farm lorries carrying roots or beasts. The land on either side was well cultivated, but the nearer one got to the outskirts of London the more apparent became the wastage of good agricultural land. Acres were lying derelict as unused building-plots or weedy garden wildernesses, surrounding disused shacks, garish villas, and rows of jerry-built houses which looked as though a few winters of wind and rain would open holes in the roofs and cracks in the walls.

However much the promises of post-war Utopia may falsify themselves, indiscriminate ribbon development and the swindling of small investors, who are induced to buy third-rate jerry-built houses on long-term instalment schemes, must be stopped.

We pulled up at the Roundabout, that great modern inn on the outskirts of Woodford kept by Charlie Brown, the King of Limehouse. Now Charlie and his old father—alas, departed to a less substantial kingdom—were both old friends of many years' standing. So to stop was the least decency.

There was a time, fifteen or twenty years ago, when, if I went on an evening, sick of the West End of London, to the simple joys of the Railway Tavern in West India Dock Road—"Charlie Brown's" to half the world—I would be sure of a drop of the true white rum, a good Dutch cigar, talk with men from half the seven seas, and songs that would lift the roof till the clock struck two and the policemen danced on the pavement. That was Charlie Brown's in the old days, a museum of men and things.

They had a double-headed pig, a six-legged calf, snakes and babies in bottles, crocodiles hung from the roof, a Chinese ivory goddess worth £7000, Louis XV furniture, a piece of plush from Queen Victoria's coffin, Field Marshal von Hindenburg's long pipe, stuffed eagles and ducks, hawks and reptiles, swords and daggers, swordfish and sharks' teeth, a piano to bang on, and anyone you liked to talk to, from 'Captain' Joe Oakley, Freeman of London River, to a Dane, a Norwegian, Chon Chu the Chinaman, or Charlie Brown himself.

Old Charlie came from my native Cambridgeshire, a fenman born and bred. He had cauliflower ears, a broken nose, and a wide and cheerful grin. His friends ranged from the Prince of Wales to the King of Spain, from skippers to donkeymen, and he had the soul of an artist. His collection of ivories was rare and beautiful. His collection of junk was fantastic and unbelievable. In all it was said to be worth more than £70,000—scattered throughout the bars and rooms of an unpretentious pub on the corner of a dirty little back street hard by the dock gates in the West India Dock Road. When he died twenty thousand people went to his funeral and the newspapers of the world carried the news.

His son, Charlie, "young Charlie," although he is nearer sixty than fifty, has inherited his father's charm and his father's friends, his ivories and his wonderful pearl pin. He carries forty-seven watches about him and was once the champion boxer of Limehouse. He sings like a cross between a bullfrog and a nightingale and could put most men out of the door with a flick of his right arm. So do you wonder that we stopped at the Roundabout to tell the time by each of the forty-seven watches, to drink a pint of ale, and talk over old days and old nights when Limehouse was gay?

ROUNDING UP SHEEP ON WALLASEA ISLAND

"A wild, flat, wide land of blenched grasses and singing winds."

Photo Douglas Went, Brightlingsea

ONE OF JACK OLDING'S SIXTEEN-TON BULLDOZERS PUSHING A TREE OVER

Photo Sport and General

When we left that genial inn a brown-paper parcel was thrust hurriedly on the driving-seat. "Don't you open that till you're out of sight!" Charlie commanded. That cheerful giant, whose heart is of gold, had christened the expedition with a bottle of whisky and one of port "to keep your clocks right on the road."

As we rumbled through Edmonton with a green thought for John Gilpin, Jim nodded sagely towards the villas, the gasometers, the lurching trolly-buses, the smoking factory chimneys, and spoke six words—"Not our country, sir. That stinks."

I thought of the minute Mrs Friedberg, perched up beside him like a canary, driving her ambulance in Hoxton through Blitzes when bombs fell, when houses and factories went up in smoke and flames, when blood ran in the streets, and women moaned under smoking bricks. "How would you have liked that job, Jim?"

"Too much of a man's job—I'd sooner be up in the air or out on a hoss. Napoleon can have it."

A lot of people have asked me since this curious pilgrimage ended how it was that we were never stranded at night for stabling or fodder. They would not believe it possible that one could travel two thousand five hundred miles through this petrol-ridden England where the saddle-horse in many districts is almost a museum piece and find a stable each night and a truss of hay or a bag of beans. That first night at Hatfield was the only night when we had difficulty. It was my own fault.

What with looking over the incredible display of the latest farming machinery in Jack Olding's showrooms and demonstration fields, choosing a suitable area of rough, derelict land for the Bull-dozers to operate on before the public the next morning, riding round to see farmers and get their permission for the film camera-men, who popped out of the blue like hawks, and answering telephone inquiries from London newspapers, it was well past nine in the evening before I began to look for stabling. I had not the slightest idea where to go. Nor had Jack. His mind does not run normally to wandering saddle-horses cast up on his doorstep late at night. He thinks either in terms of his racehorses at Newmarket or his mechanical monsters snorting on farms and airfields.

I remembered having discovered years before in Hatfield a little, low, half-timbered fifteenth-century inn called the Eight Bells. Its overhanging eaves and bedroom windows were so near the pavement that you could crack a whip against the panes. There is a legend that Dick Turpin took a flying leap from one of the windows on to the back of his black mare as the Bow Street runners swarmed up the staircase to lay him by the heels. Bill Sikes "shaped his course there" and "ate and drank alone" in a corner of the bar after the murder of Nancy.

I remembered it as a rambling, fascinating little place, with two or three little back rooms, hazy with smoke, decorated with prints of hunting and bare fist fighting, racehorses and greyhounds. One of those friendly little places whose wooden floors and plaster walls smell of that queer mixture of bees and honeycomb which is really the essence of shag tobacco and good ale slopped over. Be sure that in such a den you will always find a man with a horse, and several men with dogs to sell or buy.

So down to the Eight Bells Jim and I marched. We opened a side door, bent our heads, and groped along a blacked-out passage into a tiny, raftered parlour. There sat four or five ploughmen and hedgers of the changeless English type; a little wizened man in a striped waistcoat, breeches, and gaiters; two fat old ladies, comfortable with stout; a ruddy-faced soldier who would have looked more at home ferreting Lord Salisbury's rabbits than in battle-dress; a couple of odd dogs and a handsome wavy-coated retriever.

We ordered our beer and sat down. The company eyed us quietly. The little wizened man looked at our boots and breeches, piped up, "It's like old times to see you two gents come in like that."

"You can't tell us where to find an old-time stable, can you?"

"That I can, sir. Up by the station. Rare nice loose-boxes—haven't had a horse in 'em since the war began. I'll run up to old Bob So-and-so's house and get the key."

For an hour we three hunted Hatfield under the stars, seeking Old Bob, who had gone to ground, his wife knew not whither. Baffled, we returned to the Eight Bells. There sat Old Bob—another wizened, bent, little man with a cock-sparrow eye, a monkey quickness in his legs, and a piping voice. He produced the key, and between us we stabled the horses in loose-boxes which lacked only straw to make them perfect. We shook down a couple of bags of shavings as the next best thing. Next came the question of fodder. We had run woefully short, forgotten to load up at Goodchild's, a mistake I never repeated. So it meant a mile prowl down a dark lane into a strange field with a couple of large sacks which we stuffed to the necks with stolen hay, pulled out by the armful.

Back at the stables Old Bob, who agreed to repay the owner of the stack on our behalf, insisted that we return to a final hot toddy as the guests of the landlord of the Eight Bells. The two of them, snug in that red-curtained little back parlour with the oak table and low settles, a wood fire sputtering, were tickled to death by the thought of our expedition. Indeed, Old Bob offered to come with us on the rest of the road for no pay at all but the run of his teeth. It was the first of several offers of help and companionship which I had from working men to whom the love of a horse meant so much that they willingly offered to forgo a weekly wage—an offer I would naturally not have accepted even had I been able to have taken those grand fellows with me.

I slept that night at the Comet, a grandiloquent roadhouse on the Barnet Bypass, where Jack Olding is wont to entertain his friends and customers who may range from War Office generals or Allied military attachés to jockeys and farmers.

We were up early next morning to greet a mixed company of friends. I had bidden them at Jack's invitation to a demonstration of mechanized farming and "a bit of bread and cheese in the canteen." They arrived from the four corners of Eastern England—Lord Wolmer,[1] from the Ministry of Works and Buildings; Lord Sempill, from the Admiralty; Prince Nicholas Galitzine, from Huntingdonshire; Sir Jocelyn Lucas, M.P., from Portsmouth; Sir Richard and Lady Cruise, from Buckinghamshire; Sir Richard Cooper, of Cooper, McDougall, and Robertson, from Berkhamsted; Lord Perry, Chairman of the Ford Motor Company; Mrs Valerie Low, whose voice would charm a robin off its perch; and Mr Oswald Hickson, that eminent lawyer, looking more archiepiscopal than ever; a mixed bag of friends from Fleet Street, and local agriculturalists.

It was a varied, merry, and interested company which was motored off to a bush-grown, tree-infested stretch of quarries and miniature hills chosen as a demonstration ground for the mighty eighteen-ton Bulldozers—Caterpillar Diesel-propelled earth-shifters, whose great blades can slice hills as flat as billiard-tables. They have been used extensively for clearing bushed-up ground and levelling rough tracts throughout America and Canada. Since the war they have played a noble part in levelling and preparing the thousands of air-fields which dot Britain.

There was, I remember with unction, a stout American camera-man of Czech origin, who, surveying me booted and breeched, remarked sorrowfully, "Ach, dat iss nice. But vot a pity dat you are

[1] Now the Earl of Selborne, Minister of Economic Warfare, and a practical farmer and fruit-grower.

not dressed proper for de film. You got a hoass—if you hadt tellt me befoare I vould haf put you in a dam' nice cowboy outfit—long shaps, und a leather jacket mit beads, big silver spurs, und a dam' great hat, fit for Gary Cooper." I shall always regret that we did not let him have his head.

The Bulldozers performed miracles. Driven by one man, they charged over rough, broken ground into ash- and willow-trees eighteen inches in diameter, butted them sideways with the first head-on crack and, retreating and charging again, snapped their trunks and sent them down with a rending crash.

They ploughed up blackthorn bushes fourteen feet high and six inches in diameter as though they had been wheat. They uprooted them bodily and thrust them before them in a vast, rending, crashing thicket of tossing branches and writhing limbs. It was an impressive, almost a terrifying sight.

"There's something almost awe-inspiring about it," Lord Wolmer remarked. "One feels as though the last sanctuary of nature has gone once these machines are let loose in woods and thickets, but," half regretfully, "what an amazing saving in time and labour."

He is a notable combination of qualities, possessing the practical administrative sense of his father with the philosophic statesmanship of the Cecils through his mother.

Next, the Bulldozers moved a gorse-grown hill of earth, thirty feet high and forty yards wide at its base. The huge blades sliced into it like cake. Within twenty minutes they had levelled the entire hill. Tons of root-bound earth were shovelled into bomb-holes, and a tract of flat earth was left on which a crop could have been planted then and there.

We saw a demonstration of trench-cutting both for military and drainage purposes. The trench-cutters can dig a ditch at an incredible speed, and, what is more, the digger blades are set to give the correct fall in inches over a given area to allow for the carry-away of rain-water and field drains.

In a copse Caterpillar Diesel tractors were pulling up tree stumps at the rate of one a minute, work which would have taken two men at least half a morning with spades and pick-axes. They hauled huge logs along the road at five times the speed of a horse team. Here I noticed some of the big, rubber-tyred John Deere tractors at work. Apart from their uses in the field these tractors have a great value as haulage units on hard roads, where their speed and lightness of tread is a marked advantage. The Caterpillar can do the road work equally well, but too much of it is unnecessary wear and tear on the tracks.

Next we moved to one of Lord Salisbury's farms, where ploughing, cultivating, disc-harrowing, seeding, potato-hilling, and planting were all demonstrated behind D. 2 and D. 4 tractors.

These tractors, which are the backbone of prairie farming in America, have been known to cultivate forty-three acres of hilly land a day using ten gallons of fuel, while on hard, rock-dry land sub-soiling fifteen inches deep has been done at the rate of ten acres in ten hours, using about ten gallons of Diesel fuel. One of the up-to-the-minute business fitments of these tractors is an hour meter which is part of the standard equipment. It 'counts' and registers the number of hours the engine operates, and provides a basis for servicing on schedule. They are ideal with a threshing-drum, and can haul the tackle anywhere and then drive the drum with a belt pulley.

These tractors can disc and seed sixty acres of barley per ten-hour day on light sandy soil at a cost of about £2 10*s*., possibly more since fuel went up in price.

Ten-inch deep ploughing on flat land can be done at the rate of about twelve and a half acres every ten hours, using roughly fifteen gallons of fuel, while harvesting with a combine averages out at about thirty acres a day using about ten gallons on flat land.

I thought, watching it all, admiring the neat work of the smaller models which are used also for orchard work, vegetable cultivation and hoeing, that the day of the horse had died for ever on English farms. I said as much.

"Don't you believe it, Jimmie," grinned Jack. "We shall always need your old horses for odd jobs about the farm, for hole-and-corner work in little fields, for short haulage jobs. This merely means that instead of being the Lord of the Harvest in future the horse will have to be content with being the odd-job maid. But don't forget this—these tractors can't put dung back into the soil. The horse and the bullock can. Farming will always need them."

He showed me a remarkable photograph of six Caterpillar Diesels on the Hays Farms in Bonneville County, Idaho, pulling between them a 196-foot span of drills and seeding four hundred and forty acres per twelve-hour day at a total cost in oil and fuel of less than four cents an acre.

"Those American boys who farm on the grand prairie scale find that it pays to pull a wide string of drills in low gear, because it cuts their drill repair bill to much less than it would be at higher speed."

It is a point for the big farmers of Norfolk, Lincolnshire, and Wiltshire, who have wide fields to play in.

Finally, before lunch, I was shown a D. 4 tractor belted up to a twelve-inch centrifugal pump in a stream. On a thirty-foot lift at two thousand five hundred gallons a minute this Diesel could supply the equivalent of a one-inch rainfall on one hundred and ten acres in twenty hours. "The same Diesel can harvest forty-eight acres of corn in twelve hours," said the demonstrator, "provided the field is flat."

A quick look at the John Deere range of general purpose tractors, which seem to fulfil every need for row-crop work—ridging potatoes, hoeing beet, and general haulage work—and we went for lunch.

"Those John Deeres can do anything you like in the way of ploughing and cultivating, and, in fact, they are general-purpose tractors in the fullest sense of the term," said the demonstrator. "You can use them for hay-harvesting, and almost anything else in the way of general utility work which the horse used to do."

"You fellows will end up by driving not only the horse but the old English farm hand with all his centuries of knowledge right off the land," I retorted. "You'll have a mechanical thatcher next, a power-driven hedge-layer, a rubber-tyred shepherd, and a gang of robot land girls."

"Oh, no, we shan't! We're only giving the farm labourer a few more jobs to learn. They'll save him a lot of dirty work in dirty weather and put the farmer three jumps ahead of the weather all the time. The farm labourer is the cleverest man on earth if only people realized it—those chaps you've just seen at work are nearly all Hertfordshire villagers whose fathers walked behind the horse-plough and dug ditches with a spade. Now look at 'em. They move mountains!"

It was a pleasant lunch. Hare soup, roast partridges from Swaffham, rabbit pie from the warrens of Brocket Hall, and apple pudding. "All off our own land, shot by ourselves," said Jack, with a wink at Moray Stephenson, that harassed philosopher who runs Government contracts with one hand and manages Jack's ten thousand acres of shooting with the other.

They had dug up some claret and port from somewhere with a few bottles of white wine, so the toast to "The Indivisible Trinity—landowner, farmer, and labourer," went with a swing.

We followed it up with "The Golden Hoof" and a final toast to our host of "the bit of bread and cheese," Jack Olding.

It was Lord Wolmer who pertinently said in his speech that you cannot breed John Bulls on peptonized breakfast foods, Chinese eggs, canned meat, or bananas with a rubber stamp on. You must grow their food at home. It was Billy Sempill, that master of fact and logic, who produced methodical figures to show that Britain can grow more than enough food to feed herself always and at any time. It was Jocelyn Lucas who warned us to be on guard against the encroachments of the bureaucrats who will filch the land from its owners and tie up the farmer and the farm labourer in a cat's-cradle of red tape if we of the land are not both wary and strong when peace comes.

Then we went out into the golden light. To the busy clack and hum of combine harvesters at work on a farm across the road and the discovery that the tractor was driven by a public schoolboy on holiday whose girl assistant was an ex-London barmaid. In the field beyond, dairy shorthorns, chewing the cud in the warm sunlight, no more than flicked an ear as at an irritant fly when a four-engined bomber roared over, barely clearing the telegraph wires. Beyond the hedge four horses, glistening in the sun, drew a red-painted, blue-wheeled harvest wagon. It was built of ash and oak a hundred years ago, trimmed like a ship. Of such conflicting elements is the farming scene in England to-day.

I went up to London that night to see Mr Stowell, the Assistant Editor of the *Daily Telegraph*. That charming Fleet Street gentleman combines an old-world courtliness of manner with an alarming acuteness of news sense. The combination is rare and refreshing. Dearly though I love my Fleet Street brethren, I am compelled sometimes to ask myself whether some of the younger ones need tip their hats on the back of their heads, brandish their right fists through mackintosh pockets as though they held a gangster gun, and slip across a pseudo-American accent in order to convince one that they write news. But they are preferable to the ladylike boys of the herbaceous border breed who beatify their souls, their mothers, their dogs, and themselves in narcissus print each Sunday.

Perhaps a week out of London on the back of a horse had cleared my eyes to a new perspective.

I walked into the Savoy bar in quest of Larry Rue, of the *Chicago Tribune*, or Tommy Watson, who is Hearst's galloper, or Lorne Campbell, of Australia—anyone to whom I could listen on prairie farming. They were in other climes. All I met was Hannen Swaffer, holding court in the lounge. The Pope of Fleet Street, grey hair awash, cravat awry, thin face ascetic, black jacket ash-strewn, was cryptic.

"H-hallo, J-Jimmy—I suppose that was your ch-charger I encountered tethered in the lavatory just now! They t-tell me you got on a damn' great horse this morning to have your ph-photo taken—but you had a horse-box waiting round the corner! A fine swizz—you rubber-tyred Cobbett!"

Swaff is always dry champagne.

Later I went into the Berkeley Buttery for a solitary meal. There happened one of those odd encounters which are the peppercorns of life. One place removed from me at the black and chromium counter sat a long, thin-faced man of distinction. He had a tanned face, a beak of a nose, coldly purposeful eyes, a straight thin mouth. He looked like a hawk in tweeds. We eyed each other.

Said I to myself, "That man has either been a professional huntsman or a cavalry sergeant-major—but, by gad, I'd follow him anywhere and hate to meet him in a dark lane for a row." Presently we talked, taking in a solid, stolid naval captain who was, I think, mildly scandalized by our unorthodoxy.

Beaky-nose questioned me. He found out my name, my job, and my immediate mission in a brace of twin shakes. It was all done so smoothly.

"Here," says I, "I get my living questioning other people. I'm not accustomed to *being* questioned. Who, may I ask, are you?" Beaky-nose demurred. The naval officer, convinced by now that we were not respectable, slithered off his seat into the *Ewigkeit*.

"Come on," I said, "stump up. I was going to ask you to have a drink, but I'm damned if I do till I know who you are or what you are."

"What do you think?" he grinned.

"I said to myself when I first looked at you, 'Either a professional huntsman or a sergeant-major.'"

"You're pretty nearly right. The first guess flatters me. The second's as near as dammit. I'm a soldier."

"What's your name?"

He hesitated. The hawk looked almost shy. "Er—well—here's my identity card." I read it. "Brigadier W. D. M. Beak, V.C., D.S.O., M.C."

"Good God!" says I. "Here am I scared of a bull in a field and would think twice about jumping a five-barred gate. Have a glass of port."

We had several. We talked past the hours of all the trains that might have taken me to Hatfield until at two in the morning we sat in the lounge of the Dorchester, watching the rich and the pear-shaped go to bed. We agreed on views of people with which, perhaps, I had better not soil this immaculate page. Finally we went our ways, having lit a friendship like a spark.

"When I see you by the end of the war," says I, "I'll bet you a fiver you'll be Field Marshal Lord Beak of the Beak."

To-day, Beak is Major-General, commanding the troops in Malta against the most withering assault by bomb, mine, and machine-gun from the air that any fortress has ever endured. He is writing history in flame. His stand has been one of the turning-points of the war. All of which story is told merely from the pleasant vanity of liking to know that one has occasionally picked the right horse from the mob in the paddock.

We left Hatfield next day. We went by winding lanes through the pleasant little hills of Hertfordshire, by poppy-gay fields through Hertford and Ware, which always fill my mind with a pleasant wedding of imagined pictures of John Gilpin and Charles Lamb, through Much Hadham and Sawbridgeworth, to Bishop Stortford, which has still kept the soul and atmosphere of a town whose life was once corn and cattle. From there by Takeley, where is the remnant of a great forest, still haunted by deer; by Great Canfield, which has lovely cottages and pink and yellow old farmhouses, to Dunmow. That enchanted sleeping beauty of a little town with its pleasant streets and wooded fields has grown into a present-day Arcadia of writers and novelists. Once upon a time Mr H. G. Wells, who would do so much better if he stuck to his job as a popular entertainer and pseudo-scientist instead of trying to put the world and the future to rights, lived in that lovely old red-brick house above the fishponds in Easton Park, where Tom Devitt[1] dwelt until a year or two ago.

It was the old Countess of Warwick, that Edwardian beauty whom I remember as a charmingly vain old lady, driving about in a basket carriage drawn by white ponies or feeding her white pigeons, peacocks, and monkeys, who started the fashion for writers to live in the fields and woods of the old Maynard estates that once were twenty thousand acres.

[1] Sir Thomas Devitt, Bart.

To-day there is Philip Guedalla, that enlightened interpreter of history, living in the Old Laundry; Basil Dean in a house hard by the church; H. A. Gwynne, former editor of the *Morning Post*, in a titivated farmhouse; and R. D. Blumenfeld, the Archbishop of Fleet Street, still wise, humorous, and generous, in the manor farm of Muscombs which has been his home for many years.

But my mission to Dunmow was a mission of the stomach and not of the mind. I had hatched a cunning plot. It was a stratagem to inveigle my old friend 'Jiggs' Greville[1] into the Saracen's Head, that beamed and plastered inn which once had stabling for thirty-five horses, and there warm his heart with port till I might screw out of him permission to shoot one of his fat fallow bucks and take it with us for meat on the road.

Alas, the great herd of red and fallow deer, the finest in all Essex, one of the best indeed in East Anglia, had been wiped out at the beginning of the war. They shot them every one, down to the last doe and the mighty royals, whose antlers had clashed in the moon under the scarred oaks of that ancient park. It is a great loss, the passing of the Easton herd, for there were in it red deer whose ancestry probably went back to the Middle Ages.

So when we had drunk a melancholy pint for their passing we groped across country, by twisting by-lanes through a rich, well-farmed land, heavy with elms, beautified by old farmhouses, prosperous with great barns, to Gosfield Park. At Gosfield we stopped to eat cold beef at the end of the long lake—the longest in Essex—and I went into the tiny church in the park to see the memorials to Sir John Wentworth, who built most of this good old Elizabethan house. Ancestry is a forgivable vanity, a good ending to any road.

We halted a few miles farther at Castle Hedingham while I climbed the ramp and crossed the moat to the foot of the towering four-square Norman keep of the De Veres. It is all that is left of the mighty castle which once overlorded half Essex. Jackdaws flew from the high windows and circled protestingly about the parapets where harebells blew in the sun. Two beautiful thoroughbred hunters cropped the grass where the blood of archers and pikemen had once stained the Essex soil. The Majendie family have done a great national work by keeping this noble keep in such good repair.

It was a short run to that picture-postcard antique, the Great White Hart at Great Yeldham, one of the best half-timbered inns in the country. Its ceilings, wide fireplaces, huge beams, and the

[1] The Hon. Maynard Greville, of Easton Lodge.

cell in the sitting-room wall, in which Essex prisoners were lodged on the way to Cambridge gaol, make it worth a visit. Great Yeldham is a good farming village, full of fine old houses and lordly trees.

We unboxed the horses there to ride a few miles across country to Hosier's Farm, where Dick Plummer, business manager of the *Daily Express*, has taken to pigs, cattle, and corn. It is astounding how Fleet Street returns more and more to the earth. I prefer the pigsty breed of journalist to the narcissus bed.

Hosier's is a pretty house—pretty is the word—half-timbered, with some good herring-bone brickwork. A fine old barn footed a sweep of stubble running up to the sky, lively with rooks and partridges. A stoat slipped out of the garden, a moorhen flew off the pond, a cat smiled on the window-sill, and sweet peas talked to each other gently in the breeze. But no Plummers were at home. So back to Great Yeldham, most of the way by the headlands of fields to avoid the hard road. Before doing so I asked permission in each case from the nearest farmhouse or cottage—a practice throughout the tour. Not once was permission refused. It is a point to remember if you contemplate seeing England from the back of a horse.

CHAPTER XI

Last year a Hampshire market gardener had to grow carrots which, when lifted, were transported to Ipswich to be tinned and then sold in the village in which they were grown. This is typical of the waste which we call first-class economy.

VISCOUNT LYMINGTON

By the Roman Road to Cambridge—Where the Godolphin Arabian lies buried—The Shepherd's Soliloquy—"Yan, Tan, Tethera," and "One-erum, Two-erum, Cock-erum"—Pepys's Inn—Ghosts of Barnwell Priory—Joe Cannon's Cock-fight—Old Callaby's Ratting Parties—Talk at Histon Manor—On Yeomen—The Beginning and Meaning of the Term—The Tyranny of Bureaucracy—Chivers's, the Greatest Fruit Estate in Britain —Natural Manure, Sound Farming

AT LINTON, THAT SWEET CAMBRIDGESHIRE VILLAGE WHICH nestles in a broad valley, I bethought me of the long and rolling miles of the Via Devana, the old, forgotten Roman road which marches, peewit-haunted, over the windy hills of the Gog Magogs from Horseheath, where Sir Giles Allington had his great medieval house, to Cambridge.

A lonely road of ghosts. It sees neither man nor horse, save gipsy or plodding ploughboy, from month's end to month's end, this road where once the legions marched and brazen eagles glinted in the sun. It would, I thought, be a pretty vanity to ride those ten or a dozen Roman miles through the gold of the late afternoon into the violet dusk over Cambridge.

So we unboxed at a side road, saddled up, pocketed a map, and left the four-ton horse-box, its trusses of hay, its tackle, guns, gear, bread and cheese, and bottles of beer and port to the midget valour of the pocket Napoleon.

"She's shaping well for a Londoner," said Jim, eyeing the great van as it lumbered down the road for Cambridge straight as a die.

"I reckoned she was a rum little pocketful when you first brought her—and I don't mind telling you now I didn't like having any woman-kind on this job. But she'll do, she'll do. I'll get her on a hoss yet. She's our sort, sir." Thus, the accolade.

We rode off the tarmac, away from its heat and petrol smell, down a dusty road and into a green lane, a thin chalk track white between harebells and flowering grasses. Ahead lay the silent miles of the rolling Roman road, the chalk track hedged by blackberry, hawthorn, and crab-apple. We rode silently, watching the partridges spring, eyeing the hare on the stubble, alone with the wailing plover and the ribboned horizon of this ancient open land, bright with barley, crowned on its uplands by pigeon-haunted spinneys.

I thought of the farmers, the squires, the coachmen, and highwaymen, the humble travellers by covered wagon, the pedlars who plodded on broken horses when Cromwell was in the saddle, the gipsies whose hedgerow fires had glimmered down the centuries. We were riding in their footsteps.

It is a bold, wide, billowing land, this chalk country of the Cambridgeshire uplands. There is none of the lush richness of Essex. Its spaces are of a different quality from the spaces of the sea marshes. Big fields, rimmed by the sky or edged by belts of thin firs, dwarf the more minute beauty of Hertfordshire. It has an air almost of bleak grandeur, certainly of greater quality than the sculpted hills and graven beech woods of Buckinghamshire—that county which, because it has so little water, always reminds me of a beautiful woman entirely without character. There is space, silence, and history in these billows and slopes of Cambridgeshire barley land, wide under arched summer skies, bleak in the keen airs of winter. You begin to understand why the Great Bustard, the last of that lordly race, lingered here. The stone curlew, or thick-knee, still haunts these barley uplands, his thin whistle ghostly in the night.

Away up there on the left, where massed trees gather like thunderclouds on the brow, lies the park and mansion of Gog Magogs. There the Dukes of Leeds lived in semi-feudal state, eighteenth-century Cambridge virtually their fief and pocket borough. In the stableyard lies buried the last of that noble horse, the Godolphin Arabian, the mighty sire whose blood flows in almost every thoroughbred English racehorse of to-day.

I thought of that great horse, cantering nobly over these East Anglian downlands, mane and tail flowing in the breeze, neck arched, nostrils distended, eyes wide and liquid, sight for God or man. I thought, too, of the Darley Arabian and the Byerley Turk, of old Tregonwell Frampton, "Master of the King's Running Horses," in all his periwigged glory at Newmarket, and of the changes in history since his day. There is no longer a Duke of Leeds at Gog Magogs Park, but Mr Gray is a good squire, and the estate is well kept and well farmed. There is an Adeane still at Babraham, although Robert is somewhere in the Near East, riding a tank instead of a thoroughbred. There are still Townleys at Fulbourn, that village manor set in the plain to the right, and a Jenyns at Bottisham, where the Georgian shade of Bulwer Jenyns must surely walk the park on evenings of spring.

We dipped into a hollow. A triangle of tall firs stood by the Roman track, and a rough, flinty cart road went wandering off into the mellow dusk towards Balsham or Wilbraham Temple. A shepherd stood with a little boy by a fold at the far end of a clover field, counting the sheep as his dog herded them in. I rode idly across to ask him the local news, for it was a year and a half since I had been in my home county.

He was a long, thin man with beetling eyebrows and wide-set eyes which seemed to bridge centuries. His voice was soft, and his eyes had the unchanging look of one to whom all history was the same. He stood at the entrance to the fold. As the sheep bumped and bucketed past he talked to the small boy in a language which might have been Pictish or Tibetan. This is how it went:

"Yan, tan, tethera, pethera, pimp, sethera, lethera, hovera, covera, dik—yan-a-dik, tan-a-dik, tethera-dik, pethera-dik, bumpit, yan-a-bumpit, tan-a-bumpit, tethera-bumpit, pethera-bumpit, figgit."

"What sort of language is that, shepherd?" I asked.

"Old Lincolnshire, sir. That's the way we used to count 'em when I were a boy. I'm a-learnin' this little owd boy how to number the ship in the owd way. When I git up to dik that's ten, and when I git to figgit, that's twenty. Us shepherds hev our own language, you know. When I were a lad I were with an owd Sussex flock master, an' he used to count the flock on a tally-stick in the owd Sussex way, like this here:

"'One-erum, two-erum, cock-erum, shu-erum, sheth-erum, shath-erum, wineberry, wagtail, tarrydiddle, den.'"

"Wouldn't the ordinary way of counting be quicker and easier?"

"Ah! So that would. But I like t'owd way. Shepherden's an owd craft. I were a-tellin' this little owd boy here that us shepherds were a-goin' in Galilee when the Good Lord walked on the water. That were afore the Good Book were writ. I count 'chinery is takin' all the good sense out o' people's heads these days. They think o' nowt but the Mammon o' Unrighteousness, stiddy of the Good Lord who give 'em the breath in their body.

"This here war, sir, is a just vengeance on all mankind. They

Rooshuns and Jarmans hev made gods out o' they machines, and now the machines'll destroy 'em. Whoever the Lord will destroy, sir, he fust drives mad."

"You think a lot, shepherd," I said quietly.

"If you spend all your life with the sheep under God's heaven you *must* think, sir. I've laid rough with owd Mother Greenfield [sleeping in the open] half me life. If you live like that you know there's a God above."

We talked a little more as dusk came on, and then I turned and rode across open fields to hit the Roman road farther on. Afar off the tippity-tump of hooves broke the quiet stillness of the evening. A hatless rider, face flushed, sitting a handy little fifteen-hand thoroughbred came through a gap in the hedge just before Worstead Lodge. It was my godson, Yurka,[1] come to meet us from Cambridge, free of the earth, with a few days' leave from his regiment.

We found the horse-box looming in the dusk at the end of the road by the golf course, with Napoleon asleep on the driving-seat, unsaddled, boxed them up, and within a few minutes were rumbling into the streets of Cambridge, the town which first took my heart for all time, twenty-five years ago.

We slept that night at the Little Rose. That sweetly named inn in Trumpington Street was built when the Tudors were on the throne. It is an inn with memories of farmers and coaches, of hireling nags and hunting dons. An old rambling inn whose rabbit-warren rooms shelter undergraduates in term time as once they sheltered travellers by coach, ostlers and farmers, country wenches and travelling merchants. They say that Samuel Pepys slept in it, that his coach and four horses clattered under the cobbled arch from his family home at Impington. It has still stabling for half a hundred horses, scarce forgotten memories of cock-fights and trencher-fed foxhounds, undergraduates' bull-terriers, and illicit ratting-parties. Hobson of Hobson's Choice stabled his horses in the seventy-five stalls and loose-boxes clustered under the tumbled beauty of tiles and dovecots.

As I led Robert, hooves striking sparks on cobble stones, under the beamed archway that was built before 1400, I thought of the departed glory of the Little Rose—of the periwigged dons; of the squires from Madingley, the Hindes and Cottons; of Sir Roger, from Trumpington; Jack Linton, from Oakington Hall, and my grandfather, Luke Staples from Westwick Hall; old Squire Allix,

[1] Prince Yurka Galitzine.

from Swaffham Prior, wise village that overlooks the fens; the horse-dealers and cattle-dealers; the dog-stealers and rat-catchers; the keepers and higglers, all the motley pageant of Cambridgeshire folk from the bleak fen and windy upland, who have known this little inn, this nursery of horses.

The landlady, Mrs Bond, a fine, buxom woman, with a smile like a rising sun and a heart of gold, had set out half a ham, some cold boiled bacon, a dish of tomatoes and beetroots, pickled onions, and bread and cheese. With that and a gallon of ale we made short work.

Kolia Galitzine,[1] Yurka, and I then set out to roam the town in search of good ale in little inns, old memories of twenty years before. There was a stop at the Eagle, whose outside gallery still looks down on a cobbled courtyard. A pull-up at the Bath, old and snug, still famous for steak and onions. A look in at the Lion, with its memories of hunt dinners. A final perambulation to that tiny pub by Christ's Piece where twenty years ago Roger North, Dick Cholmondeley, George Nestle, Dick de Grey, Drewitt Chaytor, Tom Anstey of Jesus, the landlord, and I hatched a plot to trap the ghosts —seven of them—which they say haunt Barnwell Priory on the Newmarket Road. The Priory boasts a Giant Squire, a White Nun, a Disembodied Head, a Ghostly Hare, an Astral Squirrel, and a Clanking Chain. It is the finest all-round spook circus in England, with a Poltergeist to top the bill.

Whatever the truth may be, more than one tenant has left the house in a hurry. One man and his wife cleared out at two o'clock in the morning. A beautifully panelled old room on the first floor is kept clear of furniture for the very good reason that the Poltergeist is said to throw it about. So, on that night twenty years ago, with the permission of Mr Ascham, the owner, a descendant of Roger Ascham, we sat up.

The hunt began at the pub, where we met George Nestle armed with a bull-terrier, a bottle of whisky, a pack of cards, and the inn-keeper, who was a retired prize-fighter. I took a revolver, a length of chain, and a ball of string. When we arrived at the Priory, half an hour before midnight, I dispersed the company—George and the innkeeper to play cards in the dining-room, Roger North and a spiritualist to the Poltergeist room, Dick de Grey and Dick Cholmondeley to other rooms, the rest elsewhere, and posted myself at the head of the cellar stairs. All was silent, except for the snuffling of

[1] Prince Nicolas Galitzine.

At Hatfield House: Viscount Wolmer (now the Earl of Selborne, Minister of Economic Warfare) and Commander the Lord Sempill wishing the Author Godspeed

Photo Sport and General

MADINGLEY HALL, CAMBRIDGESHIRE

"That gem of its age, . . . for ever dear as the scene of a great deal of sport and good company."

Photo Country Life

the bull-terrier and the shuffling of the cards. Midnight struck. At any moment the Giant Squire might cross the stone-paved hall in the moonlight or an Astral Squirrel scamper up the curtains. In the upper chamber Roger and his spiritualist huddled close in the deep bay of the window, expecting the Poltergeist to pitch them into the garden. The last booming stroke of Great St Mary's died away. Nothing happened. Not a sound. A dozen watchers breathed expectantly.

Suddenly, in the cold, stone-paved cellar below, a chain clanked in the blackness. It clanked again. It clanked up and down the brick staircase, seeming to rattle horribly against skeleton legs. I had it on a wire which worked perfectly.

From the oak staircase, hard by the door of the Poltergeist room, came a sudden appalling hiss, a horrible deathly moan, two shrill shrieks. Dick de Grey, in stockinged feet, with a half-empty quart bottle of beer, well shaken up and then uncorked, had put the fear of God into Roger and his spiritualist friend. My chain did the rest. That was all that we ever saw or heard of the Ghosts of Barnwell.

It was enough, however, for the *Daily Express*, which faithfully appeared next morning with "Manacled Ghost Terrifies Cambridge—Clanking Chains in Ancient Manor—Moans at Midnight."

Alas, for such childish memories. When we reached the inn it was only to find that our prize-fighting, dog-breeding publican had died. His successor, an old jockey from Newmarket, was full, however, of the ghosts and the story. When he discovered that we were of the original perpetrators the sloe gin was brought up, and his heart was open. He talked of Tom Cannon and Old Joe Cannon; of cock-fighting at Lordship Farm and Exning; of the great main in Joe's drawing-room one Sunday morning when the "Red Duke" of Hamilton and a few others were gathered together to see two of Joe's birds go to it while Mrs Cannon was at church—all very fine and dandy until one of the cocks flew up the chimney and came down scattering soot all over the best carpet just as Mrs Cannon was spied returning, prayer-book in hand. Whereupon the Duke and the rest went out by the window. Poor old Joe was left to catch the birds and face the music.

We walked on, in the silky silence of moonlight, to the Fort St George. That two-hundred-year-old inn sits on the banks of the Cam in Midsummer Common, where once they held the greatest fair in all England. Even now you will see the name of Callaby, faint but defiant, painted in enormous letters on the brick wall round the inn garden.

I

Old Callaby was a sporting landlord of the old type who would stage anything from a Sunday morning's ratting in the garden with all the terriers from ten miles round to a day's duck-shooting at Upware or a private bout of fisticuffs in a barn. He was a forbear of that grand old sportsman, Horace Callaby, of the Stud Farm, Heacham, Master of the Heacham Harriers and one of the bright lights of the Hackney world. Alas, Old Callaby and his great boar-hound are snug beneath the daisies. But the Fort St George still stands, although the old chain ferry—where I once shot two chicken-stealing cats in the moonlight with a revolver—has gone.

I left Kolia and Yurka by the bridge and walked back across the Common in the moonlight where in medieval England stood rows upon rows of booths, gaily flagged, offering wares to all comers; where lines of horses stood tethered or were paraded up and down before the buyers; where spices and cakes, cloths and yards of butter, chickens and ducks, ribbons and finery, sweets and fat women, quacks and fortune-tellers, prize-fighters and tumblers, horse-copers and dog-dealers, vied for the silver pennies of the half-aquatic 'yellow bellies' from the fens and the staring yokels and solid farmers from the uplands.

It was midnight under the wheeling stars when I walked down Trinity Street, past the medieval beauty of John's, by the solemn glory of the Great Gate and tall elms of Trinity, by the airy ghostliness of King's and the ancient, crouching dignity of Peterhouse, to that little inn where once slept Samuel Pepys.

Jim roused me to a bright blue morning. "Now you're back home you can't lie abed, sir. Come on, shake a leg there. Robert's awaiting."

We clattered into Trumpington Street, that street which is as slippery to horses' feet as a glass bottle, down the paved passage of Little St Mary's Lane, wallflowers and hollyhocks gay among the tombstones, its bright, little old houses waking up like cats in the early sun, the river sliding at the bottom. We cantered at half-past six through the wispy mists of Coe Fen, dew on the grass, wild duck spattering in the Cam, under the grey walls of Peterhouse deer park, that little park which no longer has any deer. Its few walled acres were ploughed up in a futile, pathetic effort to be patriotic.

Back to an early breakfast and then through the streets, King's Chapel soaring in beauty, chiming bells chasing wheeling pigeons across the sunlit market-place. Cambridge to me is perpetually beautiful. Graciously and decorously old. It is one of those rare old ladies who grow old with feminine wisdom. They remain wise and beautiful, able to enchant to the last—wise because they have never aped man, beautiful because the wisdom and the spirit is in them. Our way was to Histon Manor to pay a visit to that courtly scholar and fiery individualist, Dr W. H. D. Rouse, an erudite historian, a master of the classics, a great horseman in his day, an unquenchable enemy of humbug, compromise, and that half-baked brand of pretentious ignorance which struts through art and literature to-day in the *ersatz* robes of 'intellectualism.'

I found him in his gracious little manor-house with its lovely ceilings, its Jacobean oak and high library, panelled from floor to roof by books. He was pottering about in a brown velvet jacket, a skull cap on his head, a bright and humorous light in his eyes. He produced sherry that winked gold in the sun. We sat and talked of the trends of the age, the bureaucracy which threatens to stamp out the English breed of values, the worship of great combines which destroy the soul, and the brittle faiths of Communism and Fascism, which have led their disciples to mass suicide.

We talked, too, of the need to save and strengthen the English yeoman, to re-create a landed peasantry, to rebuild pride and value in the farmlands.

Now this question of the yeomanry is of great present and future importance. There are many who will ask, What is a yeoman?

There was Will Goodchild, of East Horndon, in Essex, who told you that a yeoman is a man of established substance, able to educate his children in a sound manner, free enough to hunt or shoot one day a week. He maintains that such an established farmer will grow wheat before all things, beef cattle as a secondary string to his bow, dairying as a modern refuge. That is one view.

Surely, the yeoman is the man who, in a moderate way, having put his money into the soil and the hard work of his family, expects to see a lasting reward. He wants a guarantee for the fruit of his own endeavour, his invested money. He needs a reasonable guarantee not only for his children, but for his grandchildren, provided that they will live up to those sound principles of work and responsibility which are the only basis of real continuity of land ownership or proper cultivation of the soil. That, I think, is a principle which cannot easily be attacked.

Land is the ultimate bank. It is the father and mother of all production. We live by beef and bread. Whether we are born of the factory or the Stock Exchange, of the ship-yard or the middleman, the unassailable fact remains that land is the giver of food. Land is governed by weather, subject to the tricks of international fortune. But it can neither be bombed away, burned up, written off in a night, nor cast into the sea. Therefore, those who own it and cultivate it, in a responsible family sense, must always be part of the essential backbone of the nation. Of such are the yeomen, the rural middle class. When they go England goes.

Now let us look into the background and beginnings of the yeomen. What is a yeoman? The definitions have frequently been lax and sparse.

Long ago there was the Old English ye-mann or care-man, an attendant on the squire to a knight. That was merely the military sense of the yeomanry. The Yeomen of the Guard and the Yeomen Ushers of the Black Rod derive their ancient importance from this duty. They are the spiritual descendants of the bold wearers of Lincoln Green, who were retainers to the squires of the knight.

Those yeomen in peace-time and at home were no more than the small squires and big owner-farmers of to-day. They had responsibility, implemented in terms of land and service. Their younger sons and their daughters married with the barons.

Indeed, they produced, in their own way, an aristocracy of the soil which, as Stubbs says in the third volume of his *Constitutional History*, was "A body which in antiquity of possession and purity of extraction was probably superior to the classes which looked down upon it as ignoble."

The yeomen were not only men of stable property and well-founded responsibility. They were frequently farming venturers. They can be so to-day if we would only give them the chance and the money to be so.

Marshall, in the eighteenth century, speaks of a Midland yeoman farmer who had £2000 a year, which he spent in the advancement of farming as well as the upkeep of his family and his house, a modest one.

"This class of occupier," says Marshall, "has many advantages over the lower order of husbandmen. They travel much about the country, especially those whose principal object is live stock. They are led to distant markets, and perhaps to the Metropolis, and mix in various companies consisting not merely of men of their own rank or life. Men of fortune and science have of late years admitted them to their company, to their mutual advantage."

We have that sort of man to-day, fortunately left with us. They must be given the chance to "mix in various companies . . . to their mutual advantage." It is suicidal to tax the present-day farmer on an E.P.T. scale which robs him not only of the chance to rebuild his soil and buildings from the slough into which they had been allowed to fall, but will deny him those chances of betterment of his mind and experience which come from mixing with landowners and farmers not only of his own type and country but of Denmark, Holland, America, Canada, Australia, New Zealand, and others who compose the international farming picture. He can learn more from his own travels and experiments than he ever will from Ministerial leaflets.

There were one hundred and sixty thousand yeomen in the fifteenth century. They were the bridge between the peasant and the knight. They had the traditions of the first without their lacks and the security of the latter without their riches. They were rich among the poor and poor among the rich—the rural middle class. Like the middle class anywhere, they brought structural stability to society. They were oaken men.

I like that honest phrase of Sir Thomas Overbury, who says of his yeoman in Chaucer's time, "Though he be master, he says not to his servant 'go to field,' but 'let us go,' and with his owne eye doth both fatten his flock and set forward all manner of husbandry."

There you have, in a single, intrinsic sentence, the truth of individualism, of family life, as it affects the farming man of the middle sort. Mutual work and agreement between master and man enrich the soil and promote the happiness in labour of both. Mr H. J. Massingham has simply said: "If the bureaucracy has its way after the war and gets rid of him [the yeoman] crash will go one of the last pillars of the rural community."

That truth is true not only of the yeoman. It is true of the small house-owner, the small shopkeeper, and the small business-man, whom the big combines and their political hacks have put out of business, the little men who tilt a lance. If this war and the bureaucratic tyranny which accompanies it is allowed to stamp out the small farmer and tradesman the national soul of Britain will die. I cannot believe that our native common sense will allow that to happen. Bureaucrats are usually beggars-on-horseback, men of cunning but not of courage.

Dr Rouse invites and provokes such dissertations. He is of that rare breed which lives in values of the past and future, values the present accordingly. Theirs is the spy-glass of time.

From Histon Manor I went down the street to Chivers's jam factory and farms. It is a remarkable concern. Chivers of Histon own and farm over eight thousand acres. It is the largest fruit-growing estate in Great Britain. The Ghivers family began in a small way. They illustrate the essential fact that farming offers a chance for the humblest man on the land. About 1806 the family settled at Histon as small farmers, peasant proprietors. They were of good stock with sturdy bodies and strong minds. They settled down to make the Cambridgeshire land pay. By 1860 they were farming about one hundred and fifty acres, most of it down to wheat. As the agricultural depression grew worse they changed over to fruit-growing. It was a bold shot, but succeeded.

To-day Chivers's Orchard Factory employs three thousand people all the year round. The firm has a Royal Appointment as purveyors of jam, jelly, and canned English fruits and vegetables to the King. It sends thousands of tons of jams throughout the world each year.

Apart from the fruit plantations, which are unique, Chivers's have built up a great reputation as breeders and users of Percheron horses, Large White pigs, dairy shorthorns, and pedigree poultry, of which thousands of chickens are reared each year. They range the orchards and do a great deal to keep down insect pests. I was particularly impressed with the large herd of pedigree Jerseys, and by the discovery that here on Chivers's farms are some of the largest herds of attested cattle in the country. The milk is sold direct to the public from the firm's Model Dairy, via distributing depots in the surrounding district.

The vegetables grown include peas, asparagus, celery, carrots, stringless beans, broad beans, potatoes, and others, and the seed trial ground near the factory has carefully worked out and proved the varieties most suitable for canning. I advise any market gardener with an eye on growing for canning purposes to visit this factory. He can learn a lot.

For the past fifteen years Chivers have practised 'alternate husbandry'—temporary grass leys after three to five years are followed by arable crops, then returning to temporary grass. This system provides the best possible conditions for rearing all classes of pedigree stock.

The beginning of the Percheron stud is of more than ordinary interest, for it started when Mr Stanley Chivers was serving in the Field Artillery during the 1914–18 war. He was so much impressed with the clean legs, strong limbs, and hard-wearing feet of the Percherons which he saw in France and Belgium on transport work that he bought some for use in England and began the stud.

To-day the Histon young horses are broken to farm work at two or two and a half years old and put to full work at three and a half. The fillies are mated at three years, and the mares work right up to foaling. The Percheron is easy to break to work, quiet and usable. Even the stallions are so docile that most of the older Histon horses are worked regularly during the winter. Crosses with Shire mares have produced a great many clean-limbed horses thoroughly suitable for ordinary farm work on the heavy to medium lands of Cambridgeshire, Huntingdonshire, and similar counties which demand two to three horses on the plough. The Percheron is indeed an excellent all-round horse for the farmer, although personally I should never like to see the Shire suffer because of his competition.

Great horses have gone overseas from Histon. Others have made their names here in England. I think particularly of Censè, who from 1930 to 1936 sired five champions, eight reserve champions, twenty-two first prize winners, thirteen seconds, and six thirds at the Royal. Another outstanding sire was Carburateur. That great horse was champion male at the Royal in 1929 and sire of two champions, three reserves, six firsts, and two seconds at the English National Show. Histon Drayman the 10th was another noted stock-getter. Erpingham Drayman is making a name in East Anglia to-day. As a whole the stock produces quick-actioned, well-balanced, and hard-constitutioned geldings for general work.

It was good to go round these extensive farms and find so much work being done by horses. I felt that here was still not only a real pride in the land but a true sense of the fact that good comes out of the land through the animal and is thereby put back into it. The machine drops no dung. At Histon they go on the sound yeoman-farming principle that, although they take a lot out of the land, they put a lot back—through the dung of horses, cattle, pigs, and poultry.

That is a principle which some get-rich-quick Committee-farmers of to-day should bear in mind. They are flogging the land with machinery and artificials to get the utmost out of it under the spur of war. They put little or nothing back in natural manure. The land is 'gipped up' with artificial manures which are of no more lasting value than a dose of whisky to a sick man. Stimulants never yet provided lasting resistance. I shall be interested to see, when this war is over, how far the sound, permanent values of Histon, values founded on the yeoman principles of the original Chivers and the present Stanley Chivers, have outlasted the superficial, high-pressure methods of some of the so-called 'scientific' farmers and Committee farms of to-day. My money is on Chivers and their like all the time. They will stay the course. Theirs will be the enriched soil of the future. Their farms and methods will breed the winners, those who stay to last.

The genius of Histon is that whenever possible everything is grown on the place, manured, produced, graded, packed, canned, turned into jam or jelly, marmalade, mincemeat, fruit drinks, or coffee essence. It is a great English undertaking.

Fortunately it has never grown out of its village setting. It has never boosted itself with the cheap-jack methods of modern publicity —the "food shot from cannons" or "milk fit for stars" type of ballyhoo. It has relied upon quality, upon solid production; and steady sales.

The result is a village community which to-day is an asset to the county of Cambridgeshire, a steady contribution to the nation's food supplies, and a present embodiment of the honest ideal spoken by the late John Chivers when, at an annual meeting of the employees a few years ago, he said: "Success always has been and, I hope, always will be measured by the number of people for whom it can provide healthy, congenial employment."

There spoke an employer with the best principles of English landownership. Out of the soil he had made riches. He returned good living and security to those who live on the soil. His farms and factory made a healthy, happy village. He lived on the spot. He was directly accessible, directly responsible to the people whom he employed. Once responsible landownership leaves the land and dwells in London the essential heart and root goes out of the land.

There are opportunities for plenty more Chiverses in England to-day. The land is crying out for sound ownership and good leadership. Old landowners may go, but new ones will arise. If they last it will only be by work and a sense of responsibility. To counter the insidious campaign for nationalization we must produce more men of the type of Coke of Norfolk, Chivers of Histon, Sykes of Sledmere, Lord Lymington and Roland Dudley, Bakewell of Dishley, and Jonas Webb. There is plenty of manhood and brains from which to draw this essential capital of the land. It is a sound anchor for the future. We must not allow an opportunistic bureaucracy to rob us of responsible individual ownership and good cultivation of the land. Landownership is the ultimate ideal of most Englishmen who fight, who work in offices, or pioneer in distant countries. It is a sound, constructive ideal. Chivers of Histon is an example of how it may be done in the larger sense.

CHAPTER XII

Good farm and well stored, good housing and dry,
Good corn and good dairy, good market and nigh;
Good shepherd, good tillman, good Jack and good Gill;
Make husband and huswife their coffers to fill.

THOMAS TUSSER,
One Hundred Points of Good Husbandrie (1557)

Lord Eltisley's Farms—An Example of Good Landlordism—His Tribute to the Caterpillar Diesel Tractor—Weekly Costings on the Farm—Pigs, Poultry, and Rabbits—On Wages, Prices, Soil Fertility, E.P.T., and Death Duties—The Folly of too many Artificials—"Muck's your Man"—Post-war Peril of Land Exhaustion—"Duties on land should be paid not on death but on the sale of the estate"

NEXT MORNING I SET OUT TO CROXTON PARK. THERE ARE several Croxtons, but this one is that red-brick, Georgian-porticoed house which sits in its pleasant, rolling little park, gazing over a triangular, duck-haunted lake on the undisturbed borders of Cambridgeshire and Huntingdon. It looks to the south.

Croxton was the home of that good farmer and scientific agriculturalist, Lord Eltisley, who has since, alas, died, a great loss to farming and to Cambridgeshire. The last half-century of farmers remember him as Sir Douglas Newton, a one-man laboratory of ideas and practices in farming. On an estate of a little more than five thousand acres he not only carried out for many years a series of practical and progressive experiments with fruit, crops, and machinery, but proved that a landowner with ideas and moderate capital could farm considerably on his own with benefit to his pocket and inspiration to his neighbours. He was a true successor of those eighteenth-century landlords who brought individual skill and practical encouragement to the land. He married brains with capital and produced lasting results.

For years Lord Eltisley farmed between a thousand and one thousand seven hundred acres on the most scientific lines. At the outbreak of war he took over an almost completely derelict farm on which dense bushes, twelve to fourteen feet high, smothered acres upon acres of strong heavy land. The bushes were so thick and high that in places a rider could not force a horse through. Beaters, on shooting days, were completely defeated. In addition to this formidable task, he decided to plough up some hundreds of acres of grassland elsewhere on the estate.

In all he tackled 744½ acres of land, bushed, badly drained, and down to grass, bringing the area farmed by himself to more than 2500 acres.

The bushes were first cut down to within a foot of the ground. Then a small caterpillar tractor was installed with a winch and chain. This hauled out bushes by the roots at the rate of four to five a minute. The bushes and roots were then burned, putting back potash into the soil.

The land was drained by tiling and moling, given three ploughings, and by the end of July sown with wheat. The average depth of the mole draining was twenty-one inches, and each drain was six to nine feet apart. Four furrow ploughs, hauled by crawler tractors, were used. The average yield from this reclaimed stiff clay land was in the neighbourhood of five quarters an acre of the Croxton Red wheat.

The same results were got on Hill Farm, formerly a grand galloping stretch of one hundred and thirty acres of grassland, now all under wheat.

Where this heavy land required new open drains the Buckeye excavator, which he installed to the wonder of Cambridgeshire farmers just twenty years ago, was used with great success. It is a veteran of a machine still going strong.

Rabbits were reduced almost to vanishing-point—not by gassing, that horribly inhumane method advocated so fervently by officials who have never caught a rabbit in their lives, but by letting the farm labourers snare them. Hodge is the finest natural rabbit trap in the world. He has all the ancient arts at his elbow. Thus, the estate cottagers got good unrationed dinners, and the crops were cleared of the enemy.

Lord Eltisley, who was one of the pioneers of the modern tractor, had definite views about the future of heavy land.

"If I were a young man to-day and had my choice of whether I should farm light land, medium, or heavy land I should go for the heavy land all the time with caterpillar tractors," he said to me. "The caterpillar is the marvel of the age. It is a hundred-per-cent. boon to the heavy-land farmer. It ploughs five times as fast as a horse team. It runs lightly over the land and doesn't press it down unduly. It goes over land where a wheeled tractor would stick hopelessly.

And over there you can see three of our caterpillars doing a harvest job."

He waved his hand towards a group of stacks where men were at work.

"Three caterpillars are each hauling sixteen-foot long trailers, built out of old lorry chassis. Each trailer carries four ordinary cart-loads of corn. While one unloads at the stack another comes in from the harvest field, and a third goes back empty to load up again. By doing that, and by staggering the men's dinner-hour, we don't waste a minute of daylight during harvesting. These tractors are used all the year round. A rubber-tyred tractor pays for hauling loads to a station, provided it is not more than twenty miles from the farm. The result to-day is that we use only nine horses on the whole estate."

He kept weekly costings which showed the cost per acre of farming his land. These included wages, charges, and an additional five shillings an acre annually to represent depreciation. They showed that the weekly operating costs over the whole year varied from six to eight shillings an acre, plus the five shillings for depreciation. The old-fashioned steam-engine nowadays would cost about thirty shillings an acre.

He was a great advocate of the modern power-driven binder, which he considered has added 25 per cent. to the speed of harvesting. Five men were employed to each pair of power-driven binders so that the binders were kept going during meal-times.

The figures of Lord Eltisley's 1941 croppings are interesting, since they show the diversity of interests on this large one-man farm. Here they are:

Wheat, 766 acres; winter beans, 144; spring beans, 164; barley, 394; potatoes, 100; mangolds, 5; peas, 2; flax, 41; brussels, 19; onions, 2; trefoil in wheat (to cut), 69; clover in wheat (to cut), 41; fallow, 16; new land fallow, 30; fruit, 106; permanent grass, 127; rough grass, 232.

Every one on the estate worked—from Lady Eltisley, who is almost as good a farmer as her husband, to the butler, who drove a milk-float between meals.

Lord Eltisley, in common with every farmer and landowner I have spoken with, considered that far too much land, unsuitable for arable cultivation or capable of giving better service as pasture, was being ploughed up.

"County War Agricultural Committees have done a good job

of work," he said to me. "But the time has come when they should set up a consistent policy to guide farmers into a settled course of food production.

"The Huntingdonshire Committee have given a lead by laying it down that the average farm should consist, generally speaking, of two-thirds arable and one-third grass. I agree. We need fixity of policy for the next few years, instead of Whitehall and the County Committees merely claiming credit for ploughing up large areas. They make impressive entries in ledgers—but that is not always good farming policy!" I wondered what Mr Hudson's reaction would be to that truth.

From all these facts and philosophies of the past few weeks there emerge five major problems which stand out like lighthouses. They will govern the immediate future of farming. They will determine the long-term future of landownership and cultivation. Those five points are (*a*) wages, (*b*) prices, (*c*) soil fertility, (*d*) excess profits tax and farming profits, and (*e*) death duties on agricultural land.

Let me take the present-day facts. This was no bumper harvest of 1941. It was not even a record. It may suit the book of Government publicists to proclaim it as such, but the plain truth is that this harvest was fair to average. If anything it was below 1940's yield per acre. Wheat, on the whole, did well. Barley suffered from the wet. It was a poor crop in most places and not more than average at the best. Live stock has depleted. It hovers now on the verge of approaching a serious shortage. The rationing of chickens and pigs is a major problem. The ban on them should be lifted. Each farmer should be allowed to produce as many as he can. *Leave it to his own resources and his common sense.* He knows whether he can feed them off the farm or not.

At present the average farmer is restricted to keeping fifty chickens. Yet on any arable farm he could keep far more and feed them from the farm itself. To-day I rode over a ten-acre stubble field. At least five sacks of loose grain were lying, ready to rot, on that field. A hundred chickens could have been turned out on it by day, penned up at night, and fattened for the autumn markets. Chickens are natural gleaners of any farmyard. They will scratch for a living where a living is to be found. At this moment of harvest thousands of sacks of loose corn are going to waste on the harvest fields of Britain (*a*) because the chickens are not there to pick and eat it up, (*b*) because the village women, with rare exceptions, are not willing to go out to glean.

Pigs could be raised in far greater quantities if they too were allowed the run of the farm. Farmers in old days kept pigs and chickens as natural scavengers, pickers-up of unconsidered trifles, gleaners and delvers of the fields and the hedges, the woods and the stackyards. Whitehall must lift the restriction on pigs and poultry production at once if we are not to face a serious shortage of eggs and the loss of much potential pork.

Farmer after farmer has pointed out the consequences of this meddlesome, short-sighted piece of bureaucratic interference. These two thousand five hundred acres of farms at Croxton could comfortably produce two thousand one hundred pigs a year, fed exclusively on home-produced food—this without taking stocks of corn or other produce which would normally be for human consumption. Yet Lord Eltisley was reduced to a third of his pre-war pig-production figures. The same applies on the Fordson farms and on countless smaller farms.

Let us consider the five major problems I have indicated. First, wages. No responsible farmer grudges the labourer a decent living wage. All would like to see him earn more money. None that I have met pay less than 48*s*. per week.[1] Most pay overtime. With one exception all face the prospect of having to pay more with serious forebodings. Those forebodings are based on the fact that present prices of wheat do not keep up with the present increases in wages and certainly not with the proposed increase. In the old days it was a farming maxim that a sack of wheat paid a man's wages for the week. To-day it takes nearly two sacks to pay a man's wages. The farmers complain, quite justly, that they cannot face the mounting wage bills unless the Government raises the price of wheat. The problem is simple and straight. I have not yet met an agricultural labourer who denies its justice.

Actually, on many farms, labourers receive more than the minimum, since harvest money and overtime add their quota. Horsemen, cowmen, and shepherds are, in any case, paid more.

The only unpleasant fly in the rural ointment is the undoubted fact that here and there one finds men who will not work overtime because once they get beyond the three pounds a week level they become liable to pay income tax.

"I don't see why I should work in the evenings just to earn money for the Government when I might work in my own back garden growing stuff for the missus and kids," was the plain ultimatum

[1] The national minimum is now 60*s*. a week.

given me by one labourer. His views are typical of many, though not of the majority.

Maintenance of soil fertility is another problem. It is all very well for learned pundits, for professors and the research scientists of agriculture to laud the uses of artificial fertilizers. Ninety-nine farmers out of a hundred will tell one that artificial fertilizers are all very well as a stimulant, but that they do not impart a robust and lasting richness to the soil.

"Muck's your man" is as true to-day as it was when "Turnip" Townshend and Coke of Norfolk were putting English farming in the vanguard of the world. "Where there's muck there's money" is as true now as then. But farms to-day lack the muck—the natural farmyard manure which is nature's own medicine for the soil. It is as important on a farm as pure milk and fresh fruit and vegetables are to the human body. But with the killing off of cattle, the restrictions on chickens and pigs, the dwindling flocks of sheep, and the threatened exit of the horse, muck is becoming gold.

It is no use continuing to feed the land on artificials. One might as well dose an invalid with repeated nips of whisky. We must get back to sound farmyard manure, to leys, and, to a lesser degree, to green manuring. The latter depends on the rainfall. Every farmer, without exception, whom I have interviewed in the last three weeks admits that artificials have their uses. Nine out of ten good-humouredly accept the wordy advice of the professors and rural scientists who bombard them at N.F.U. meetings and through the Press. Under it all is the growing conviction that grandfather's methods of manuring were the best, and that the sooner we get back to them the better for the land.

If this matter is not taken seriously in hand now the end of the war will find many parts of England suffering from lowered fertility and land exhaustion.

Lord Cranworth, that wise man of Suffolk, who knows more about practical farming than most people, is of this opinion. So was Lord Eltisley. So is Lord Perry. So are such sound farmers as Robert Fuller, of Spinney Abbey, Cambridgeshire, Hector Buchanan, of Downham Market, Norfolk, Tom Mann, of Virley Hall, Essex, and a hundred others.

"When an industry has a by-product it can't make use of, it shoves it in a bag, gives it a fancy name, and dumps it on we poor mugs of farmers," was the latter's summing up. "Most of it ought to be dumped in the sea if it wasn't for the fact that it would poison the fish."

The most cogent criticism of the average artificial is that although it is a distinct help provided rain falls after it has been placed on the land, to distribute its goodness, it lies like sand in the soil if the weather is dry. Wet farmyard manure disseminates itself. You can very often plough it up and turn it over the next year. It not only gingers up the soil, but it becomes part of it and *adds* to it.

One hard lesson is that many small farmers to-day are not an asset to farming. They farm a small farm with one horse—take everything out of the soil and put little back. They are largely the victims of the last twenty years' neglect of farming, which has robbed the land of its capital, impoverished the farmer, and let down the high standards of cultivation which are the pride of our industry. The result is that on many small farms the yield per acre to-day is about half what it was thirty years ago.

There is much resentment against the levying of excess profits tax on farming profits. That is not because the farmer is an unpatriotic person. It is because for twenty years the majority have farmed either at a loss or with the barest profit. Many had to live on capital. Others had to borrow. Some jobbed off odd bits of land for arterial roads, bungalows, villas, bathing huts, or sand and gravel. They lived as best they could, a miserable, hazardous, scrape-ha'penny existence. There was no money for a new roof on the barn. That is why we saw derelict farms, roofless buildings, and tumbledown cart-sheds all over rural England before the war.

Least of all could the farmer afford to buy new machinery. To-day, when he is urged to plough every available acre, to grow more wheat and yet more wheat, he needs new machinery—caterpillar tractors, combine harvesters, crop-dryers, potato-spinners, silos, and a dozen ancillaries. America, under the Lease and Lend Bill, is flooding rural England with farming machinery, new and marvellous. How can the farmer buy it if 80 per cent. of his excess profits are paid to the Government while the remaining 20 per cent. vanish into a doubtful limbo of repayment after the war? He needs the money *now*. He does not want it to put into his own pocket. He needs it as present-day working capital. It must be put straight back into the land if the land is to grow more food. To rob the farmer of his excess profits at this present juncture is rank suicide, folly of the worst description. One might as well expect a cow to give extra milk without more food.

Death duties on land are in much the same category. For over thirty years the heavy incidence of death duties has paralysed the land. They have broken up estates, destroyed security of tenure, and robbed the land of the landowners' working capital. They forced the farmer to buy often when he could neither afford it nor wished to do so. They destroyed much of England's most beautiful scenery. They encouraged the middleman land jobber, that city parasite who flourishes by buying estates as a whole, chopping them up and jobbing them off to the wretched tenants afterwards. The result to-day is that the National Trust has to beg for money to buy up beauty-spots and ancient houses, and expensive committees are set up to suggest laws against speculative development. Death duties on agricultural land rob the land of one-third of its capital each time an owner dies. Yet they contribute an infinitesimal amount to the national exchequer.

Surely, since land is our Fourth Fighting Service, it should be placed above the wretched class consciousness and factitious politics which were responsible for its main burdens. Duties on land should be paid, not on the death of the owner, but *on the sale of the estate*. That would be fair and just. It would help to stabilize the future of English farming for ever. Land would become once more a sound investment for the man with money. And farming needs money.

We talked of these things that night in the big dining-room at Croxton under the portraits of bygone Leedeses and Newtons. It was here, and at Elveden, in Suffolk, that my host's family, sound, responsible squires, produced the strain which bred those twin bright lights of English science, Sir Isaac Newton and Professor Newton. Lord Eltisley waved the stump of his cheroot—"Can't offer you a cigar nowadays as I do without them in war-time"—towards the portraits and said:

"Why not treat land for death duty purposes precisely as the Revenue treats those pictures or any other works of art—that is, pay tax on them *when they are sold*, but not while they remain in one's possession? That would be fair to the land and fair to the landowner. The State would tax him when he sold out, but would allow him to keep his capital intact so long as he kept his land and used the capital for the improvement of the land and farming.

"If an estate is to be farmed properly there must not be continual breaks in ownership or policy. If they can make this provision in favour of pictures and works of art, which are non-productive, surely it's a hundred times more necessary to have such a guarantee for land, the mother of all production."

CHAPTER XIII

A time there was, ere England's griefs began,
When every rood of ground maintained its man;
For him light Labour spread her wholesome store,
Just gave what life required, but gave no more;
His best companions, innocence and health;
And his best riches, ignorance of wealth.

But times are altered: trade's unfeeling train
Usurp the land and dispossess the swain.

OLIVER GOLDSMITH, *The Deserted Village*

Partridge-shooting at Kimbolton Castle—"The Perfect English Village"—A Home of Sport—Lord Mandeville and Frank Cowlard—The Boar which brought over £1100—Madingley Hall, "A Gem of its Age"—"Capability" Brown's Landscape—Talk at the Three Horseshoes—On old Pigeon and Rabbiting Days—On Foxes and Anti-Sport Cranks—Farewell to the 'Pansies' of Cambridge—Her Value for the Future

I WAS UP EARLY IN THE MORNING AND IN A RIDE ROUND THE HOME farm saw an original method of protecting mangolds in the pit from frost—*i.e.*, by pitting them between walls made of baled bean straw. They are completely frost-proof and, because of their thickness, need no earthing up. This method has been used at Croxton with great success for four years. Women workers at the potato pits are protected from prevailing cold winds by large portable wind-screens which are also used on the lorries at harvest time.

After a little horse exercise in the park, on we went to Kimbolton Castle, in Huntingdonshire. Kimbolton, the principal seat of the Dukes of Manchester, is, like Hinchingbrooke Castle, near Huntingdon, one of the great Montagu strongholds which were built on the verge of the undrained fens to keep the fen-men in order—much as the Lord Wardens' border castles guarded the Marches of Wales against the unruly Celts.

For some years the estate with the neighbouring family property of .Brampton Park, a lovely old Elizabethan place just outside Huntingdon, has been administered by Lord Mandeville, the eldest son of the present Duke, that wickedly amusing Bohemian who came into one of the greatest fortunes in England at the age of twenty-one and went through more than a quarter of a million. He is the best story-teller I know, a most amusing companion, and a man of great, unused, intellectual powers.

It has been left to 'Mandy' to pull the estate round. For years he has been his own steward, estate agent, and farm manager, living on the spot and giving every day to the care of his farms and woods. The result is an estate which combines the best of feudal traditions with neat cottages, good farmhouses, well-farmed land, and excellent forestry in its big woodlands.

Kimbolton is the perfect English village. A long, straggling, sunny street, bordered by neat, gaily coloured houses. There is the cream and black of Elizabethan half-timber and the warm red-brick of Queen Anne, white porticoes of Georgian doorways and the pink and yellow plaster work of fenland cottages.

At one end the Castle, towering above its great red-brick wall and stone gateway, dominates the scene. That cosy old inn, the George, a nest of foxhunters, faces the Castle green. At the other end of the street the slim spire of the church overtops elms, busy with rooks in spring, murmurous with bees in summer. The Elizabethan grammar school turns out scholarship as sound as the home-made bread which they bake in a brick oven in the village baker's shop. I have never eaten better bread elsewhere in England.

Kimbolton is a home of shooting, foxhunting, and high farming with a little pike-fishing, dog-breeding, and coursing thrown in. From it a man can hunt with the Oakley, the FitzWilliam, the Cambridgeshire, or the Pytchley. Go into the George any spring evening or any cold night of winter, and in the little parlour with its mahogany tables, its warm red curtains, grinning fox masks, and historic brushes you will hear talk of great runs and great horses, great steeplechase riders and great hounds; talk of shooting and coursing, farming and dogs, the sound, simple values which make country character.

My visit to Kimbolton that autumn morning, however, had neither to do with hunting, horses, nor farming. Mandy was home on a precious few days' leave, enough to fit in one day at the partridges and collect a few old friends round him. We met at the bridge over the tiny stream of the Kim in front of the Castle, a gathering who had not seen each other since war began nor indeed had dreamed that we should handle a gun together before peace dawned.

There was Hugh Duberley, from Great Staughton Manor, who has made the Hunts War Agricultural Committee a model for others to learn from; Reuben Farley, from Kimbolton, a pioneer of ballooning in the days when the aeroplane looked like an orange-box; a couple of naval officers; Mandy, fresh from his aircraft carrier; myself, and Frank Cowlard, the head keeper. Now Frank is a great character and a big man. He looks and stands like a bull. He will walk all day and never tire. He is a true naturalist, a lover of beast and bird, a man to whom woods and the hedges are not solely nurseries for pheasants or sanctuaries for foxes. He has a quality which Thoreau would have put into prose, this Herculean ex-soldier whose kingdom is the woods, the open fields, the pike ponds in the park, and the fox coverts on the hills. Mandeville and his keeper are the perfect combination.

One day's partridge-shooting is much like another, but I shall not soon forget that start in the wispy mists of early sunlight. The walk among cattle feeding on the slope in front of the Castle; the tall woods on the rise ahead where the red-brick ruins of the old Tudor priory are now a keeper's cottage with a view for a king; the sight of the Castle, asleep in the hollow, blue smoke curling from its chimneys into a sky full of rooks and pigeons.

We walked and shot through fields we had known in the golden days of peace. Then all England had seemed prosperous, too prosperous, and the countryside was the mere playground of city men with money enough to take a gun in a syndicate. Thirty and a half brace of partridges, a hare, and one and a half couple of rabbits—what a contrast from only four years before when eight guns killed over fifteen hundred rabbits in a day on a farm so eaten up by them that Mandy remitted the entire rent for the year to the tenant. This destruction of the rabbit on an estate formerly swarming with them has been achieved, as at Croxton, almost entirely by allowing farm labourers and villagers to have a free crack at them.

We lunched at Reuben Farley's house. Home-smoked ham, great bowls of salad, potatoes in their jackets dug from the garden an hour before, beetroots pulled fresh from the soil, baked apples from the orchard, Northampton ale, and Norfolk cider. I would not have changed it for the best that Claridge's or an army of Frenchmen could provide.

I slept that night at the George and nearly set the place on fire by putting a match to the paper blackout round the electric light, which was full of wild bees.

Next morning we set off on our various travels—Mandy for Colombo and the Indian Ocean, one of the naval officers for Scapa

Flow and another for Iceland, Hugh Duberley back to the farmers of Huntingdonshire, and we to our English pilgrimage.

I stopped for a glass of beer at the Leeds Arms, in Eltisley, where the landlord still treasures a golden sovereign on his watch-chain given him by King Edward VII when he stopped, while out hunting one day, for a brandy and water. Past Dry Drayton, home of Terah Hooley's famous herd of Large Blacks where, in the pig boom after the last war, I saw a boar sold for over £1100, a gilt for nine hundred and fifty guineas, and a total of—I think it was sixty-two lots fetch over eleven thousand guineas. Those were the days when money was free, pig prices were at the North Pole, and everything in the farming garden bloomed gloriously. I could not help wondering whether that brief South Sea Bubble will grow and burst again when this war is done.

At Childerley Hall, hard by Dry Drayton, a pleasant old Elizabethan, moated house, built by Sir John Cutts about 1520, the Brooks family farm on a large scale, soundly and well.

Next door, across the brook, is Madingley, the loveliest Elizabethan house in all Cambridgeshire. It is a gem of its age, for ever dear to me as the scene of a great deal of sport and good company. So I unboxed Robert, got on his back and rode round the outside of the park belt, putting up partridges and three-quarter-grown pheasants at every step. The ground was baked as hard as a brick, but the corn, mostly cut, looked well, full in the ear and long in the straw.

On the corner of the road as I came out of a field gate I saw a familiar back, bent, weeding in a cottage garden. The hair on the head was white, but there was no mistaking a form and figure I had not seen for twenty years or more. I gave him a holloa. He slowly straightened himself, cupped a hand over his eyes, stared long and hard. "Why, blest if that ain't Master Wentworth. Come you in, sir, and have a glass. Lord A'mighty, that's twenty year since you were round here."

It was White, that remarkable countryman who for more than a quarter of a century has been keeper, farm bailiff, estate agent, carpenter, dog-breeder, and even thatcher to the estate. A rare one-man combination of rural virtues and arts. We found our way to the Three Horseshoes, that enchanted little inn by the pond, shadowed by rookery elms and flanked by thatched and plastered cottages. Its sunny face gazes towards the mellow Elizabethan grace of the Hall, one of the most perfectly proportioned Tudor houses in England.

The sweep of the park from the front down to the pond where I once caught a two-and-a-half-pound roach at midnight, over the sunken road by the main gates, a glory of ironwork, to the shallow valley, dotted with forest oaks and mighty elms—this was the work of "Capability" Brown, that sound country-house gardener whose motto was common wisdom, "Every garden has its capabilities." Whatever he may have done to redeem other country-house gardens from the Frenchified formality which aped Versailles, here at Madingley he achieved genius by using the everyday qualities of grassland contours and old trees to give the Hall a perfect English setting.

We talked of the old days, sitting in the parlour of the Horseshoes, with its kipper-coloured settles, its smell of bees in honey, an old spaniel philosophic on the flags. The days after the last war when that shrewd old man, Colonel Walter Harding, an uncommon combination of business-man, squire, and historian, gave me, an impecunious young man at Cambridge, the freedom of the estate with rod and gun. There were wonderful rabbiting days and high festivals of rook-shooting, standing knee-deep in cow parsley splashed white with their droppings, in the tall, windy elms of the park belt. We shot them with ·22's, for he who shoots rooks with a twelve-bore should himself be pelted with bad eggs. They took a lot of hitting as they swayed and swung against the bird's-egg blue of May skies, half seen in the green haze of bursting buds.

There were rough, hot days of walking up partridges on the Dry Drayton side. Midsummer nights fishing the pond, alone with the stars and barking foxes, with only the chimes of the stable clock to tell you that humans were alive in the rest of the night world. There were great rudd, fighting perch, slab-sided roach, and writhing eels pulled out among the rushes in those silent small hours between midnight and the dawn.

Best of all there were the great rabbit shoots in Mill Plantation. Days when rabbits, grey and black, rabbits in scores and hundreds, nipped across the rides like lightning, urged by the neolithic cries and caveman gutturals of a horde of village beaters and boys.

"D'you recollect that arternoon when you and Master Richard Cholmondeley stood back to back in that top ride with sixty-nine dead rabbits laid out round you and scores more fleein' across in front of both on you—and you'd run out o' cartridges? Lord, how you did swear!"

There were bitter, windy, winter nights, crouching in a hastily made hide of fir branches under the lee of a holly-bush when the pigeons came in from the fen stubbles in clouds. Never, surely, had there ever been so many pigeons on the wing and never would there be so many again. Pigeons as artful as foxes; as big, so they seemed, as turkeys; as tall as little Gabriels; as swift as rockets; pigeons darting in, swooping, side-slipping on the wind, whirling overhead against the snow flurries like blown leaves. Pigeons climbing high against the angry sunset.

"That were the night you brought out that great owd eight-bore duck gun o' yours. My heart! That did thump when you let her off. But I count you'd 'a' done better with a handier little gun. Them big 'uns fare to swing behind all the time. Why, damn, that weighed over a stone."

We talked of foxes in war-time. White, like every other keeper, with the knowledge and support of the hunt, has trapped them, shot them, and dug them out. "But still I can't keep 'em under. They're artful as sin. Hounds don't meet above once a week, and they foxes get about the country like greyhounds. I ketch 'em every way I can—but, Lord, you need the sound of a horn and a pack of hounds on the track on 'em. That'll clear a fox out of the parish quicker than anything."

I told him of the jaundiced letters from Nonconformist parsons and others which had appeared in a London daily, accusing fox-hunters and sportsmen generally of preserving foxes in war-time to the injury of the poultry-farmer. A listening farmer joined in.

"Them owd wimmen! They allus set theyselves up to find fault with sport when better men than them are out o' the way, doin' a bigger job! There's not a man in this county would harbour foxes now if he could get rid on 'em. We kill 'em down all we can, but there'll allus be foxes. They're the artfullest animal that run. If the poultry-farmers lose their hens that's because they don't lock 'em up at night or keep an eye on 'em in the day. What's to stop settin' a trip wire with an alarum gun round a hen-field or havin' a dog with a slip noose on a long wire to run round the pen? These hen farmers don't think, half on 'em!

"I wonder," he added musingly, "if some o' these humanity-folks would fight as good a battle out in that African desert or up in the air as some of our lads from hereabouts, that used to like their bit o' sport. I doubt it! They wouldn't have the heart. They used to come to us huntin', steeplechasin' farmers' sons for the best of the cavalry. Now they get 'em mewed up in the tanks—still wi' heart enough to fight the devil, but I doubt if they like theirselves in tin so good as they would on a hoss!"

We talked on of the old, gay days at Madingley "when the owd Colonel were about." That trim, shrewd little man wore a white Vandyke beard and walked about the park and the farms in a yachting cap, like a rural Sir Thomas Lipton. We talked of names and faces which made the memories—Eddie Russell, Arthur Cotton, whose forbears owned Madingley a century before, Victor Raikes,[1] Dick Studholme, Dick Cholmondeley, Basil Marsden-Smedley, David Pollock, Dick de Grey, and that extraordinary Arab sportsman Cherif Haddad, who pirouetted on one leg when shooting driven rabbits—far more dangerous to his neighbours than to the rabbits—and Charlie Searle, cheerful and ruddy, the Cambridge doctor who was later to achieve an unfortunate fame in the "Helen of Troy" case. He put trout into the upper river with the result that a five and a quarter pounder was caught that summer (1941) in the mill pool above Queens'.

Back to Cambridge to dine with Pam Fox[2] in an excellent new restaurant on K.P. which I remembered as a highly Victorian haberdasher's shop administered by a gentle, Gladstonian old gentleman most beautifully named Mr Lavender. They produced a first-class beefsteak and a bottle of Burgundy which at this brief vista of time stands out as a now unattainable pinnacle.

But first there was a visit to Gallyon, that excellent gunsmith opposite the Round Church, one of the best craftsmen at his trade in all England. Alas, old Gallyon with his parchment face, his beetling black eyebrows, his penetrating eyes, and incisive knowledge of his craft, has gone. There are, fortunately, able sons to carry on. May the day be far off when the craft of the individual English gunmaker, foremost in quality throughout the world, the fine flower of four centuries, is swamped and absorbed by combines or mass-produced factory weapons. They are, of their kind, as notable and precious as the sword-makers of Toledo or Solingen, the watchmakers of France and Switzerland, or the diamond-cutters of Amsterdam.

We talked late that night, for Pam Fox is one of those younger men who have the right ideas and the ability to carry them out. I walked back to the Little Rose under a canopy of swinging stars. Cambridge at night, in its white beauty, is a queen among towns.

These few days in Cambridge, the town which I love more than

[1] Now M.P. for South-east Essex. [2] Sir Gifford Fox, M.P.

any other in Britain, whose soul and spirit is not only of itself but of all men, have given me good reason to think.

Twenty years ago, after the last war, the average undergraduate was either a man who had joined the Army or Navy at seventeen or eighteen, fought his whack, and thereby learned sense, or he was a youngster fresh from school, with the stern lessons of war dimly planted in his young mind. The result was not bad. It was, indeed, at Cambridge, exceedingly good.

There were, it is true, a few willowy-minded and willowy-bodied intellectuals who, lacking any reason for faith in themselves or their abilities—as is true of most 'intellectuals'—postured and postulated an immense superiority to the ordinary breed of their fellows. They did not cut much ice or get very far. They wrote a few bad poems. They produced a little inconsequent literature, if that is not a derogation from the word, acted in a few shallow plays of their own callow world, and talked wordily in those little societies which are the safety-valves of universities. On the whole they were pretentious, gaseous, and disregarded. They made little mark on the world then or since.

Many times, since those early twenties, I have revisited Cambridge, observed and listened to its undergraduates. It seemed that the breed was becoming more pansified. They talked more in their debates of Russia and less of England. Internationalism was of more consequence than their fathers' achievements. They dwelt on vague Communistic possibilities rather than on accomplished facts or a determined future. Some of the dons were to blame. The trouble with 'intellectuals' is that they are so seldom intelligent, frequently perverts, and almost invariably conceited.

I was beginning to lose a little faith in Cambridge. For Cambridge, of all universities, has always combined a sense of beauty with one of reality. It has married tradition with achievement, belief with resolution, a flavour of the past with constructive thought for the future.

Those last few days in war-time Cambridge showed me that all that Cambridge ever stood for is still true to-day. The loose destructiveness of the neo-this and the pseudo-that, the brittle Communism and laziness of thought, have been swept away. The scum is off the pot. The pot is boiling strongly. The Cambridge University Air Squadron has a magnificent fighting record, a new knighthood of up-to-date chivalry. Cambridge men have made a new Roll of Honour to add to past lustres.

The town itself, full of the Air Force, girdled by airfields, its night skies noisy with the throb of engines, its laboratories contributing mightily to the practical defence of England—this Cambridge has put a new edge on its ancient blade, dipped it keenly in the blood of the Hun.

We of the fens have a more than personal love for this spired town of grey colleges and chiming bells, of buttercup meadows and daisied lawns, which sits beside the slow Cam. There are many sons of Cambridge in the four quarters of the world to whom she gave, in a few impressionable years, the gift of beauty and enduring values. They are her debtors. We of the fens—so we like to think—are the native owners, the patriarchal tribesmen, of this Witan of learning which adorns our otherwise undistinguished county.

So do you wonder that I turned into bed, my mind fastidiously affectionate to this old town of learning which has given strength and construction to the English world? We need those strong, straight values for the future. There is as much danger in pretentious intellectualism or bureaucratic tyranny as in the crude, disturbing barbarisms which masquerade as Communism and Fascism. England must preserve, as Cambridge has cradled, the strong English middle course.

CHAPTER XIV

And give me that best of bounties,
A gleam of November sun,
The far-spread English counties
And a stout red fox to run.

WILL H. OGILVIE

The Last of a Primeval Fen—On "The Company of Adventurers" and the Drainage of the Fens—A Mighty Achievement—Wicken Fen—The "Fen Tigers"—Pout Hall and its Sheep-stealers—The Murder of Peacock—My Wildfowl Sanctuary and Shoot—Bitterns, Montagu's Harriers, the Great White Heron, and Black-necked Grebes—One Thousand Wildfowl a Year—Cattle Egrets and Garganey Teal—Gay Shooting Days—"Swan mere's ploughed up"

WE WENT NEXT MORNING TO ATTEND A FUNERAL. A SECRET WAS laid bare, an old value violated. We went, in fine, to see the draining of a unique re-creation of the old fens of England, a bird sanctuary, home of bittern and harrier, garganey teal and grasshopper warbler. It was my own especial pride.

We went on this sad journey by way of the Newmarket road, turning left at Quy, whose tall, lonely church stands bleak as a peel tower on the treeless upland. Thence, by hedgerow and stubble field, down through the thatched and whitewashed houses of Quy, Swaffham Prior, and Swaffham Bulbeck. Those wise, leafy villages crouch at the foot of the Newmarket uplands and overlook the flat fens. Their cottages and great pink-washed farmhouses, their halls and thatched barns, were built when the fens ran, misty and immense, mere beyond glittering mere, mile beyond mile of soughing reeds, to swampy islets gay with yellow marigolds in spring, green with willows.

Those old villages have seen the fens shrink and wither from their watery wilderness. Carolean drainers renewed the work which the Romans began and Canute continued. The Gentlemen Adventurers, led by Francis, Earl of Bedford, achieved more. For a hundred years they laboured mightily to drain the greatest swamps in England. Every Jacobean squire for miles round who had a taste to gamble his money in the reclamation of that quarter-million acre morass which was the Fenland, earned his reward. The Duke of Bedford's great twenty-thousand-acre property at Thorney Abbey was the tangible prize to the Russells for the million pounds which their forbear sank in the Cambridgeshire bogs.

As we rode by the brook at Bottisham I caught a glimpse of Bottisham Hall in its park of woodland and water, an oasis of "pheasants and feeding things" in this bare and windy country. The first Jenyns of Bottisham, Thomas, son of Sir John Jenyns of Hayes in Middlesex, was of the fourteen prominent men who formed the first Company of Adventurers. The others included Sandys, Gorges, and Thynne, who, apart from that Fenland venture, were of the Virginia and New England companies in America.

Thomas Jenyns, of Bottisham, laboured all his life at the drainage of the fens and, with the rest of the Adventurers, received four thousand acres of good land for his share of this immense work. For two hundred years successive squires of Bottisham have sat on the Board of the Bedford Level. Soames Jenyns, man-about-town, political essayist and versifier, who was Member for Cambridge in Horace Walpole's day, was Squire of Bottisham. I doubt if he spent much of his time in this lonely parish between the wildfowl-clouded fens and the windy heaths of Newmarket where Lord Orford coursed hares and drove his carriage with a team of stags. Sarah Jenyns, Duchess of Marlborough, and the famous Duchess of Tyrconnel were of the family, though not born here.

I thought of those early adventuring squires of Bottisham, of the immense labour which they and their kind accomplished when they drained the fens in an age when practically all work was done by hand. Machinery hardly existed, and motors and steam-driven pumps were unknown.

The State, its engineers and its War Agricultural Committees think themselves mighty clever to-day when they drain a few odd hundred or thousand acres of swamp. Let us give the greater glory for the greater task to the Earls of Bedford, to the squires and the labourers who, in the Bedford Level alone, drained a hundred thousand acres of swamp, mere, peat bog, reed bed, and willow holts. They dug great lodes, threw up miles of huge banks, erected windmills, and planned outfalls to rivers and sea. Their banks were broken by floods. Their lock gates were blown up by the indignant, semi-barbaric fenmen. Their watchmen were shot by 'fowlers who came spritting silently through the foggy reeds in their punts to fire half a pound of slugs from a long-barrelled duck-gun.

It was a rough, turbulent, murderous, and nobly creative era of

English history. Private enterprise, epitomized by the Russells and their squires, accomplished a task which would cause a modern English Minister of Agriculture to quail in his office.

They robbed no one but the poor, ague-stricken, yellow-faced men and women of the fen isles—the 'Eys' of Ely, Stuntney, Stonea, Manea, Whittlesey, Thorney, Denny, Wentworth, and Wicken.

The "yellow bellies," "fen tigers," or "Cambridgeshire camels," as they were called, lived by fishing and fowling. They walked upon stilts, herded geese, netted pike, rudd, bream, and eels in slithering, shining boat-loads, drove moulting mallard into nets in summer and punted at them with great crazy punt-guns in winter. They skated on the ice on bone skates made from sheep's leg bones, planed flat—I have a pair somewhere at home—and drank poppy-head tea and laudanum to dull the 'shivers' which racked their miserable frames.

Their heritage was steaming swamps where the will o' the wisp danced in the summer dusk. Shining meres were thunderous with the thousand wings of mallard and widgeon. Greylag geese nested in the sedges, bitterns boomed on indigo nights of spring, and marsh harriers and fen eagles patrolled the waters on lordly wing-beats.

The Adventurers drained these wild wildernesses, pregnant with fever and death, and gave in their place the richest corn lands in all England. My own ancestor, Sir Hugh Myddleton, "that sly fox and subtle citizen," the Carolean engineer who dug the New River, the first of London's pure water-supply, was, with Sir Cornelius Vermuyden, the Dutch drainer, among those chiefly responsible for turning mere and marsh into cornfield and potato land. We have been in the fens ever since.

While the fen squires and distant earls and barons gained land from the waters, while the villages rose in wealth and health, poor Vermuyden, greatest engineer of them all, was shockingly treated. The Carolean kings had bribed him with a promise of ninety-five thousand acres of land to plan the drainage scheme which is the basis of the Ouse Drainage Board system to-day. Vermuyden planned and drained. He succeeded and laid the keel for greater successes. He faced bitter opposition, sabotage, murders of his Dutch drainers, riots, and blowings up of his banks.

When his work was done and the fens had become the granary of all England we made war on the Dutch. The Dutchman was obliged to sell his fen property. He died abroad, ill, old, and poor.

An unknown poet of 1629, when the fenmen were fighting the

Dutchmen, the drainers, and the Adventurers, rallied the "fen tigers" in verses which endure to this day:

Behold the great Design, which they do now determine,
Will make our bodies pine, a prey to crows and vermine.
For they do mean all Fens to drain, and waters over master;
All will be dry, and we must die—'cause Essex calves want pasture.

Then, having rallied the fenmen against these frightful plans to drain their meres, rid them of their fevers,[1] enrich their lands and fill their purses, the unknown poet invoked the "yellow bellies'" God of that day, our terror in the fens to-day, and cried:

Send us good old Captain Flood to lead us out to Battel,
Then tuppenny Jack, with scales on his back [2] will drive out all the cattle;
This noble Captain yet was never known to fail us,
But did the conquest get of all that did assail us:
His curious rage none could assuage but, to the world's great wonder,
He tears down banks, and breaks their cranks and whirligigs asunder.

To-day the Ouse Catchment Board area embraces two million acres of land, worth anything from £15 to £100 an acre. The annual rateable value is £3,000,000. It is the richest area in all England, equalled only in fertility by little pockets of land at Ormskirk, in Lancashire, and Watchet, in Somerset. This two-million-acre sweep of upland and dyke-ruled fenland which runs into the flat skyline like the waves of a silent sea is drained by five hundred and sixty miles of rivers, all feeding and comprising the Great Ouse. It meets the tide at Denver Sluice and empties into the sea at King's Lynn.

It was an ironic reflection on our egoistic modernism that although in the days of the Stuarts and afterwards we reclaimed most of these two million acres of upland mere and fen, we allowed no less than two million acres of arable land elsewhere in England to go out of cultivation between 1919 and 1939. A pretty commentary on the boosted efficiency of democracy!

In March 1937 the bungling bureaucracies of Government and the County-Council-ridden plans of engineers nearly succeeded in putting the clock back three centuries. Thousands of acres of fenland in that month were flooded when the banks 'blew' at Soham Lode, and the waters swept over Soham Mere, that vanished lake of the

[1] When the Bishop of Ely presented the Reverend Dr T. S. Whalley to the living of Hagworthingham-in-the-Fens it was with the stipulation that he should not live in the parish, as the fever-ridden air would kill anyone but a native.

[2] The great fen pike.

Saxons through whose bending reeds and watery channels Canute rowed in a boat, "to hear the monks of Ely sing so merrily." If the banks had gone that March at Denver and Littleport, as they went at Soham, a hundred thousand acres of fen would have been engulfed. There would have been drowned cattle and men, babies bobbing among the sodden corpses of sheep, women marooned on cottage roof-trees and wailing in the night. Only a turn of tide and wind at King's Lynn saved the situation.

Three years ago hundreds of acres of derelict swamps were half-dry in summer and lakes in winter. In addition, there were thousands of acres of dry, reed-grown cattle fens dotted with thorn-bushes, sallows, willows, and creeping brambles.

At Wicken, my old home, we still preserve the last large area of primeval fen in England. Wicken Sedge Fen, now largely the property of the National Trust, with the adjoining St Edmund's Fen, runs to some hundreds of acres. Dense reed beds, sedge which cuts to the bone, thickets of sallow-bushes, dykes, and pools make it an enchanted sanctuary for reed-warblers, grasshopper warblers, sedge-warblers, doves, shrikes, red-polls, snipe, redshank, a few duck and herons, with an occasional bittern and Montagu's harrier. Both the latter have nested on and off for many years.

My grandfather was largely responsible for preventing this fen from being drained about a hundred years ago when plans were on foot to do so. He pointed out that it was a valuable catch-water area in time of flood and would always provide sedge for thatching in summer. He gained the day, although I rather think that his interest in birds and wildfowl shooting may have had quite as much to do with his zeal for saving the fen.

Most of my childhood was spent roaming its reed beds, wading its pools, punting silently up the dykes, staying out half the night to listen to duck and otters, owls and reed-warblers, waders and wild geese. In those days it was a wild and lovely spot, full of rare birds and insects. To-day the National Trust has drilled and regulated it, cut droves or rides through the sedge; thrown most of the old village place-names overboard, and called every paltry ten acres by the names of its various benefactors, until the fen is a mere show-place, a donnish playground.

I determined some years ago to try to re-create some part of the old fen in its natural wildness and glory. There were to be no paths for professors afraid to get their feet wet, no signposts to show mollycoddle 'students' where to catch a beetle or pursue a butterfly, no planks over the ditches with handrails to stop the girls falling in, and no conducted parties of peering, precious adolescents, shepherded by pompous dons or nose-led by museum naturalists whose closest acquaintance with a bird is usually by a coloured plate or a dried skin.

So I bought a few hundred acres of wet, reed-grown land in Burwell Fen. It was under water six months of the year, a steaming swamp in summer. Its soil was black, and its ditches stunk. A few half-wild horses and bullocks roamed its reed beds. They bedded in meadow-sweet and grasses and had to be hauled, half-choked by ropes, out of its bogs and dykes. This land lay between the high banks of Burwell and Reach Lodes, a V-shaped area embracing with other drowned properties perhaps seven hundred acres. In the past some had been dug for peat.

In my grandfather's day an old reed-thatched, black-boarded inn with an earth floor and horn panes in the windows stood at the far point where the two lodes meet. Its bedroom windows peered under poke bonnets of thatch down the shining water of Burwell Lode to the old Anchor Inn at Upware Sluice. Pout Hall it was named because of the burbots, or eel pouts, caught in the lode—odd fish shaped like a thick, short eel with a skin instead of scales, a species of lamprey.

The old inn was a haunt of sheep-stealers and corn-thieves, eel-catchers and poachers, turf-diggers and sedge-cutters, duck-shooters and plover-netters. That rough, native crew of fen tigers were unable to read or write, distrustful of strangers and contemptuous of the law, but they had great qualities of heart and courage. As a race they are almost extinct. You will find their recognizable counterpart in the broadsmen of Norfolk, and their marine cousins among the fishers and fowlers of the coastal mud flats.

They recognized no authority but that of their few fen squires and farmers, men not only of local property and prestige, but ready to fight for it with their fists if need be. My great-uncle, Isaac Aspland, who stood six feet two, was broad in proportion, would ride any horse that walked, and fight any man who asked for it—a man of great generosity of heart and first-class intellect—was one of the few who claimed their respect. Old Cole Ambrose, of Stuntney Hall, was another. He and Squire C. P. Allix, of Swaffham Prior Hall, Fred Johnson, of Wicken Hall, and old Dr Lucas, of Burwell, were perhaps the only men for miles round for whom those fen tigers would doff their moleskin caps and say 'Master.'

Pout Hall was their stronghold. When my maternal grandfather,

Luke Staples,[1] was snipe-shooting in the fens, poling over the floods in his duck punt, or leaping dykes with a twelve-foot long jumping-pole which his man carried behind him, he sometimes called at Pout Hall for a glass of home-brew or that strong mead made from fen honey, which would turn most men upside down.

A lot of sheep-stealing at night went on from the farms round about Burwell, Reach, the Swaffhams, and Exning. The sheep were brought down to Burwell or Reach at dead of night. Their carcasses were loaded into barges and then taken by water to Pout Hall, where they were shorn, skinned, cut up, and parcelled out among the gang. At harvest time the fen tigers would go on to the upland fields, steal the short, sickle-cut heads of corn by the sackful, and bring them by boat to Pout Hall. There they thrashed out the corn with wooden flails on an outspread sail-cloth. Who was to know what went away from that lonely marsh inn in the holds of the barges which every now and then called on their way from Burwell or Reach to Cambridge, Ely, Littleport, or even as far as Lynn on the Wash?

Things got so bad in the end that a squadron of Dragoons was sent into the fen to break up the gang, and the old inn was pulled down or burned down.

That was before or just after they had killed Peacock, the first policeman we ever had at Wicken. He was set on one dark night in a back lane, his head bashed in with a bludgeon, and the body wheeled on a turf barrow down to the fen, where it was thrown in a pool—to be recovered thirty years later with the skull smashed like an egg-shell.

In the triangle of rough fen and sighing reeds at the back of the tall poplars where once stood this old fen inn I began my wildfowl sanctuary in 1934. The whole seven-hundred-acre triangle was a natural catch-water area for the winter floods from Burwell and beyond. The only draining windmill which worked was blown down in a gale. The other had been burned down some years before.

That first August when I became owner of part of the fen five of us set out from Cambridge at two in the morning. We motored through the Swaffhams to High Town Drove in Burwell Fen where, in the blackness, we bumped and bucketed over a rutted, grassy fen drove, as uneven as a prairie trail in Canada. The previous winter, when the fen had been flooded, I had seen scores of duck on the

[1] Then of Landwade Hall, Newmarket. He was an Ulsterman, a collateral of that remarkable old man, the late Sir John Molesworth Staples, Bart., of Lissan, Co. Tyrone.

wing. I baited my friends accordingly with promises of the mighty bag of wildfowl we should get that morning. We had a shilling sweep on it. Mandeville, sceptically, said eight duck; Galitzine, twenty; Jocelyn Lucas, twenty-five; Robert Adeane, the same number, while I was wildly optimistic with forty. The total bag was four duck! The place was as dry as a bone. Nigel Holder, it is true, killed about thirty doves which came in to feed on the seeds of grass and reed. That winter the draining mill blew down. The floods came. The water stayed. It grew and waxed.

Within twelve months I had a hundred and eighty acres of permanent water in summer. In winter anything from three hundred acres to the whole lot was under water. One January reed-stacks were sailing about like ships.

A year later, it was a paradise of wildfowl. The bittern nested each year, usually two pairs of them. The Montagu's harrier returned. The hen harrier beat the levels like a setter in winter. Short-eared owls rose from the rough grasses as we walked to our butts by the side of the meres. The sweet little garganey teal was a regular summer visitor. Sometimes six or eight pairs nested. In 1936 the rare black-necked grebe, which had not been known to nest in Cambridgeshire for eighty years, returned and raised a family.

The fen was cut in half about the middle of the V by a rough track, a boggy cart road of black peat, grass- and reed-grown, which had led from the Priory Cockup Bridge over Burwell Lode to that vanished, forgotten, old thatched cottage which once stood on Reach Lode bank. It was called New Zealand a hundred years ago, when New Zealand was new on the map, a distant and savage place as was this lonely fen cottage.

This old track roughly divided the two principal meres—Swan Mere of about forty acres on the Reach side and Pokers' Mere which, with a succession of pools, ran on down towards Pout Hall. Now Swan Mere was a natural small broad, studded here and there with large clumps of sedge. Its shores were fringed with tall reeds, mare's tails, and 'litter' which, on the banks and shallow edges, merged into meadow-sweet, purple loosestrife, white horse-bane, arrowheads, water plantains, and water violets. Two or three pairs of swans, many of which nest in the fens in a semi-wild state, made it their home the first year and gave it its name. Before long I had seventeen of them sailing its waters like a fleet of yachts. They were a magnificent sight on the wing, the beat of their great pinions making windy music in the wide fen sky.

Wooden butts, rough platforms with reed sides, were put up here and there in the meres. Pools, from half an acre to two acres, were cut out by scythe in the dense reed beds towards Burwell Lode. The reeds were so thick and high that more than once a man was lost in them for half a day. In places they were twelve to fourteen feet in height.

Duck of all sorts flocked in to the fen, made it their home, nested, and brought up their young. Contrary to the doctrines of the pundits of Wicken Fen, who refer scornfully to 'gunmen'—whatever they may be—as the enemies of bird life, I not only allowed but encouraged shooting on about two hundred acres of the whole fen, setting aside the rest, with the exception of a few acres owned by the National Trust, as a private bird sanctuary.

My rule was not to shoot the fen more than once a fortnight; to discourage guests from shooting any birds which were rare, uncommon, or not easily identifiable, or which might fall in dense reeds where they could not be found; to cease shooting after the morning flight until at least midday; and not to shoot at all in the evening. That was partly because of the difficulty of picking up and partly to inculcate in the birds' minds the idea that the place was a sanctuary. The result was extraordinary. On an average we killed eight hundred to a thousand head a year, including duck, snipe, coots, moorhens, redshank, plover, various waders, pigeons, and a few partridges and pheasants. I should say that anything between a thousand and fifteen hundred duck were bred on the fen each year. It became an extraordinary reservoir of wild life. Not only was it the largest area of water in Cambridgeshire, but it became comparable in interest and variety of bird and plant life to almost any Norfolk Broad.

The duck soon got to know where they were safe and where they were not. I have sat in my punt, hidden in the reeds on the edge of a mere, while the morning flight was in full swing with six or eight guns banging off over an area of less than half a square mile, and seen ducks pour over my head in scores, straight into pools and waterways, perhaps only a hundred yards from the nearest gun. They knew they were safe, and there they stayed for the rest of the day.

My guns were meticulously careful to see that no rare or uncommon birds were shot, and that, in case of doubt, it was better not to shoot at all. The result was that although probably a score of young bitterns were reared on the fen during the five or six years when it was in its glory, only two were shot by mistake, one in the mist of morning by Sir Jocelyn Lucas, who mistook it for a goose, and one, I regret to say, most inexcusably by myself.

Mr Nigel Holder shot a bean goose in the winter of 1936; Captain D. K. Wolfe Murray ("Fish-hawk," the bird artist) saw and identified the Great White Heron in August 1937; Prince Galitzine and I both saw six Egyptian cattle egrets in September 1938, probably escapes from Whipsnade or Lilford; Dr E. A. R. Ennion, that practical ornithologist and charming bird artist of Burwell, who spent half his spare time studying birds on the fen, recorded the garganey, gadwall, black-necked grebe, and greenshank as nesting and was of the opinion that the rare bearded tit, or 'reed pheasant,' had returned to us; Captain Aubrey Buxton and myself both saw the hen harrier on several occasions, while the Montagu's harrier was as regular a yearly visitor as the bittern. Marsh harriers were seen by Mr Basil Green, of Hill House, Newmarket, who also recorded about a dozen of the uncommon Black Terns, or 'Blue Darrs,' as regular spring visitors and one Arctic Tern which he saw sitting on a post "very tired" in May 1940; also five "pure white" terns in the same month. Waders which dropped in to feed and rest included ruffs and reeves in spring and autumn, curlew, curlew-sandpiper, green sandpiper, common sandpiper, greenshank, and bartailed godwit. Little grebe or dabchick nested, and I saw the Great Snipe once.

The great crested grebe, which I always hoped would visit us to nest, was never seen, but nesting duck included mallard, teal, shoveller —of which twenty to forty pairs bred each year—pochard, tufted duck—quite common—garganey, and gadwall, which were often shot in winter. Pintail and golden-eye were shot once or twice. Widgeon put in a regular appearance in numbers in stormy weather. Wild whooper swans came most winters, and pink-footed and grey-lag geese were seen in small numbers each winter. One Canada goose was seen.

It was a rare, enchanted place. Its meres and pools, fringed by tall bulrushes and tasselled reeds, starred by water-lilies and sweet with water-mint, where dragon-flies darted in the sunshine, herons fished, and swifts, martins, and common terns hawked, were perfect in spring and summer. Two or three hundred black-headed gulls began a gullery on Swan Mere and the Cottage Pool. Their great untidy nests and white-splashed droppings fouled the reeds and stained the peaty-brown waters. I could not find it in my heart to drive these clamouring, wheeling multitudes away. They may have taken a few eggs and fouled a few water-ways, but they were a constant airy delight of beauty. Their wings etched fantastic patterns against the high blue skies of April, the white cloud masses of May. Their voices made clamorous the sunny solitudes of reed and water where reed-warblers sang, coots clanked, ducks spattered and bibbled, snipe drummed, peewits wheeled black-and-white, and the redshank sprang on quivering wing, ringing their million bells.

An enchanted place when autumn turned the reed beds to deep gold and rusty red. Seas of purple grasses on the dry marsh turned more purple yet and the bulrushes stood bold and brown. On any morning, wading thigh-deep through dewy rushes, one might flush the harrier from the top of the old reed-stack, a sparrow-hawk from the ruin of the mill, or a carrion crow from the tall trees by Pout Hall. Those were the mornings when the shoveller flew on creaking wings, grunting like pigs, making up their minds to go south to Spain. Mornings when, long ere Burwell or Wicken chimneys were smoking or cottage fires were kindled, I poled the punt in the half-dark from butt to butt, from reedy island to squelching hummock, dropping a gun here and a dog there, whispering injunctions to keep quiet—"And don't shoot them flying over the reed beds!" Finally all were in their places, and the dark sky was lightening in the east.

When the first streak of dawn spread above the Newmarket upland there would come a mighty rushing sound of wings, an immense chattering and clattering in the reeds. Starlings in tens of thousands would rise up out of the great reed beds, swing back and forth in the green-grey dawn, and pour out over the lode banks for their morning forays in stubble field and stack-yard, at the heels of cattle and on the edge of flood waters.

I have seen them come in to roost at night, a great, wavering, soughing bank of birds half a mile long and a hundred yards deep, sweeping in with a roar of wings like the rush of sea waves on a shingly beach. It was an incredible, almost awe-inspiring sight. Once or twice, when they threatened to ruin acres of reeds which I wanted cut for thatching, I fired point-blank into these rushing masses of birds. The double shots cut a great hole, as though through a curtain. Birds dropped in dozens. The ranks closed up. The bank of birds swept upward. They dived, swooped, and came with an irresistible rush, chattering like a million spindles, into the reeds. I believe if you had fired a score of guns into them they would merely have closed up the holes and flown on.

David Wolfe Murray has recorded in his carefully noted and beautifully illustrated *Birds through the Year* the extraordinary phenomenon which he saw on this fen one morning when a vast host of sand-martins, which he estimated at over fifty thousand birds, rose from the reed beds and scattered themselves over Wicken and Burwell Fens in the dawn.

There were bitter winter days when the skies were black and heavy with snow. Mornings when leafless poplars and tousle-headed willows stood like ghosts of trees against a blood-red dawn, and the frozen grass crackled under foot. The meres were edged with tinkling ice, and the windy side of the bulrushes was white with thin snow. The widgeon came in then like bullets, from the far seaways of the Lynn and the leaden waters of Cowbit Wash and Earith. Pochard whizzed by like hock-bottles on wings. Mallard plunged in, heavy-bodied, on determined wings. Teal sprang and circled sharply, their thin whistle delicate between the gusts.

Those were the mornings when perhaps half a score of great grey geese would come lumbering off the bitter stubbles of Spinney Abbey, lords of the sky, planing down to spend a day on the reedy waters of Swan Mere or the Bitterns' Pulk.

One remembers those days, the essential Englishness of them. The gay companions, the sight of birds and clouds, the wind in the reeds, herons fishing the pools, peewits dancing like ballet dancers in summer shallows, gulls clamorous against clouds, the whistle of winter sleet like shot into the water.

There were odd accidents and humours. The day when, cold as only January can be, I was poling Nigel Holder and his dog in a narrow punt across Swan Mere, slipped, and went overboard up to my waist. I had to push the punt to land, wading sometimes up to my armpits, for a quarter of a mile with the knowledge that at any moment I might step into an old turf hole and go over my head. Nigel had the laugh.

There was that other winter afternoon when a rotten plank over the flooded main drain broke as I was walking it, and I went in, over my shoulders, clawing frantically at a sallow-bush to stop myself from total immersion in fourteen feet of water and mud.

There were grand shooting breakfasts at the Swan, in Reach. That ancient fenland pub hides two hundred years of humble history behind a grey-brick exterior. Tatem, the landlord, small, spry, dapper, and black-eyed, would have looked equally well as an eighteenth-century ostler or a present-day jockey, as indeed he was in his youth. He would discourse on cock-fighting, racing, and pike-fishing, while his wife bustled upstairs with enormous platters of bacon and eggs, fat Cambridgeshire pork sausages, chops and beer, a great brown earthenware teapot, and a jorum of port to top up.

Good and bright companies were drawn by the magic of that primitive fen—men honoured in sport, great in achievement, some of them makers of modern history. Lord Lloyd, gay, dark, and incisive, that most compelling personality, perhaps the greatest proconsul of our age; his son, David,[1] and young Jellicoe, son of the great Admiral of the Fleet; Billy Sempill, fresh from conquering new airways of the world; K. K. Horn, of Thurlow Park, one of the "War Birds"[2] of the last war; Robert Adeane, urbane and cheerful; Kolia Galitzine, invariably wet, tireless, and indefatigably well-mannered; Jocelyn Lucas, Member of Parliament, Master of Hounds, fireman, and driving force of the Overseas League, the man who has never grown up; Peter Ackroyd, then joint-Master of the Belvoir, huge-shouldered, craggy-faced, with a booming voice and a devoted retriever; Nigel Holder, who helped to make motor-racing history at Brooklands with "the Bentley Boys" in the roaring twenties; Tony Heckstall-Smith, that amusing, impudent, and erudite yachtsman who crowned an insouciant youth by winning the D.S.C. for outstanding gallantry at Crete; 'Chub' Leach, the Newmarket trainer, son of old Felix Leach, 'father' of the racing Athens; David Wolfe Murray, dark, enthusiastic, perpetually sketching and watching birds; Ralph Curzon, who thought it the most enchanting place in England; and our twin local archangels, Eric Ennion, who combined doctoring fen tigers with a delicate artistry of birds, and Ernest Parr, the keeper.

I have an abiding affection for Ernest. That quiet, sunburned little fenman, tough as wire nails, with an eye like a hawk, has a remarkable knowledge of rare birds and a love of natural history. He is a rare dog-breaker and trainer, an amazing shot with a disconcerting habit of shooting driven partridges with a double four-ten. That, I think, is the apogee of fine shooting.

Alas, for these memories. As we cantered on to the village green from the sunny slopes of the Devil's Ditch Ernest was waiting at his gate, his face as long as a sea-boot.

"That's a rare shock you'll have. There ain't a drop o' water on the place. They've bored a great tunnel under Reach Lode—one man got killed doin' it—and they found a lower level in Swaffham

[1] The present Lord Lloyd.

[2] The famous flyers who figure in E. W. Springs's *War Birds and Ladybirds*, an epic of the R.F.C. in 1914-18.

Drain, so all the water's run off. The ducks has gone. Swan Mere's ploughed up, and there 'on't be a snipe on the place or a reed to set behind a month from now. Come you and see. That'll break your heart."

We rode from the village down High Town Drove. Where a year before had been a rutted grass track, with holes a foot deep where partridges dusted, was now a long glaring ribbon of concrete road. It pointed straight as a sword into the heart of the fens. A symbol, cold and hard, of the mechanical values which slew that last sanctuary of reed and bird, flower and fish.

At the end of that mile-long rapier of concrete I came to the fen. Another concrete road was being laid. Once it had been an old green drove, fringing the flower-starred waters of the mere. Flowers and waters had gone. Reed and sedge, meadow-sweet and bulrush, had vanished. Where duck had paddled and the coot clanked, where redshank had hung on quivering wing and the pike swirled, a caterpillar tractor pulled a four-furrow plough. Great slices of chocolate-coloured soil turned relentlessly over behind the spitting, chuffing passage of the tractor.

As I reined in Robert, my horse, and stood a moment on the corner of the mere my mind went back. By that thorn-bush on the edge of the drove, over the bulrushes, I first saw the hen harrier. Twenty yards to the right was the little dock in the reeds where the gun-punt had lain, grey-painted, its bottom boards littered with empty cartridge-cases, stray feathers, dead lily roots, the sudden starry shine of fish-scales. But the thorn-bush had gone, hauled up by the roots. The bulrushes were a memory. The reedy dock was a quadruple furrow of black-brown soil.

Where Swan Mere had spread its open waters, where pochard and teal had sprung on sudden wings, lay furrow after furrow. Beyond, the tall battalions of reeds, rooted in dry soil, their stems water-stained five feet from the earth, rustled in the September wind. No water gleamed. All was dry, silent, robbed of its quick virtue. The beauty and the birds had gone.

A gang of men in blue dungaree trousers, some in the old-fashioned corduroys, tied below the knee with string, looked up from their road-making at this sudden apparition of a man on a horse. You do not see horsemen in the fen very often nowadays.

"I reckon that don't seem like home te ye," said one toothless grin. "If yewd 'a' towd me a year agoo that this here fen could 'a' bin draínded I'd 'a' towd that man he were a liar. Now, do yew look at it—that's a masterpiece. They've runned all the water off. But I don't doubt the land'll git up an' blow away on 'em one o' these here days if they make it too dry."

He spoke the essential country wisdom which knows, particularly in the fens, the danger of over-drainage, of dry, friable soil which may get up and blow away in black clouds, leaving the roots of wheat, mangolds, and turnips bare.

I rode on. Here and there, for sheer contrast of memory, I put my horse through reed beds where the reeds grew so high that their tasselled flags overtopped my cap. His hooves trod the dry stems of bulrushes, yellow irises, and water plantains. They churned the dust of dried plants which had made brief beauty in shining waters.[1]

Excavators had sheared new dykes, cleaned out old ditches. A few inches of water gleamed in the bottoms. The sides flared outward, sliced clean, showing a rising fall and depth of peat, lying on the blue clay like thick chocolate. In places it was six and ten feet deep. In others the blue clay rose in billows within a foot of the surface.

The peat was stippled, like currant cake, with shorn-off stems of reeds and rushes, pale yellow. White shells, tiny but perfect, of pre-Ice Age, water-snails, and shellfish starred the cut surface. Two thousand years of history was laid bare to the eye of a geologist. Within a year hundreds of tons of potatoes, wheat, beans, and mangolds were grown on that one fen alone.

Mr J. A. MacMillan, Chief Executive Officer of the Cambridgeshire W.A.E.C., tells me that his Committee has drained or reclaimed seven thousand acres of fen at a cost of (*a*) drainage, £3 to £6 an acre, (*b*) removing bushes, bog oak, etc., from nil to £10 an acre, (*c*) cleaning the land, £3 to £6 an acre. His Committee now farms about 7500 acres.

[1] To-day (1942) this fen is growing crops of potatoes, mangolds, and beet, and has been visited by the King and Queen.

CHAPTER XV

The happy horse is the tranquil one. The one that will go at any speed the rider asks without question and without excitement.

LIEUTENANT-COLONEL M. F. MCTAGGART, *Stable and Saddle*

A Fen Oak One Hundred and Ten Feet Long—The Prehistoric Man in the Peat—Badcock's Hut—"A Supper Mess o' Water-rats"—Village Aristocracies—"The Five Miles from Anywhere: No Hurry"—The Upware Republic—Black Shuck—Henry Cromwell at Spinney Abbey—The Tale of a Five-hundred-acre Fen Farm—Fields which blow away

OVER THE LODE IN SWAFFHAM FEN THE DRAINERS HAD RAISED A more notable prehistoric relic—the trunk of a black fen oak a hundred and ten feet long. Thousands of these prehistoric trees lie beneath the black fen soil. For two hundred years we of the fens have dug them up. Some are quite black, others dark brown. All seem to lie in the same direction, pointing south-west as though to prove the old theory that they are part of a prehistoric forest which was swept down by a sudden avalanche of ice from the north-east.

This Swaffham oak—or, by the length of it, I should say a pine—gave the reclamation people so much trouble to bring to the surface that they were obliged to call in the sappers who blew it up in three parts. Hundreds of tons of such fen oaks lie useless to-day—occasionally used as posts, more often burned for firewood.

They, however, are minor relics compared with the skull of *Bos urus*, the great ox, dug up in Burwell Fen in my father's day with a flint axe embedded in its skull. A pretty trophy of Stone Age hunting.

Before that there was the savage man whom they found years ago, while draining near-by fens, sunk in the peat, standing upright in his dug-out canoe. A haunting figure, the skin still on the bones, stained brown with peat. Hair, lank and black, hung over his shoulders, the remnants of a leather jerkin and cross-garterings about him, the right hand upraised as though to cast a spear. It was a remarkable example of preservation by the peat, preservation which lasted all too shortly when exposed to the open air.

I rode on across the fen, Robert's hooves kicking up dust where a year before I had rowed a boat, to the high Cockup Bridge over

Burwell Lode. Beyond Priory Farm I rode left down Harrison's Drove, a sea of autumn reeds on either side. A few tall poplars ahead, a draining mill at the head of Norman's Dyke, were landmarks in the lonely fen, a sighing reedy solitude without sign of plough, stubble, or potato.

This old Adventurers' Fen has been no-man's-land since the dawn of history. When Wicken Fen was embanked as a catch-water area, Adventurers' Fen was left, not as a primeval waste but as a low-lying swamp. It was peat land where the men of Burwell and Wicken dug turf to warm their houses and make their ovens glow. A rough wild place, haunt of snipe and redshank, of Montagu's harrier and fen pigeons, cut up by turf diggings which, when flooded, were full of small pike six or eight inches long. Mallard came there in winter. Teal used it in wary, springing wisps. Green plover came in white-waistcoated battalions. No house stood. The mournful poplars on a hillock in the midst of these watery wastes marked only in memory the site of Badcock's Hut.

When my mother, that gallant woman who is now seventy-two, was a young and beautiful girl of seventeen she was sent for one winter night to go to that earth-floored, reed-thatched hut in the savage fen. She was of the proper Victorian sort which considered that the inheritance of a little property or dignity conferred a lasting sense of responsibility towards those less fortunate. A point of view which some of our modern 'intellectual' sneerers at the Victorians might apply to their own rabbit-warren lives. So, in the frosty moonlight she set out. Guided by a ragged boy, she went through the sleeping village, along the soggy towpath of Wicken Lode, across the wooden cattle bridge over the Runawater, by the high bank of Wicken Lode, a trackway in a sea of mist. She left it for a winding, intricate runway through the reeds, twisting by pools, edging along dykes, through a blanket of frosty fog. Thus she came to Badcock's Hut.

Thatched, turf-walled, scarcely ten feet high, the wretched dwelling had neither windows nor wooden door. Its door was a hurdle thatched thick and dense with reeds. The floor was beaten earth. In the one room with its rough, wooden settles, its guttering, home-made candles, with a central fire which smoked through a hole in the roof, she found a child lying on a sheepskin, yellow and shivering, thin as a rat. It was in a high fever.

She took the child to her bosom in that wild, half-savage hut and nursed it all the night. When she asked the mother what food it had been given the mother answered, "Same as us, miss—a supper mess o' water-rats."

When old Dr Willis, of Soham, came ten hours later, having driven by dog-cart, been rowed by boat, and walked the rest in thigh waders, he found the child in the throes of typhoid. My mother was nursing it. Not a breath of fever touched her. God had watched over that lonely fen hut for ten hours of the winter night.

It is odd how village history repeats itself. I rode down the peaty track towards the poplars of Harrison's Spinney, fifty years after that notable night of duty. Half a dozen men, shirt-sleeved, in high water-boots, stained with mud and fen water, were dydling out the bottom of a dyke. A little farther a caterpillar excavator, mounted on railway sleepers to stop it sinking into the soft soil, was scooping up the black, spongy peat with a great grab. One of the men peered up from the bottom of the dyke, straightened himself, shaded his eyes, and exclaimed:

"Why, I know you, master."

"All right—who is it?"

"Alec Johnson, from the Hall, eeain't it?"

"No! Guess again. You're near enough. I'm his cousin."

"Har—Master Wentworth! Damn, boy, I ain't sin yer since yer were a little owd boy, gittin' up tew yer backside in this here fen! My owd Dad pulled you out o' the dykes more'n once. Blarst, he said yew was the pesk o' his life when he were turf-diggin' here. Yew know me. That's Bert. How are yer, sir! How are yer!"

He climbed out of the dyke. I leapt off Robert. We shook hands, as old friends do, pump-handling up and down for half a minute, grinning and mumbling.

It was Bert Bailey, that long, dare-devil, raw-boned fenman, a hero of my youth, a rare man with a long dog, hawk-like with a fish spear when the pike darted from the bows of his turf-barge, quick as a heron with an eel glaive. Bert is one of the last of the true old breed of real fenmen. In any other age or sphere he would make an ideal cavalry soldier, a great scout, a Dominions pioneer. Such men are the marrow of life.

There have been Baileys, Simpkins, Marshalls, Scriveners, Rumbelows, Fullers, Houghtons, Badcocks, and Treens in Wicken and Burwell since the Middle Ages and earlier. They were there when the Saxons chased the Normans out of Ely and roasted them screaming in the blazing reeds on Aldreth Causeway.

Cottagers, farmers, and fenmen—theirs is a true aristocracy of the soil—as true to tradition, as sound in principle and humble endeavour as the old nobility, Stanleys, Cecils, Russells, De Greys, Grevilles, Percys, and the rest in their wider spheres.

There is more true aristocracy to-day in the farmhouses and cottages of England than in all the ranks of our newly minted peers, that vast caucus of middle-class mediocrities—chain-store proprietors, lawyer-politicians, Labour 'intellectuals,' Liberal schoolmasters, brewers, soap-boilers, shipbuilders, and Back Bench nonentities who have ennobled themselves and their dreary posterity by opportunism or cheque-book.

Looking into Bert's honest, grinning brown face with its even teeth and quick smile, I could not help thinking that were I a soldier in the ranks I would rather follow such an honest man as sergeant-major than tote my tommy-gun at the behest of some of those less English men of new honours..

We talked old times, boyhood days, a little. We talked of his father, old John "Bunyan" Bailey. He got his nickname, as all village nicknames arise, from an accident of living. When old John Bailey was young, seventy years ago, he left Wicken and travelled to Soham, four miles away, where he served as houseboy to old Dr Willis. It was a long journey in those days. He was more or less in foreign parts. When he returned, at last, moneyed and travelled, to settle down and marry, he was christened "Bunyan" Bailey because, like the immortal evangelist, he had been on a long pilgrimage to strange places in the company of the ungodly.

Beyond Bert, where the excavator clanked and grabbed its mouthfuls of soil, I found a little, old, bent man with a leather face, blue eyes, and white whiskers. He wore a leather jerkin, a butcher-blue shirt, one of those narrow, blue-and-white, glazed collars with a brass stud and no tie, which the fenmen affect. He looked as though he had grown, gradually, out of a clump of reeds. Brick cottages, iron stoves, brass door-handles, and cheap carpets do not know such men. They belong, when they are at home, to white-plastered cottages with thatched roofs and low-ceiled whitewashed kitchens, cosy with the smell and glow of turf fires in fireplaces built of chalk blocks and brick. Fireplaces where the oven runs into a great white belly of bulging wall. Bread is baked on the creamy ash of turf from the fen. They belong to the age of mead and fen honey, of eel stew and baked pike, of pigs' fry and broad beans, of goats' milk and paigel[1] tea.

[1] Cowslip.

We took a long look at each other. We looked at the excavator, grabbing its voracious lumps remorselessly from the primeval soil. The little man raised a forefinger, bobbed imperceptibly, spoke shyly.

"You're Miss Staples's boy, aren't you, master? I'm Badcock—used to live in the old housen under them poplars." It is gratifying still to be regarded as a boy when you are forty-three, and a compliment to a woman that she should be remembered by her maiden name half a century after her marriage.

"Yes, I'm Miss Staples's boy. Are you old Daddy Badcock's son?"

"That I am. Seventy-three this Michaelmas. Why, that was your mum that come down here and nussed my sister time she was took ill o' the fever, 'fore she married and got you. She's a good woman, the missus is. A good woman. D'you give her my best respex and love."

We talked of the change in the face of the fen, of the new draining, of the proposals to plough up and sow corn where turf had been dug and the goldfinch had swung on the thistle. He did not think much of the chances.

"Rare good land, rich as any in the fen, but that howd the water. That allus did, and that allus will. That'll cost a mint o' money to drain and 'on't ever arn a penny." We shall see.

I rode on to the Runawater Bridge by Malting Pits, past Ragamoor, the lonely hut, to try to get to Wicken. The bridge was too narrow. The lode was too wide. The bottom, of clay and stiff mud, was too sticky. It would have been suicide for man or horse to have tried to swim or jump it.

So back we rode by Wicken Lode bank in the warm glow of sunset, by carrs of sallow-bush and whispering reeds, where the grasshopper warbler was tuning up his reeling song, back in the yellow and gold of sunset to Upware. At that sanctified inn of boyhood, white-walled, red-roofed, its feet in the Cam, its roof shaded by great willows, that inn most happily named "The Five Miles from Anywhere: No Hurry," we stopped for ale.

It is an immortal inn. Undergraduates for a hundred and fifty years have known its magic. Arthur Gray,[1] the Master of Jesus, in his *Cambridge Revisited* tells of the "Upware Republic" which flourished there about the sixties. A rumbustious, riotously healthy gathering of sporting, talking, argumentative undergraduates who rowed by boat or hacked by horse the ten or twelve miles from Cambridge, set up their mock republic in the inn, fished for pike,

[1] Since, alas, dead.

and shot duck and snipe in the fen. They poached hares and partridges on my uncle's farms, fought the bargees for fun and pint pots, and started steeplechase races through bottomless barrels for the girls of the hamlet or set them afloat in a skiff on the river with a gallon of ale to drink and nought but their bare hands to row themselves back to bank. John Eldon Gorst was one of the leading spirits.[1]

I drank a pint with Jolly, the landlord, to the memory of those twin stalwarts of Upware who maintained its last traditions until a few years ago—H. M. Finch, tall, broad, bearded, scholarly, and pugnacious, "the Fighting Barrister" who was of the time of J. K. Stephen and W. S. Gilbert, and Charlie Crisp, the unlettered, honest, cheerful cottage sportsman of Upware, a great snipe-shooter, a champion skater, a merry beer-drinker, a master of the gun. Charlie is an immortal memory. I see him now, ruddy-faced, mischievous-eyed, with his whiskers greying, his clay pipe glowing, leaning back on a wooden settle in the bar, his feet stuck straight out in front of him, his long-legged spaniel snoring, while he declared solemnly to a sucking undergraduate:

"Lor, bless you, sir, that were so hard here one winter and that many geese up the river that they come over the house-top one night like a troop o' hosses. I no more to do but stuck me owd gun up the chimbley and fired her off when I heerd 'em honkin' over. Blarst, boy, when I run to the door I couldn't git that open. Shut fast."

"Snow?" inquired the innocent.

"Snow! Blarst! No. Dead geese! A cart-load on 'em. Them what I shot out o' the chimbley."

And so, by the hard high road to the haunted bank of Spinney Fen where they say Black Shuck, the ghostly hound of Thor, runs by night. We picked our way, delicately, by that rutted thistle-grown track, bordering the Sedge Fen on one side and the cattle marshes of Spinney Abbey on the other, with one eye on a roving bull, the other on the treacherous track. It was dusk when we came by Breed Fen Drove, through the aromatic turf smoke of the Lode cottages to Wicken, to that thatched Elizabethan house which is my home, its great white Tudor chimneys smoking among the sycamore leaves, its dormer windows with a motherly eye on the village green. It is now as it was when Sir Henry Jermy built it as a hawking and fishing-box in 1540.

It was pleasant to put horses in loose-boxes which had not known a thoroughbred for years. Good to hear them stamp and snort in

[1] Later Sir John Eldon Gorst, British Agent and Consul-General in Egypt.

the night, to listen to the clink of stable buckets and the hiss of rubbing-down in the morning. We have lost a lot that is precious, good, and healthy by the motor values of the last twenty-five years. Old men and children gathered in the stableyard as we walked the horses round in the morning. One ancient man evoked memories of when my uncle and Joe Blanton trained Robert the Devil secretly in the village a year or so before his immortal fight for the Derby in which he was only beaten on the post by a nose by Ben D'Or.

I rode over to Soham by the Horse Fen next morning and had a day's partridge-shooting the following day with Cowley, the policeman, a good sportsman who used to be a keeper at Sandringham. I gave him a great muzzle-loading four-bore out of my curious battery of wildfowl guns, wherewith to shoot duck on the flooded 'washes' of the Cam in winter. On Sunday I rode by Padney and Fordey Gate to Ely, finding my way by old grassy tracks and droves across black, peaty, stubble fields. I came finally to that cathedral city of the fen, its great fane like a fairy palace upon its little hill, by riding along the top of the high river wall of the Great Ouse.

My mission was to take a leash of partridges to old Mr Nicholls, the lawyer, at the Cutter Inn. It was a Sunday, a hot morning, and nine miles by horse to go. I got to the City of the Fens almost too late for the pint of beer which sun and exercise had warranted. A plump woman, locking the door of the Crown, spied me and cried, "Are you dry?" I nodded. "Bring that hoss in the back-yard then, and you shall have a pint. That does me good to see a gentleman on a hoss again. In me dad's time the half on 'em went about that way."

There, again, as in a score of other towns and villages, I found the open sesame of a horse's hooves to an English heart.

I went on the Monday to Spinney Abbey, that monastery farmhouse, grey and alone in its thin firs, a mile out of our village. It broods on the ancient glory of its day when Henry Cromwell, Lord Protector of Ireland, retired there to spend his declining days in the ample peace of a farming gentleman. We have three of his family buried in the church. Charles II, when the throne had come again to its own in a roisterous, bawdy reaction, was hunting the hare on Fordham Moor. It led him, by the open fields, through Wicken to Spinney Abbey, where they killed. It was just such a hot, dry September day, and the King craved claret or a quart of ale.

"I know of a country gentleman living quietly at yon house who will be honoured to welcome your Majesty," said one of his suite.

He clattered ahead into the stone-walled farmyard, to bring thence the embarrassed person of Mr Henry Cromwell. Before him the courtier marched, bearing aloft a muck-crome.

"What is the meaning of this foolery?" demanded Charles, sympathetic for Mr Cromwell.

"Merely, Sire, that I bear before this gentleman, Mr Henry Cromwell, the symbol of his present agricultural pursuit as I once bore before him the mace of England when he was Lord Protector of Ireland," replied the cavalier.

It is a pretty story, true enough in substance, crowned by the agreeable fact that Charles, who, whatever his faults, was a man and a good friend, put the shy Cromwell at his ease and drank with him, ate his cold mutton and, I do not doubt, talked of casting hawks at the heronshaws and mallard on the fens of Spinney and Wicken.

This day at Spinney I took a sandwich and, for old time's sake, cracked a bottle of champagne with Robert Fuller, whose family has farmed land in Wicken parish for two centuries.

"I farm five hundred acres now," he said. "We reckon a good harvest at twelve to thirteen coomb of wheat an acre and an average harvest at from nine to ten coombs. I get that by using plenty of farmyard manure—cattle, pigs, and sheep. You can't do without sheep. Your uncle had the best flocks of sheep hereabouts—yet he gambled away a whole flock on one race at Newmarket. Crazy days, trying to put your acres on a horse's back! He had the best land for miles round, but racing killed it.[1]

"This farm runs to a bit of everything—black fenland, heath, London clay, and what they say is the only outcrop of coral-rag, or marl, this side of Oxford. You know that—it's by the side of the old Roman green road, between High Fen and Upware."

Nine generations of Fullers have owned and occupied Padney Farm since John Fuller bought it in 1695. Robert bought Spinney Abbey and Thorn Hall farms in 1918, when Lloyd George declared speciously, "Never again shall agriculture be allowed to fail."

"That was all right as far as words went," Robert Fuller mused, "but by 1930 farmers were going broke in all directions. Not here at Wicken, though, because our wives, sons, and daughters worked all the hours of daylight. Most of us managed to weather the storm, but it was impossible to employ enough men to cultivate the land properly, as the foodstuff we produced couldn't sell for enough money to cover the cost of production. The result was that hundreds of men were driven off the land into other jobs.

[1] This was true of many another local squire and farmer in Edwardian days.

"I invited our M.P. to tea one Sunday, and my brother-in-law and I explained how matters stood and asked that farmers should be paid prices high enough to cover the cost of production. As a farmer he knew the position, but as a politician he said it wasn't practical politics! Our suggestion would be opposed by the Labour Party in the House of Commons!

"Wheat went down in price to twenty shillings a quarter and malting barley to twenty-two shillings, until finally we laid the heavy clay lands down to grass and went in for more cattle, sheep, and pigs, feeding the cattle and the pigs on wheat, which was by then down to seventeen shillings a quarter. We mixed it with Russian barley, which we could buy at the same price. In this way and by growing beet, we were able to exist. But it was the life of a slave—to produce cheap grub for the towns."

He recalled the disastrous harvest of 1879, when, by winter-time, half the corn crops were under ice on Spinney Fen. Five hundred fenmen turned out on Spinney Fen to see the champion skater of all time, old "Fish" Smart, of Welney, race and beat Bert Dewsbury, of Oxlode, Ely. That was in March 1880, and fields of barley, mangolds, and turnips were clear under the ice as the skaters raced along. From that day to this Spinney Fen has been down to inferior grass until, in 1939, a new pumping plant was installed, miles of drains were deepened, and the heavy clay and the fen were once more brought back to cultivation.

"Give us more money and more men in farming, and we can feed most of England," said Mr Fuller. "But most of this reclaimed fenland will be useless for corn-growing unless it's properly clayed with the blue clay which underlies it. If we had had strong winds this spring half Newmarket would have been suffocated by black clouds of peat dust blowing off the fens. Clay is the answer to that."

He remembered that his great-grandfather used to haul his carts from Padney Farm to Wicken High Road with a bull straining in the lead of the horses, so deep was the mire.

"A man who killed his wife in those days," said he, "was charged with sheep-stealing. When the evidence was looked into they couldn't find that he had stolen any sheep. The prosecuting party, although they knew he had killed his wife, could find no proper penalty in the book for womanslaughter, although there was one for manslaughter. But they knew he would be hung if they had him up for sheep-stealing. So sheep-stealing it was, and hang him they did."

CHAPTER XVI

"London's a charming place," ejaculated Miss Watkins, "but I can never get Par and Mar to go there."

"I don't think so," replied our Master. "Give me the country—give me huntin', shootin', and fishin', and Oi'll give moy share o' Lunnon to anyone who likes it."

R. S. SURTEES, *Mr Facey Romford's Hounds*

Newmarket, the Town of Kings—Felix Leach, the Gamecock in Human Form—The Man from Swaffham—To Euston by Barton Mills—The Vulgarity of Elveden—The Triumph of Euston—Farming on Sandy Land—The Duke of Grafton's Experiments—An Extraordinary Object-lesson in Reclamation—Ten Sacks of Barley to the Acre

I WENT BY HORSE-BOX TO EUSTON HALL IN SUFFOLK TO STAY WITH THE Duke of Grafton, for no one but a fool would take horses on such hard roads. I stopped at Fordham Abbey for a word with George Philipson. He was away soldiering. So I talked with his wife and mourned inwardly at the manner in which Cyril Dunn-Gardner's one-time park was cut up by the wheels and boots of soldiery. Like every other country house, Fordham is a cross between a barracks and a school, a stamping-ground for hobnail boots, rifle butts, caterpillar tracks, or evacuee children, school-teachers, and mucky habits.

In this case the soldiery have left no traces other than the honourable scars of war. A very different story from some of the houses, great and small, where irresponsible evacuees, some of them incredibly filthy, have either knocked the place about or so fouled the rooms and passages as to make them a disgrace. Fortunately, those examples have been comparatively rare. None the less they exist. As such they are a reproach to our social system. It is an attitude of mind which must be remedied—an attitude which never existed in country villages but is too prevalent in towns where slums are allowed to grow up. Rural Conservatism often finds it difficult to imagine the depths to which urban slumdom can fall, but if Conservatism is to endure as a leading principle it must remedy this disgrace—a disgrace partly fostered by Victorian slum landlords, who should have known better, and partly by factory owners who themselves were working men grown rich. The landlords were bad or unthinking. The factory owners merely exemplified the old truth that "Jack's a bad master."

I went upstairs to have a look at a converted flat in the top floor of the Abbey, where Daphne Philipson is living with the children. She took the view, as most women of responsibility do, that although her house might suffer some mutilation, it was the least that she could provide, apart from her own efforts, towards the defence of the country.

"After all, if you've got a fair-sized house nowadays," said she, "you can't either expect, or afford, to live in it by yourself. You have to put it to the best use. I'm bound to say I shudder occasionally when I think of the way the staircase or the walls may be knocked about, but, after all, we might have been blown up. We are lucky."

That is the view of any responsible householder I have come across in the Eastern Counties, where, after all, they are in daily danger of being bombed sky-high.

I stopped for lunch in Newmarket, the town of kings and horses, and called on Felix Leach—seventy-two, very spruce, very upright, terrifically smart in a grey suit, grey bowler hat, blue bow tie, and an enormous pair of race glasses. He is the gamecock in human form, a great character in a town of characters. That morning he had been breaking and jumping young horses! We went round the Meddler Stud, saw some great sires, and I found in the house oil paintings of game chickens and terriers, bred by my father fifty years before—"a great sportsman and a scholar, he was," said Felix. "He loved all old things and old-fashioned sports."

We took a glass of sherry at the Rutland, where I met an amusing rough diamond who was evidently a parish councillor from Swaffham Prior. No collar, no tie, but a shrewd eye and a pleasant sharp face. He was holding forth about "Wicken chickens," so I chipped in and asked him what was wrong with my native parish.

"Call us fen tigers, yellow-bellies, or Cambridgeshire camels," I said, "but not chickens. Wicken men were never chickens. Why, damn it, they caught the first policeman we ever had and buried him in the fen."

"I know, I know! I take it all back. Your Wicken men are too tough for us fen-siders. But you must agree that Wicken is fifty years behind the times, even to-day."

"Thank God," says I.

He told me, which I did not know, that Lode men are known as Lode monkeys; Quy villagers as Quy jackdaws, because they chatter so much, and Swaffham—"They as don't know nawthin'." I had always thought that this applied to Swaffham in Norfolk, and not to Swaffham by the Fen.

Two or three other men joined in. We discussed the reclamation work in Burwell, Reach, and Swaffham fens. All were local men, and they gave it as their opinion that my land will be worth up to £100 an acre in a few years. They told me that fen oak burns like coal and cuts up into beautiful wood for furniture, but you must have a bench saw to cut it. It blunts an ordinary saw and defeats an axe. I shall try to corner some of it! Hundreds of tons of fen oaks are lying about by the drove sides and stacked up by the Lode banks.

I had a look at the old stables by the Rutland—beautiful red brick with dogs'-tooth eaves. I should say they are Charles II or thereabouts.

We left Newmarket and went on to Euston by Barton Mills. The Bull was very lovely in the September sunlight. Walls newly cream-washed, geraniums blazing in the window-boxes, pigeons cooing on the tiles, a jumble of roofs, chimney-pots, dormer windows, and good, broad, bow windows, white painted, with a vision inside of oak and mahogany, silver and glass. This pub is a perpetual joy to return to. I have memories from 1910 of its stuffed fish, its wildfowl from the Lark in cases—probably shot by old William Howlett in the nineties—and its copper and brass. The Lark was full-bank, swirling under the mill. A trout jumped as we went over the bridge.

Thetford Heath looked very scarred by tank tracks, and the entrance to Elveden Park a little down at heel, but the village still very smart, modern red-brick and staring white paint—Tooting villadom dumped down in the midst of the Norfolk heaths. A maharajah and a brewer fathered it. I had a vision, through the trees, of the Hall, yellow Bath stone, with that monstrous central dome overshadowing everything. It really is a vulgar building—Lambeth Baths translated to the country.

We went right, by Barnham Heath, another great open warren, criss-crossed by tank tracks, empty of rabbits, musical with stone curlew and peewits. Not a partridge or a pheasant to be seen. But the fir woods on either side were tall and lovely in the afternoon heat-haze. We were in the sandy lands of heath and sighing pines. Miles of rusty bracken and broom, a land empty of house or man, silent in the sun and wind.

As we crossed the invisible boundary on to the Euston property, I could feel somehow an indefinable difference at once. Tidy, whitewashed, thatched cottages looked very demure, like middle-aged dairymaids. Great elms by the field sides. Rough meadows here and there with cart mares and colts out to grass. No Shires to be seen, but some very nice-looking Suffolk punches. We turned in over the bridge to the stable front of Euston Hall. The house, square, with turrets at either corner, overlooks a narrow lake made by damming up the Little Ouse. Faintly it reminds one of a less ornate, less pretentious Audley End.

We unboxed the horses and put them into two of the best loose-boxes we have so far come across on this tour. It was good to walk into a well-appointed, old-fashioned stable again with plenty of warm wheat straw in the boxes, and good, big, wooden mangers. Jeffcott, the groom, being hunted out of the engine house where two or three vast machines were purring, remarked as Robert was unboxed:

"I'd sooner see one of his sort, sir, than all those engines put together."

The Duke turned up with a car full of keepers just as we had stabled them. A pleasant, quietly humorous, unassuming man with intelligent eyes and the enthusiasm of a boy for farming. Five guns had just got sixty-three brace walking up, which is not so bad in war-time when usually half your guns cannot shoot. We had a cup of tea and went round the farms with Archer, the farm manager, a Norfolk man from Wells, with a red face, terrific enthusiasm, and a gift for long sentences.

We picked him up at his cottage gate just as he was about to have tea.

"I'll take the kettle off, damp the fire down, and leave tea until we have been round, your Grace," he said. "I'd miss any amount of tea to show this gentleman what we have been doing up here."

My instinct was to get out the horses and ride round. But the Duke would have none of it. There were only two hours to dinner, and in that time he was determined to whisk me into a motor-car, shoot me round the farms, and show what had been done. This agricultural duke, who spent a great deal of his life as a land agent before he succeeded, is an excellent example of the up-to-date country gentleman. He combines the best of responsible traditions with a determination to experiment. His point of view is that of the best of the eighteenth-century landowners—a type which put English farming and stock-breeding at the head of the world.

We have taxed that tradition almost out of existence. To-day democracy seeks to substitute State-run farms and hordes of inspectors and paper-wise clerks in its place. Fortunately the process has not gone too far. But it is not until you go round a great feudal estate, like Euston or Holkham, or a great yeoman-bred estate, such as Histon, that you begin to realize how strong, good, and rooted is this individual Englishness of the soil. Townspeople would learn a lot if they paid more attention to native values.

Euston is a remarkable example of triumph over natural difficulty. The estate includes some of the poorest land in England. Land which, before the war, was almost worthless, fit only to breed rabbits or be let as a pheasant- or partridge-shoot. The Euston land, which Bloomfield, the Suffolk plough-boy poet, knew well and put in such delightful antique verse, is so light that "whole fields hereabout get up and blow away." It is finer than sea sand. It runs through the fingers like sand through an hour-glass. We kicked it up in clouds which whitened us to the knees.

Yet here, on what is probably the poorest land in England, the Duke of Grafton, who farms twelve hundred acres of his fourteen-thousand-acre estate, has performed miracles. He has reclaimed virgin heathland, where the bracken grew six to eight feet high. In two years he has grown ten sacks of barley to the acre, and ten sacks of rye—"which," he remarked to me, "is more rye than I have ever heard of anywhere." I am inclined to ask if this is not indeed a record.

What the Duke has done at Euston is an object-lesson to every owner of sandy bracken land elsewhere. Norfolk, Hampshire, Dorset, and other counties can show tens of thousands of acres of similar land at present waste.

He began four years before the war by ploughing up five acres of rabbit-infested land covered with gorse-bushes. It was horse-ploughed at first, but this was a failure owing to the fibrous mass of roots which extended six to nine inches deep. A tractor ploughing a foot deep was next used. This thoroughly broke the land. Then followed a magnificent crop of marrow-stem kale which was folded off by four hundred ewes for six weeks. The land was then ploughed shallow by tractor, and barley put in. The result was the best barley on the whole farm. The yield was fifty-two sacks to five acres—just over a sack an acre on almost pure sand, having a chalk subsoil, and with no record of its ever having been ploughed before.

Then, in the winter of 1939–40, a one-hundred-acre block of similar gorseland, the Leys, was reclaimed. It had been cultivated only once before, in 1918, when it grew one good crop of rye and was then allowed to go back to rubbish.

The Duke estimates that it costs £3 an acre to reclaim this land from bushes and bracken, and up to £2 an acre to plough it a foot deep, using a special single-furrow tractor plough. This does not include the normal cultivation costs. His secret of success was a liberal dressing of potash, but no potash is promised the farmer for next year. Old turf is the main source of humus.

Next followed the reclamation of six hundred acres of park land where the bracken grew taller than a man. The Duke began on a hundred acres just before the war. The War Agricultural Committee is now tackling five hundred acres next door to it. The bracken was first rolled, then ploughed straight into the ground, using an old International tractor, pulling a specially made single-furrow plough a foot deep. The first crop was oats and rye. Practically no bracken was cut with the first harvest. Another thirty acres was put down to roots, seeds, kale, and white turnips. All were good crops, and all were fed off by sheep.

The root land was then ploughed shallow following the sheep, while the corn land was again ploughed a foot deep and sowed with barley.

In both cases the land was then smothered with a new growth of bracken. So sixty East End schoolboys, some of one hundred and forty who are staying in the Hall, hand-picked it in the evenings. They picked it four times during the summer. In spite of this the bracken grew so fast that when the barley was eighteen inches high they had to stop picking, as the bracken was ahead of the barley. When the crop was cut it was completely smothered by bracken. Yet the yield was eight sacks an acre of good malting barley!

The Duke believes that the bracken germinates again from blackened roots, apparently quite rotten, and that it will take three, possibly five, years to get it out of the soil. Deep ploughing and potash is the secret. He intends to lay all this land down to lucerne four years after the first ploughing, keep it down to lucerne for five years, put it down to two corn crops, and then continue with lucerne again. Sheep are the keynote.

On another field of one hundred and seventy-six acres of lucerne the whole is folded by four hundred Suffolk-Cotswold cross-bred ewes once a year. The second crop of lucerne is made into hay, and the third crop put either into the silos—he thinks wooden ones are best—or hay or both. It produces three crops a year.

Lucerne will grow in any season, almost anywhere, wet or dry, but whereas the Duke considers that its roots go at least six feet deep, Mr Archer, his farm bailiff, astonished us both by saying that he had actually traced its roots thirty feet below the surface during excavations in a gravel pit at Walsingham.

The lesson of Euston is this—that land once let at 2*s.* 6*d.* an acre, so rabbit-infested that four to five were killed per acre, is now growing first-class corn crops and magnificent roots, feeding sheep, and paying its way. I predict that the Euston system of light land farming will in time become as historic a common-sense venture as the Euston system of rearing partridges was in more leisurely and less dangerous days.

In the quiet of the evening, bucketing in a motor-car on a rough cart-track round the headland of an enormous field, by the side of a fir belt lively with clattering pigeons, the Duke suddenly stopped, with a grinding of brakes, and said with momentous pride:

"Look at that furrow. It's a mile and a quarter long—straight as a die. That was ploughed by a youngster using a tractor and a straight eye. So I think we can say that some of these young mechanical ploughmen are going to be as good as their fathers who followed a horse."

We drove back, by great barley fields, golden in a Hobbema evening light; by sunset-gilded haystacks which would have given Old Crome time to pause; by ragged, tall hedgerows whence finches flew and sparrows chattered in cascades, until we came to the Hall:

Where noble Grafton spreads his rich domains,
Round Euston's water'd vale, and sloping plains,
Where woods and groves in solemn grandeur rise,
Where the kite, brooding, unmolested flies:
The woodcock and the painted pheasant race,
And sculking Foxes, destin'd for the chace.

Euston is a quiet, spacious, glowing house. The square hall has Lelys, Knellers, Van Dycks, Hoppners, a Viviani, and one or two Jervases, mostly of Fitzroys and Nell Gwynn. She is the Duke's fifteenth great-grandmother by Charles the Second. There were others of Charles himself, his Court, Queen, and concubines, Castlemaine, Cleveland, and the rest. A magnificent Kneller of Thomas Wentworth, Earl of Strafford, who was beheaded, caught my eye. It brings out all the slumbrous, fighting quality of the man. A strong, rather dour face with a direct, sincere look in the eye which redeems its bellicosity. Looking at it, one can well imagine him as a faithful servant of the King, a strong Viceroy, and an implacable enemy. I was reminded of that unconsciously great epitaph, "This morning saw my Lord Wentworth pass on his way to execution at Tower Hill. He looked not so much like a man about to go to his death, but rather as a victorious general leading his army to victory."

The whole house is like that inside—like walking into a page of history, muted, still alive, half-forgotten. The servants are all old friends of the Duke. We waited on ourselves at dinner. On the walls there were nice water-colours of South Africa painted by him. He is a pleasant artist.

After dinner we went to a concert in the dining-room, given by the troops. There are eight hundred in the Park and one hundred and forty East End boys in the house who take their lessons in the morning, work on the farms in the afternoon and are paid for doing so. They live ducally, study academically, and are rewarded agriculturally. It almost pays one to be an orphan and a poor boy nowadays. Apparently these Barnardo boys are looked after, trained, educated, and put into jobs until they are twenty-one—a great work which deserves better recognition.

The troops' concert was extremely good. The high light was when two comedians sang, "It's a Long Way to Tipperary" and "Pack up Your Troubles in Your Old Kit Bag" simultaneously, dividing the audience into two equal halves, with the injunction to follow the competing songs lustily: "Right down the middle line," yelled a pink-faced little comedian. "Straight down the middle of Nell Gwynn—my side take the oranges." That brought the house down. Nell Gwynn at the end of the room, satinly beautiful, seemed to enjoy it.

In the morning I saw two cock pheasants bowing to each other on the lawn, necks out, tails out, rather like two game-cocks. A poor imitation of a challenge. In between defiances they picked up worms. They made a noise like shovellers on the wing.

CHAPTER XVII

The old squires were rich—rich in the fewness of their wants—but the new squires have found wants that their forefathers were ignorant of. We strongly suspect, however, that squires will find no safer or better speculation than in draining and improving their land.

R. S. Surtees

Across the Norfolk Heaths—The Merman's Grave—Singing Ghosts of Thetford—Lord Fisher's Blackcurrants and Asparagus—The Folly of gassing Rabbits—By Ring Mere and Fowl Mere—Chicken-plucking for a Bet—At Swaffham Market—The Seal which drank Beer—The Rich Land of Lincolnshire—Land of the Tractor and Potato—Thompson and Dennis

We rode out from Euston, asleep in its valley of great oaks and shining waters, with its memories of Charles and Lady Castlemaine, and took the grass road from the bridge over the lake to the west, up a rise where partridges barely scuttled from beneath our horses' hooves. Under a tall eighteenth-century archway and then with the sun on our cheeks there was nine miles of the Duke's Ride, dead straight as a sword, running into the west.

It crosses heath and warren, by neolithic flint-pit and Danish barrow. It skirts the edge of lonely pine woods where the peregrine stoops like a bolt at the sudden pigeon.

A wide, empty land of lonely beauty, old as time. Flint-strewn heaths, dappled by rabbit scuts, rusty-red with bracken stretched for miles like waves of an autumn-coloured sea. Fir-trees, their giant trunks reddened by the suns of countless summers, mourn in the wind. The wild whistle of the stone curlew quickens the night.

They will tell you that on these wild warrens and lonely heaths ghosts of the Stone Age, grim shambling figures in woad and skins, haunt the great flint-pits under the white moon. Fewer people than almost anywhere in England live to the square mile on these ancient wastes.

For an hour we cantered over Barnham Heath by Little Heath to Barrow's Corner and Shelterhouse, between the singing trees which make this ducal avenue where no duke ever rides and only the rabbits play.

I saw a hobby hawk, graceful as a dream. I heard the high whistle of Norfolk plover, saw them flick by, quick as scimitars, their great round eyes amazed at this odd sight of two horsemen on a heath where no horsemen ride. At Barrow's Corner we turned right-handed by the park belt of Elveden Hall, centre of the great twenty-five-thousand-acre estate of which these heaths are an ancient part. It was here that the Newtons lived when Sir Isaac was young and unknown. Here too lived Dhuleep Singh, in princely retirement, killing pheasants and partridges by the cart-load in the days when such vulgar records were thought worthy.

In Marmansgrave Wood, beyond the park, there is a lonely tumulus, grave, so they say, of a great Marman or Merman, a man of the sea, perhaps some forgotten Danish prince who met his death here a thousand years ago when these lonely heaths from Thetford to Fornham in the South rang with the clash of swords and the cries of fighting men.

At Elveden Gap we rode into the main heart of England's greatest, yet unknown forest. Thetford Chase and the woods and plantations which come within the power of the Forestry Commission extend to more than three hundred thousand acres, growing forests not yet a quarter of a century old, yet greater than the forest of William Rufus, in Hampshire.

It would be very easy to lose oneself in these dense alleys of dark Germanic pines, of spruce, larch, and fir. Their scent is heady, strong as wine on the wind. The long rides which cut them into squares are grand gallops. But there is little beauty in this new woodland. The trees are too close together, dark, dusty, and cobwebby, breeding places for magpies, jays, carrion crows, rats, and every kind of vermin. Many of the trees are of poor quality.

For two miles we rode through half-grown timber, the ride-sides choked with thistles, blue- and red-headed, tangled with long grasses and tall flowering weeds. Beneath the rows of trees on either side as far as the eye could reach lay long lines of dry and dusty brash—dead branches and undergrowth. A dozen incendiary bombs could set square miles of this forest blazing for days. I have never seen greater criminal neglect of such an elementary fire precaution. True, wide fire-breaks, ploughed up and free of weeds, separate the different blocks of timber, but this brash should be cleared out.

We came in the late afternoon into Thetford, cantering softly over pine needles by the edge of a twisted line of ancient firs, the white-gold tower of its church standing dream-like in the evening sun. Thetford, once the city of twenty churches, "Metropolis of the

Heptarchy," is a town of narrow streets and ancient houses, of monastic ruins and quiet glimmering waters.

We clattered along the hard road above the green river valley with, high on the far skyline, the ruins of the old Leper House, gaunt against its great sunlit wood. Through a gateway, by a thatched and dormered lodge, under the towering shadow of a mighty monks' barn, and into the forecourt of "The Canons," that low and lovely house which crouches in its bright garden, like an old spaniel warm in the sun. The ruined walls and high windows, the barns and refectory ruins of the once great Priory of the Canons of the Holy Sepulchre, climb grey and ghostly on the brightest day. On the other side, towards the river, the monks' fish-pond lies dreaming of great carp and wallowing tench.

There we found stables and a welcome, a glass of wine in a low, mellow room full of good pictures, a garden glowing with flowers, geese moving solemnly in an orchard and, beneath the immemorial grass of the lawn hard by the ruins, a lighter patch in the grass which marks the last resting-place of the mighty Hugh Bigod, one-time Lord of half East Anglia, a man strong enough to defy the King.

It was in this old house, sitting one bright May morning at eleven o'clock, that my host and hostess, Dr and Mrs Jameson, heard in 1937 the sweet singing of ghostly monks. It was so clear on the air that they thought at first that the wireless was turned on. But there was no wireless. And for half an hour the monks of seven hundred years ago sang sweetly. Then came slow reading by a man's voice. Silence, and then the ringing regular footsteps of a man walking on a paved floor where now there is no paved floor. There are green grasses, fig-trees lucent against roofless walls, and a white pigeon and his mate nesting beneath the hollow, windowless, great west window.

That is a strange story, but no stranger than was told me a week earlier by Robert Fuller, of Spinney Abbey, in Cambridgeshire. He, his two sons, and a maidservant at breakfast on Low Sunday morning after Easter seven years ago, under a blue sky, heard suddenly the sweet, unearthly singing of monks in Latin. They too, at first, thought it was the wireless. But there was no wireless.

"It was high up in the air, ten or fifteen feet above the ground, the sweetest singing I have ever heard," said Mr Fuller. "I know no Latin, but I do know English, and this was not English. It was over there," and he waved his hand.

"And what was once over there?" I asked.

"That's where the old chapel once stood. We've traced out the walls and the foundations."

I thought of these two sweet hauntings of music in sunlight when we rode out next morning, from the courtyard of that five-hundred-year-old, enchanted inn, the Bell, with its cheerful, ex-cavalry landlord, Captain Edwardes, its timbered gallery, and good cellar. The way was across the river, through the gaunt magnificence of the Abbey ruins, pearl-like in the morning, up a dusty farm road and then full gallop across barley stubble where partridges sprang like bomb-shells, and into the tall tapestry of woods that lead to Croxton Park, lost in heaths and coverts.

Even there, where men for a hundred years have lived by timber and pheasants, by partridges, hares, and rabbits—for the land would grow no better—they are ploughing up the sand and bracken. Hundreds of acres which for centuries knew first the bustard and then the pheasant are now under the plough.

At Kilverstone, across the road, Lord Fisher grows some of the finest asparagus and blackcurrants in the country. The wise son of the great Admiral of the Fleet one day, some years ago, saw a shoot or two of wild asparagus growing on a heath where no cultivated food of man had ever grown. He took the hint. To-day Kilverstone, many of whose fields are almost pure sand, grows corn, roots, carrots, asparagus, blackcurrants, and the rest. The Duke of Grafton, in Suffolk, and Lord Fisher, at Kilverstone, between them have set shining examples to the owners of light sandy land.

The rabbit trade, which a few years ago and for a century before was the staple industry of this land of heaths and warrens, is almost dead. Major Ashley-Dodd, the squire of Croxton, told me that this season his party of nine guns killed only twenty-five rabbits in a day's shooting. A few years ago they could have shot over a thousand. The Forestry Commission trappers, netting, and, above all, gassing, are to blame. True, you cannot have rabbits where there are young trees. But it is folly for any Ministry or self-constituted, so-called humane society to advocate the gassing of rabbits.

A gassed rabbit suffocates slowly in his underground prison. No one can know his agonies. He is wasted as food when shops and housewives are crying out for him. His skin is lost when the fur markets demand it. Gassing is the most inhumane and wasteful form of the wanton destruction of wild life ever devised by man and shrilly sponsored by women. These rabbits could be frozen, canned, turned into brawn and rendered down into tinned soup. They are the best invalid diet, equal to chicken and costing one-third of their price. Why waste them?

We rode round by the lost, unknown meres of Ring Mere, Lang Mere, where the teal sprang suddenly and the plover lifted into the wind, by Fowl Mere, where bitterns have nested, along the old Drove Road. Men of the Stone Age laid this most ancient English trackway across the wide and windy heath, older than the Romans, æons before the Dane.

And so back to Thetford, city of ghosts and ancient history, brooding sunlit in its valley. There, at dinner, I was approached by the landlord, who said:

"There is a gentleman here, a squire from Coney Weston, Mr Moore, who would like to have a word with you. That one-armed gentleman over there."

I approached Squire Moore, who, being younger than I, very properly addressed me as sir, beginning, however, with:

"You're writing about farming in this part of the world. Forgive me being blunt, but I don't think you're a damned farmer at all. You're just a journalist. Why, I don't believe you could catch and pluck a chicken."

"Have a glass of port," says I, for I liked the look in his eye, "and I'll bet you a pound to a shilling that I'll catch a hen quicker than you will and pluck it into the bargain."

"Done!" says he, and slapped down two half-crowns. "Landlord, three glasses of port. Let battle begin!"

Ten minutes later, Moore, Jim Rodd, and I invaded the inn hen-run. We hunted those unfortunate chickens in a clucking, chattering, scuttering cascade through cart-sheds and loose-boxes, from hay racks into lofts, from lofts down to pig-sties until we caught three hens and wrung their necks. I horrified Moore by biting the head of mine, an infallible means of disgusting the onlooker, and the quickest way of killing a bird.

Then we sat down to pluck. Feathers flew. Down mounted into the air in airy spirals. The loose-box wherein we sat was a dust of feathers, its silence punctuated by the stertorous breathing of three duellists who had looked on the port rosily. Those three hens died nobly. I won by thirty-three seconds from Jim, who led the one-armed squire by a quarter-minute. Three months later, escorting a girl into the Berkeley, I was hailed in broad Norfolk:

"Damn, here come our chicken-plucking champion—howd my hoss while I bite his head!"

Next morning, a pearl-grey morning which mounted into china blue, I went early after breakfast to call on an old friend of other days, Sir William Gentle. Portly and white-haired, with an inextinguishable cheerfulness, he was walking the gravel path outside Ford Place where the Thet flows at the bottom of the lawn, trout jumping. Ford Place is one of those pleasant houses built within the confines of a town yet with the views and pleasures of the country. You will find a good many such, clinging like jewels to the skirts of the better sort of English country town.

At Ford Place you look over green lawns and shining river to buttercup pastures and barley fields, to green willows and shady oaks. The partridge walks on the lawn. Moorhens scutter through the flower-beds, trout jump under the road-bridge, and the otter leaves his seal in the kitchen garden. The ghosts of monks walk with vanished kings to whom Thetford was the capital city of the Heptarchy.

Under an oak by the town road-bridge a trout jumped noisily. A moorhen swam out from the reeds, its red-pated head bobbing knowingly, white tail flicking.

"Do you know that a town youngster, a boy about ten years old, caught a six-and-a-quarter-pound trout on a half-crown rod under that bridge last year," said old Sir William suddenly. We had been talking about trees and apples, about pheasants and the great days when he had Croxton Park, where I once killed nineteen rocketers with twenty-one cartridges—and grew a foot taller.

"You and I could fish all our lives and never do that. He hooked it this side of the bridge, played it right under the arch—and back again! How he missed letting it get round the middle arch is beyond me. My gardener went down with a landing-net and after five minutes manœuvring got the fish into it. Then the net broke. Do you think he cut the line on the net rim—not a bit of it!

"The fish got away again. That blessed boy played it under the bridge and back again until we'd sent a fellow on a bicycle to borrow a net from a quarter of a mile off. Then it was landed. Just three-quarters of an hour after he hooked it. What a fish! What a boy!

"I paid to have the fish set up as I thought the boy deserved it. But oh! what I'd have given to have caught that fish myself on a light rod with a fly. 'Out of the mouths of babes——'" he mused.

We lunched in a high, pleasant, sunlit room, at a pretty Sheraton table, looked on by those good sporting rural paintings by Hardy,

Thomas Blinks, and Dendy Sadler, of dogs, shooting, fishing, and harvesting, which you will find in country houses of the old sort. They may not be great art, but they are good companions.

I boxed up the horses after lunch and left for Swaffham, that sunny, sleeping metropolis of West Norfolk. I doubt if it has ever been called a metropolis before in its life. But in the days of Horace Walpole and Coke of Norfolk it had Assembly Rooms, routs, balls, dances, and dinners. Every local squire and lord had his town house in Swaffham. It was a little local London. London was too far by rutted roads, by lumbering coach, pregnant with the danger of pistol hold-ups by highwaymen or capsizings into ditches. So Swaffham, like a proper country town, fulfilled its duty to its neighbouring gentlemen and villagers even as a good city such as Norwich will largely take the place of London to-day.

In Swaffham they have an open market. A market sprawling gaily under the harvest sun between red and yellow houses of Queen Anne and the Georges.

Jim and I parked the horse-box, watered the horses, and strolled over to the Athenian-looking market-place. Under a little open temple of graceful pillars a Norfolk auctioneer was hawking tea, honey, sugar, apples, butter, chickens, jam, tomatoes, blackberries, and onions on behalf of the Red Cross.

A cheerful, ruddy-faced audience of fat mothers, complacent fathers, giggling young women, gaping children, and gawking boys bid him up by pennies and shillings.

All bids were overtopped by the undefeatable broad Norfolk of an aircraftman who bought recklessly. We bid against each other for a pound of tea, a yard of butter, a jar of pickled onions. He won each time.

"We shall have to overtop him. That man's out a-huntin'," said Jim. He plunged into a fine frenzy of disregarded pennies, defeating the aircraftman on a hot run for a string of sausages by one-and-ninepence.

Whereupon the Air Force grinned tremendously, edged his way through the crowd, caught Jim by the elbow, and said:

"You look a proper Norfolk boy. Come home to my mother's and have a real Norfolk high tea. I'm Eric Winner, of Beachamwell. This is my leave, and I'm spendin' my money layin' in a few things for the old people at home. I've got 'em enough tea to give 'em tannin pisenin' for the rest o' the year." The two pump-handled.

It was a pretty scene, in the afternoon sunshine, beneath that

SWAN MERE IN 1939

"Where herons fished, terns hawked, and pike swirled."

Photo Sport and General

SWAN MERE IN 1941

"Great slices of chocolate soil turned over behind the spitting tractor." A concrete road is beginning on the right.

Photo Douglas Went, Brightlingsea

THE AUTHOR SHOOTING DUCK ON SWAN MERE IN 1939

"A rare, enchanted place where bitterns boomed, coots clanked, reed warblers sang, and the redshank sprang on quivering wing, ringing their million bells."

pillared little market-place of that fine, bland little town, with its eighteenth-century dignity of architecture. The Norman church tower, grey and graceful, topped by a slender steeple on which a great golden cock winked boldly in the sun, looked down upon the scene. Farmers and their wives passed in dog-carts and pony-traps. A keeper or two stood about in whipcord coats and leggings.

In the Grapes, in the dusty sunlight of a panelled room, Mr Lane, the baker—white-coated, double-chinned, and bland—puffed at his pipe. Mr Perkins—thin, quick, brown-faced, and full of local antiquarian lore—talked of houses and churches, the Swaffham Pedlar, and the folly of evacuees who closed their eyes and minds to the autumn beauty of the country and the warmth of the East Anglian heart. I have seen enough and plenty of that.

Mr Winner, of Beachamwell, ordered beer and blew a hunting-horn for sheer lightness of heart.

Perhaps it was the note of the horn which called in the farmers. They talked of the vast new Government drainage works in Feltwell Fen and elsewhere about there. It is a fine job to look at, a great job to talk about—but who in the end will pay the cost? The owners, impoverished by years of poor farming, crippled by drainage rates levied on land that was never drained, want to know, here as in Cambridgeshire, who is to pay the cost of reclamation. For it is more than hinted that when the land is handed back to the owners after the war they will have to pay the costs of these highly expensive undertakings—undertakings so costly that few private individuals, certainly no working farmer, could ever have afforded them.

The costs may work out at anything from £10 to £50 an acre—anything from ten times to twenty times more than the land will be worth if farming is let down again by post-war Governments as it was after the last war.

We talked of this boding thundercloud of trouble in that ancient inn on Swaffham market day. We talked, too, of the thin ribbons of concrete roads laid on no more than six inches of sand and gravel, which stretch into the fens like narrow swords. Shrinkage of soil caused by drainage, two or three wet winters, heavy frosts, unheeding tractor drivers trundling iron-wheeled tractors along them—all these may break up these bright experiments within a few years. Who again is to pay? I foresee much warfare in the fens to come when these twin pigeons come home to roost.

They told me of land so grown up with reeds, brambles, ragged robin, and meadow-sweet, land between Setchey and Wormegay, that a man could lose himself in it for hours. It was full of wild pheasants, duck, snipe, and renegade partridges from the surrounding farms, a shooter's paradise. But there were adders writhing among the roots or sunning themselves in open patches—so many adders that more than one party of guns refused to shoot over it. The snakes were not only a deadly danger to the dogs, but there was a fair chance of the shooters being bitten. For I have more than once known an adder lie curled up on a bent, blown swath of reeds or long grass, so high above the ground that he had only to launch himself to strike a man in the hands or even the face.

Riding round those heaths and lonely West Norfolk villages, from Methwold to Beachamwell, from Cockley Cley to Nordelph, on those hot September days I recaptured memories of high days after the last war when peace stretched fair to the clear horizon of youth.

There were those big rudd caught in the lake at Stradsett Park at the hour when bats were hawking and owls began to hoot. There were grand shooting days, setting out early from the Swan at Fincham to walk all day on the fens below Marham, killing wild pheasants, duck, partridges, and hares until we came to the river Nar. There the trout were rising, trout which Sidney Gowing used to stalk with the art of a Skues. There were gay parties in the Swan and in that inn at Downham Market which was full of stuffed Norfolk birds, or at the Crown at Mundford with its archæological landlord and his wonderful collection of flint implements—Kolia Galitzine and Yurka, the one sardonic and self-possessed, the other irrepressible and electric; Alastair McKinnon with his fantastic handlebar moustaches. They now wave furiously in the rear-gunner's turret of a bomber.

There was a hot, slogging September day on Stoke Ferry Fen, where once Ralph Hare and Jimmy Luddington killed a fantastic bag of mallard and teal at flight; a windy day on the wildfowl-haunted lakes at Didlington, into which I upset Eve Manningham-Buller from a sailing-dinghy when a squall caught us. Longer and earlier days fishing on Thompson Water or Stanford Mere with old Lord Walsingham rowing the boat and singing the "Eton Boating Song"—gay and young at seventy odd.

Days shooting round the park at Merton, the keepers in green coats and hard felt hats with gold cords. Other days alone with the rabbits and the stone curlew on the high dry heath at Mouse Hall when the heather seemed to glow and swim in the hot sun. Lonely

Scotch pines stood silent in the heat, the hot scent of resin sharp in the nose. Carrion crows *craa*-ing, pheasants skulking in waist-high bracken, and Dick de Grey producing marvellously, unexpectedly, from a bracken stack, a horn of cool ale.

Norfolk is full of such memories. Rich, good, English memories of open-air days. Long hard walks on wild heaths. Partridge-shooting over acres of shining turnips. Tiny fire-crested wrens slipping like sudden jewels from the dark aisles of fir wood before the first bouquet of pheasants came over. The vision one day of roe deer like ballet dancers in the Cardigan Belt. Geese flighting over Stanford Mere on winter nights of stars. Norfolk plover and red-shank playing in the shallow edges of flinty pools by stranded farms on forgotten heaths. The smell of bean-fields on summer evenings when we walked to Clermont or Threxton. Castle Acre Priory, gauntly magnificent, alive with rooks and chacking jackdaws, in the wet meadows of the Nar.

And older, inherited tales of my grandfather's time when they went hawking with peregrines and gyr-falcons from East Hall, Feltwell, and from Hockwold Hall in the days when Edward Clough Newcome, Lord Berners, and old Tyssen-Amherst were keeping the most ancient of all sports alive, and the Old English Hawking Club was great in the lands of East Anglia.

I thought of these memories of precious days and good friends in Swaffham, the old West Norfolk town which has seen their like come and go for centuries. In Norfolk values do not change too quickly.

At Wereham, in an inn by the pond where they once kept a tame seal which drank beer out of a bottle, I heard a man say of Sir Ralph Hare, of Stow Bardolph:

"Our young Ralph's a good 'un. Pity when 'owd Tommy [the late Sir Thomas Hare] died he couldn't leave our Ralph two or three more estates. And why did they hev tu bury owd Tommy up in Scotland, where he died? He should hev laid here along o' us where he b'long."

Of James Luddington, of Wallington Hall, he said:

"Our Jimmy's in the Army. He'd better by far ha' bin left on the land what he know than faddlin' about in brown boots and britches. He's the boy to grow corn on the land stiddy o' corns on his fitten."[1]

That is the way they talk of their squires in West Norfolk.

[1] East Anglian for 'feet.'

Of another man who had gone broke through bad farming he said:

"He jist got on the thatchin' ladder and flew." And, of another, about to divorce his wife: "He's agoin' ter sell her and git a new 'un." There is, you will observe, no nonsense in the language of these farmers and men of the villages which crouch on their uplands looking across the black fens to the flat, fat, rich land of Lincolnshire.

An hour away by car next day—for I would not take the horses to hammer on the hard high road—we saw the richest land in all England. Land in Holbeach Marsh; at Kirton and Frampton, where Mr Frank Dennis farms ten thousand acres or more on a mighty scale; at Algarkirk and Gosberton, at Whaplode and Moulton Chapel and round about Spalding is worth anything from £70 to £150 an acre. It grows the best potatoes in England. Its wheat, roots, bulbs, and fruit are unimpeachable. You will not see a stone or a weed for miles. It is the land of the tractor, of the highest form of mechanized farming and the most intensive types of cultivation.

Its churches are magnificent, cathedral-like. Their tall towers gaze on wide, flat fields that run to the skyline and the sea. A bold, free, big country of few hedges and fewer trees, ugly cottages and scattered, fine old Georgian manor-houses. It is bleak, unbeautiful, and unbelievably rich. Old farmers ride in Rolls Royces and young farmers drive Bentleys—not all, but a noticeable plutocracy. The Romans first drained this rich land and the Goths have followed them.

I found only two farms so badly farmed that they might have been called almost derelict, and those two Mr F. S. Myers, of Spalding Grange, had transformed within a few months by using the latest form of agricultural machinery. One farm which had broken three previous tenants had been ploughed a foot deep, subsoiled to a depth of nine inches, and turned into a property worth at least £70 an acre as it stands.

"I sold my tomatoes at two hundred pounds an acre," said Mr Myers. "They would have fetched five hundred pounds in the Black Market."

Freddie Myers is the "Caterpillar King" of Lincolnshire. Farmers from all over the Fens go to him for tractors, lorries, other agricultural machinery, and repairs. His Spalding workshops cover five and a half acres of floor space and carry a permanent stock of £200,000 worth of spare parts. He employs one hundred and fifty mechanics for nine months of the year, has seventy men out doing repairs on farms or travelling the country with mobile workshops, and does an average of twenty-five major repairs to tractors every week at Spalding. This gives some idea of the growth of the agricultural machinery business to-day.

In the forging and welding plant I found men working at the forges who were the sons and grandsons of local village blacksmiths. The craftsmen of the villages have been swept into the central web. The serious shortage of lorries and their spare parts has led, on these Lincolnshire farms, to a widespread use of the John Deere tractor, which burns paraffin instead of petrol, hauls loads up to twelve tons at an average speed of sixteen miles per hour, and is reckoned to pay on its haulage cost anywhere within twenty miles of a railway station.

Old bus and lorry chassis are converted every week at the works into trailers for farm purposes. An old Dennis lorry, twenty feet long and seven feet wide, which would normally have been rusting on the scrap heap was just ready to leave the yard, having been converted to carry fifteen tons of potatoes. Hundreds of these old chassis are still lying about the country, derelict, some of them in fields as aircraft obstructions. They should be salvaged and converted.

I was interested in a dipper ten feet long and five feet wide which will carry three and a half tons of loose potatoes, up to ten tons of baled stuff, or an acre of corn in a normal harvest. Nowadays, of course, the difficulty is tyres, but, when peace comes, these dippers, trailers, and high-speed, rubber-tyred tractors for haulage work will undoubtedly play a far bigger part in farming than they do to-day. Another machine with a great future is the potato digger or spinner. These diggers raise 56 per cent. more potatoes a day than can be done by hand labour. One man only is needed to work them. It is estimated that one digger will do the work of twenty women in a day. Having seen them at work at Euston, and again in Lincolnshire, I can believe it.

Talking at lunch with Freddie Myers I was interested to hear that on some badly farmed land which he had taken over, ploughed up, and cultivated he had covered his cultivation cost of £15 an acre by selling onions at the controlled price. Last year several Lincolnshire farmers made a thousand pounds an acre out of onions, and, to show the fertility of this land, even that which Mr Myers virtually reclaimed showed four and a half tons of potatoes an acre at the first lifting. Like any good farmer he believes in plenty of live stock and runs Irish-bred Herefords and large white pigs on his farms.

This Lincolnshire land is a revelation. Some of it is so rich around Freiston that it can carry two crops a year—early potatoes followed by broccoli or sprouts. The main crops are wheat, sugar-beet, particularly round Spalding, potatoes, celery, and mustard, with, in peace-time, large areas of bulb land.

In Holbeach I thought naturally of those two romantic figures of modern farming, James Thompson, the bankrupt farmer of South Lincolnshire, and Bill Dennis, the wagoner of Kirton. These two men started the potato-growing industry locally in 1880. Up to their time, although a few potatoes were grown, cultivation was bad, practically no manure was given, and yields were low. Thompson and Dennis first tried Magnum Bonum and then Up-to-dates, going on the principle that heavy manuring and good cultivation were needed. After one or two failures they were tremendously successful. Then one day a Kirton gardener who had accidentally left a few potatoes in a basket through the winter found them sprouting beautifully. He planted them. The result was better and bigger plants than ever before. Hence the beginning of 'boxing' the seed before planting.

There have been various other experiments and developments since those days and occasional wild booms. Potatoes in Lincolnshire are the equivalent of race-horses at Newmarket, prize dairy cattle in Ayrshire, sheep on Romney Marsh, or pigs in Staffordshire. Potatoes have made more than half the fortunes of that rich county. Some years ago when a new Lincolnshire variety of potato, El Dorado, was introduced, the price of its seed mounted so astronomically that in the end it was sold for more than its weight in gold. The average yield for the country is seven tons, but in Lincolnshire they think nothing of ten or twelve tons.

Potato-growing is a great art in this flat rich land. Much manure is given, cultivation is excellent, varieties are chosen to suit markets and conditions, each is set in the field that suits it best, and sowing is done in sequence to suit the lifting and delivery season. Altogether, more than 30 per cent. of the arable land round Holbeach is in potatoes. The Isle of Ely follows closely with 25 per cent., the Ormskirk district of Lancashire with 20 per cent., Cheshire with about 12 per cent., while Bedford, Norfolk, Durham, Stafford, Essex, Devon, and the West Riding all produce from 10 to 12 per cent. a year.

The Thompsons to-day probably own about twenty thousand acres of land, while the Dennis firm at Frampton has one of the best-administered estates in the country, covered with a network of light railways and cultivated to the hilt.

So rich is this Lincolnshire land that the ordinary principle of using live stock for soil fertility hardly applies. The Holland Division, for example, carries only 2·5 cows per hundred acres, a low level which is beaten only by the Isle of Ely with 2·2 per hundred acres. Compare these figures with twenty-six cows per hundred acres of cultivated land in Cheshire and roughly the same numbers in Lancashire and Somerset. Very few counties show less than five cows to a hundred acres of cultivated land.

If anyone wants to see English arable farming at the highest peak, an object-lesson to the world, let him go to Lincolnshire. He will find rich land and rich farmers. But do not expect conventional beauty. There is beauty in the bulb fields, glorious, unbelievable splashes of colour; beauty in wide skies, glimmering lines of silvery poplars, vast sweeps of stubble field and glistening roots, beauty in piled cloud masses that roll in like galleons, full-sailed, from the Wash; a soaring beauty in magnificent churches which stand like cathedrals above the flat land.

It is a bold, big, wide, and windy country, fit nursery of Hickathrift the giant, the hero of Lincolnshire lads.

CHAPTER XVIII

Come, spur away,
I have no patience for a longer stay,
But must go down
And leave the chargeable noise of this great town:
I will the country see,
Where old simplicity,
Though hid in gray,
Doth look more gay
Than foppery in plush and scarlet clad.
Farewell, you city wits, that are
Almost at civil war—
'Tis time that I grow wise, when all the world grows mad.

THOMAS RANDOLPH,
An Ode to Master Anthony Stafford to hasten him into the Country
(1605–35)

St Peter's Lodge in Marshland—The Monson Greys—Borrow's Tale of Old Shales, the Kingly Horse—A Memory of the last Norfolk Witch—The Difficulties of the Farming Squire—How we brought the Big Grey out of Norfolk—From Lynn to Hillington—The Valley Village of Hillington

WE CAME ON A DARK NIGHT OF STARS, BY HEDGELESS ROADS, edged by gleaming dykes, through a country of squares and parallelograms. There are few corners and fewer contours on the road from Spalding, the centre of last minute farming methods, to that ancient home of farming, beef cattle, horses, and dogs, St Peter's Lodge by Walpole Highway in Marshland, which is part of West Norfolk.

There I was to stay with an old friend, Claude Monson, a name famous in Lincolnshire annals. He has kept alive two of the finest breeds of horses and dogs in all England—the Monson Greys and the old English curly-coated retriever.

Bleached red and gabled, with stone mullions and twisted chimneys, the old house is monastic in its dignity. Sheltered by oaks and set in a park of brilliantly rich grass, it gazes on a cobbled stable-yard. Its green-painted loose-boxes were once the home of what George Borrow described as "the wondrous horse, the fast trotter, the best in Mother England." That horse was the wonderful old Marshland Shales, who was said to have been foaled in the archway beneath the altar of the magnificent church of Walpole St Peter a hundred and thirty years ago.

Travellers in those days rode to church on horseback and tethered their horses at the iron rings still in the archway wall. A local farmer, Mr T. Jenkins, had a mare called Hue and Cry which he rode to church. It is said that Hue and Cry dropped her wonderful foal there while Jenkins was at prayer.

George Borrow wrote of this horse in *Lavengro*:

> So it came to pass that I stood upon this hill [Castle Hill, Norwich] observing a fair of horses . . . an old man draws nigh: he is mounted on a lean pony, and he leads by the bridle one of these animals; nothing very remarkable about that creature, unless in being smaller than the rest and gentle, which they are not, he is not the sightliest look; he is almost dun, and over one eye a thick film has gathered.[1]
>
> But, stay, there is something remarkable about that horse; there is something in his action in which he differs from all the rest; as he advances, the clamour is hushed. All eyes are turned upon him—what looks of interest, and respect—and what is this? People are taking off their hats—surely not to that steed? Yes, verily! Men, especially old men, are taking off their hats to that one-eyed steed, and I hear more than one deep "Ah!"
>
> "What horse is that?" said I to a very old fellow, the counterpart of the old man on the pony, save that the last wore a faded suit of velveteen and this one was dressed in a white frock.
>
> "The best in Mother England," said the very old man, taking a knobbed stick from his mouth and looking me in the face, at first carelessly, but presently with something like interest.
>
> "He is old, like myself, but can still trot his twenty miles an hour. You won't live long, my swain—tall and overgrown ones like thee never does—yet if you should chance to reach my years you may boast to thy great-grandboys thou hast seen Marshland Shales."
>
> Amain I did for that horse what I would neither do for earl or baron —doffed my hat. Yes, I doffed my hat to the wondrous horse, the fast trotter, the best in Mother England, and I, too, drew a deep "Ah!" and repeated the words of the old fellows around, "Such a horse as this we shall never see again; a pity that he is so old!"

Dreaming of Borrow and the scene on Castle Hill, I woke to a morning of rooks, black against a sharp blue sky, cold air off the Wash. Jackdaws chacking among the walnut-trees, a cow mooing at the park gate. The smell of frying bacon rising in a heavenly eddy from distant kitchen quarters. A small girl screaming at her nursery bath.

[1] The old horse was then thirty years of age.—J. W. D.

Out in the yard the steady *clickety-clock* of the stable pump, rattle of pails, and neigh of horses in the sharp morning light. A rime of frost on peony leaves in the borders beyond the lawn.

I came down that beautifully sweeping staircase, which preserves the lost charm of the eighteenth century, to a stone-paved, carpeted hall, swept by all the winds that blow through the Norfolk sky. These Norfolk people live hardly, with grace, with endeavour, with a sense of old beauties. They are of another England, an older, stronger, and better England than this mechanical world which drags at the skirts of London and the grimy North.

I believe that if all the rest of England were sunk beneath the sea to-morrow and Norfolk left alone, islanded, it would endure. There are many in Norfolk happy to know no greater city than Norwich. They need no more urgent port than Lynn, no busier sea-mart than Yarmouth with its fussy, tempestuous trawlers, its come-and-go of coasters. In Norfolk they breed, make or catch most of the things that matter—bread and bacon, herrings and beer, mustard and pheasants, barley and sheep, sailing-ships and good horses that trot upon the roads or gallop the fields.

In the hall of St Peter's Lodge, the sharp wind whistling, the bacon sizzling, I looked at the water-colours of old cowboy days in Montana and Wyoming, painted by Claude Monson when he was young and leather-limbed. For like many another son of an English squire he went out to the West in the old, gorgeous days of the early nineteen hundreds when Buffalo Bill was a living inspiration, Custer was a potent memory, and Annie Oakley, "Little Sureshot," was breaking glass balls with shot-guns at Earl's Court in spectacular feats which rivalled the performances in the field of Walsingham, Ripon, Huntingfield, and Payne-Gallwey.

He lived a rough, hard life under the stars in the sage-brush, riding to cattle, herding and branding, living on fat bacon and beans in the bunk-house, his music the creak of saddle and clink of spurs, the thunder of hooves and milling cattle. The scent of sweating horses and the sharp smell of burning hair were his daily perfumes. He has put those memories of the last of the bison and the Indians, of crags purple in the morning light, of bucking horses and high-pommelled saddles, into delicate water-colours. For these sons of England who adventure by saddle and sail, on foot and in the air, have often the seeds of beauty.

I walked across to the harness room. Robert's lean, intelligent head, leaning over his half-door, followed questingly. Jim was hard at work boning boots, in a welter of tack and saddlery. He pointed to a great Mexican saddle, long-rowelled silver spurs, to coiled lariats and gay Mohave blankets.

"This is a rum harness room. We've landed up among the right sort here. I never run across a cowboy foxhunter before! The Captain's been up all the morning, and me pumping him since the last hour about the Indians."

Borrow would have rejoiced, as I did, had he walked with us the next minute and seen a score of young horses, wild ones, foaled under the stars, ignorant of stall or loose-box, milling round the riding-school, a tossing sea of manes and flowing tails. Unshod, full of blood and fire, these handsome young greys, great-grandchildren of Old Shales, thundered round Claude Monson. The old cowboy stood inscrutable in their midst, blue eyes narrowed to humorous slits. The immortal Tamzen, velvet cap perched on fair hair, straight as a die, clasped his right hand. The wondering eyes of youth following unblinkingly, the imminent, deadly peril of tossing hooves within a yard of her nose.

Tamzen is among the memories of little girls who will endure for all time. A child of spirit, of charm, she has that East Anglian reticence which regards you with solemn, unblinking discernment for at least three days before it admits you to the confidence of its heart, the warmth of its friendship. For that is the Norfolk way. Young or old, they take not readily to men or things new or unknown, but once worth is proved, you are a friend for life.

"A nice young lot, aren't they?" said Claude. "I've just got them up from off the fen. They've been running wild for months with the cattle. Nothing but beef cattle here, you know. You can't expect an old range-rider to have dairy cows about the place." He grinned.

We went in to breakfast, to visit afterwards the kennels where that famous Calgary strain of old English curly-coated retrievers had been bred, of whom Calgary Grizzly was the peer. These descendants of the earliest "water dog" have been bred for hard work first and prize-winning qualities afterwards. There is no inbred, snipy-headed show bench fatuity about them. They are dogs with broad heads, big stops, jaws strong enough to carry a hare, legs fit to gallop all day, swim a river, or plug through a marsh. They are full of bone and brain, breeding and quality. They work and win.

That ten days at St Peter's Lodge stands out as a high light of memory. Good, gracious days, riding over miles of Lincolnshire farms, trotting down old, grassy, fen droves, Tamzen's locks bobbing in the breeze; days spent wandering the narrow, windy streets of Lynn, sweet with the sharp sea wind; pilgrimages to old churches, lovely as dreams; Lovell's Hall, sixteenth-century and mellow, full of soldiers, its heritage of surrounding meadows bartered by some speculator for a rash of 'bungalosis'; afternoons on the windy, lovely verge of the Wash, alone with the curlew, the shifting shadows of clouds, the change of light on blue sea and purple marsh, with the red sails of distant smacks creeping up Lynn Channel.

I have a memory of that old house in Lynn Tuesday Market Place where dwells Mrs Chaplin, Alex Monson's mother, the old Georgian house, white-panelled and graceful within, on whose red-brick front you will see the sign of a heart, cut deep in the brick beneath the eaves.

That is because when they burned the last Norfolk witch in the market-place she cried out, with a dreadful scream, as the high flames leaped at her throat, "If I am an innocent woman this day may the heart fly out of my body." Fly out it did, and there is the mark of it, cut in the brick above Mrs Chaplin's bedroom window. So who am I to disbelieve the tale?

St Peter's Lodge provides a perfect example of the difficulties under which the average, conscientious, stay-at-home, farming squire has laboured, albeit on good land.

Claude Monson farms four hundred acres on sound practical lines, one hundred and sixty acres of it down to rich permanent grass which makes the sweetest butter imaginable, and the rest on the four-course system. He is a working farmer, living in a roomy but not over-large house, a business-man, and a man who has roughed it in the toughest life on earth, the cattle ranges of the West.

Yet even he, farming some of the best land in England, owning more, admits that had he not had private means it would have been impossible before this war to have kept his land down to corn, his men in employment, his cottages in repair, his children properly educated, and his home reasonably provided for. That is the plain tale which I have heard on every farm I have visited with the exception of a few men owning and farming vast areas in the Fens or in Lincolnshire, growing not only corn, but supplying peace-time markets with fruit, flowers, potatoes, currants, beetroot, and asparagus.

They tell a tale at St Peter's Lodge that the first of the Monsons to come there, a hundred and thirty years ago, was banished by the then Lord Monson from Burton Hall, in North Lincolnshire. Banishment it must have been, for there was no hard road to this abbey-like house set down in the bleak flat fields within three miles of the sea-walls of the Wash, where the winter tides grumble, and the gale brings the spume stinging over the marshes.

"My old Dad," said a village ancient, "used to tell me that in his young days a great gentleman in a vasty big yellow carriage with a spotted dog runnin' a'hind and men in fancy jackets ridin' the hosses, used to travel down from some'ere up in the Wolds once a year to see the squire Monson that lived at the Lodge in them days. He was all in finery and wore a cocked hat and none on us nivver know'd who he were or where he come from. That was a mystery."

Which perhaps explains the cocked hat, laced and ancient, which they found in a rusty tin box in a loft above the stables, long disused, home of a snoring white owl.

I left St Peter's Lodge one sad morning, full of that pleasurable melancholy born of leaving good friends and a warm, old house.

With us went a great, prancing Monson Grey, a noble six-year-old who had known neither shoe nor hard road. I doubt indeed if he had seen a dozen motor-cars in all his life, of a certainty no city streets. This great-grandson of Old Shales, Marshland Smokey, is a horse fit for an Emperor to ride, to carry a de Bouillon to battle.[1]

When you come over the great bridge across the Ouse into Lynn, leaving behind you that tag-end of West Norfolk called Marshland, which physically is Lincolnshire, you enter a new country—a country of big upland fields, of great woods, of sandy heathland bright yellow with gorse, purple-streaked with heather. Thin fir belts sough in the wind. From folds in these swelling hills you look to the grey vastness of the North Sea, to the curlew-haunted wastes of the salt marshes which run from Lynn by Wells and Blakeney to Weybourne Gap.

It is an older, bolder, more beautiful country than the flat, reclaimed, rich levels of Lincolnshire. It is part of all English history, a part so old that the very names of its villages and houses, its squires and labourers, bring back echoes of Saxon and Norman. There are L'Estranges still at Hunstanton Hall; Bedingfields at Oxburgh—that moated gem with its high hall and tattered banners; the ghost of Anne Boleyn to haunt the stately walks of Blickling; ffolkeses at Hillington, where they have been for half a thousand years; Hamonds here and there; De Greys, Cokes, and Walpoles. There are on the manor rolls freemen and farmers named Macro and Kettle, names which came here with the Norsemen when the longships grounded

[1] Alas, he fell victim to tetanus in November 1942, and had to be put down.

on the beaches, their raven flags drooping at the mast, when there was shouting and the clash of steel, hollow in the mist.

It is an ancient, noble, self-contained county, where men have kept their heads and values. It led the van in English arable farming, bred fine beef cattle and grand sheep. It showed the way with beet-sugar and barley. It is a cradle of old values, a nursery of new ideas. The kings of England have made their private home at Sandringham, the house which is neither too large nor too small, not too grand nor too old, crouched beneath a tapestry of woods with its face to the groaning North Sea and the sharp winds of the North, its back to the rolling barley stubbles and the yellow wheat.

We came from Lynn, with a fond farewell to St Peter's Lodge, by way of Gaywood and Castle Rising—the great Norman keep, jackdaw-haunted and sunny upon its green mound—then by side roads to Anmer, to leave a letter, and so to Hillington. For at Hillington lives an old friend, a squire among women, a woman of quick brain and immediate charm, one who loves land and preserves old values. She is Dorothy, Viscountess Downe, Norfolk-born and bred.

This valley village of Hillington, which lies on the skirts of the King's estate, is English of the English. I like to think that it is of the sort that Washington Irving loved. Thackeray knew its kind, and Surtees, had he been a Norfolk man, would have hunted from it. Americans dream about its like, and, for that matter, there are plenty more like it.

The village lies in a shallow valley within smell of the North Sea, the park wall girdling the road, the Elizabethan hall standing, red and glowing, among old trees and grazing cattle.

Through the park runs the Hillington river, which some call the Babingley Brook, the river where King George V caught his first fish and Queen Mary learned to throw a fly. It is not the sort of river that you would ever hear much of, for it is quiet and little. It runs through tousled woods of oak and ash, willow and fir, which sprawl at the foot of wheat and barley fields. A broad, shallow valley, chequered with cloud shadows by day, night-musical with snoring owls and the high voices of thick-knee plover.

It is a tiny river. You can almost jump across it. Gay in spring with tasselled rushes, cheerful with red-robin and yellow irises, it slides and chatters through the valley, its waters aquamarine above the bright green of silky weeds and the yellow of sandy runs.

Wild duck quack softly and teal whistle sibilantly in the dusk. Even as we came over the bridge cock pheasants strutted like jewelled rajahs on the high bank against the sunset skyline, crowing imperially as they bustled up to roost.

On either side of the valley the fields swing up to the skyline, big and bold, full of the promise of high farming. Fields of swedes and kale, of stubble and plough, run up to the rising moon, hare-haunted, plover-musical.

Little round fir coverts, full of clattering pigeons, crown the roll of the ploughland. Overhead the gulls drifted seaward in superb aerial unconcern, swinging down the long air-currents of the sea wind. Their underparts were lacquered with a golden pinkish glow, unreal to England. The mind flew back to a vision of flamingoes seen in just such a wave of reddish gold, straggling against the sunset of the Upper Nile.

Lower in the valley, where we came down the road from Anmer, the river chatters quietly under a bridge. By the gatehouse in the park wall, turreted and battlemented, you step from the matter-of-factness of fields and woods to the indefinable peace of an English park. The little river ceases its chatter and slides into a broad calm lake. Oaks, jackdaw-haunted, stand shaggy and alone. Rooks straggle home across the sky.

In the distance the Hall broods, battlemented and mullioned, its windows winking the sundown back from the quiet lake.

Across the water, keeping a rectorial eye on the Hall, a little church, grey and demurely old, stands on a rabbit-drilled scarp. A few windy firs sing to it in the sea wind. An arm of the lake sweeps right up to the foot of the bank on which it stands. The water is alive with birds. Egyptian geese, an exotic importation of George Dawnay's, cronk throatily.

The Hall was noisy with soldiers. Stone passages echoed to their nailed boots and rifle-butts rang on oaken floors that knew the footsteps of English kings. Under the painted ceiling of the library the sergeants sat at mess, while Elizabethan and Cromwellian squires gazed from large gilt frames on a class of red-faced youths painfully mastering the mathematics of searchlight practice.

By the park gate stood the keeper, so I got down, leaving the box to go on, and walked with him across the park. In his hand swung a mallard, three pigeons, and a snipe. "Please, sir, what are those birds?" A young London sergeant, eager and a little shy, stopped us, avid for the elements of natural history. So we talked.

Now it is a notable thing that, in spite of the fact that there were many men in the Hall and scores of rabbits in the park, fallow deer in the wood, unconcerned pheasants pecking on the lawns, and aldermanic ducks on the lake, not a feather or a foot had been poached. The troops, honourable successors of a famous battalion which made history on three fronts in the last war, accepted these manifestations of wild life as they would accept the ducks in St James's Park or the animals in the Zoo.

We walked across the park, through the Wilderness where the old decoy pond gleams sullenly in its ring of shaggy firs and reeds. Ducks started suddenly on clamorous wings.

"D'you know, sir, that King George, the present gennelman's father, and that old German Kayser, and one or two gennelmen with them, shot seventy-three ducks one day off this owd pond? That were a snowy day and the ducks cum in sudden off the sea. The Kings and gennelmen left their lunch to goo after 'em. The ladies were rare put out. Some of the owd keepers still talk about it."

We walked on, dusting the memories of 1910 when thrones and empires stood splendid and unshaken. The main gatehouse, castellated, loomed stark and imposing against the sunset.

The village lies half without and half within the park walls. Some of the cottages are on one side of the road and some are built into the park wall itself, their gardens running out into the park. It is as though they had snuggled within the paternal wall for protection and warmth, as though the Hall had reached out its ancient hands to gather them in and guard them. Even the cottages on the opposite side of the road have each their little earnest of feudal protection in the shape of little brick snuggeries built into the park wall. Each has its little archway, and if you look inside you will find dog-kennel, pigsty, wood-shed, and tool-house with the village pump sitting in a little courtyard of its own.

The whole parish is on the estate. There are carstone farmhouses and cottages; an inn, the ffolkes Arms; a post-office attached to the inn; one shop which sells currants, aspirin, electric batteries, tobacco, tinned fruit, cheese, flour, candles, paraffin, bootlaces, cartridges, and chocolate. There is a petrol pump whose owner mends punctures, hires out a car, carts pigs, farms twenty acres, and is a great man with chickens and runner ducks.

There are two hundred or so inhabitants. Twelve young men are in the Services, and fourteen are waiting to be called up. Those who have not put their names down for the county regiment want to get into the Royal Air Force.

There are no unemployed, one policeman, my friend the game-

PEDDAR'S WAY

"We went by the Peddar's Way, that ancient road of ghosts, from Castle Acre."

Photo Sport and General

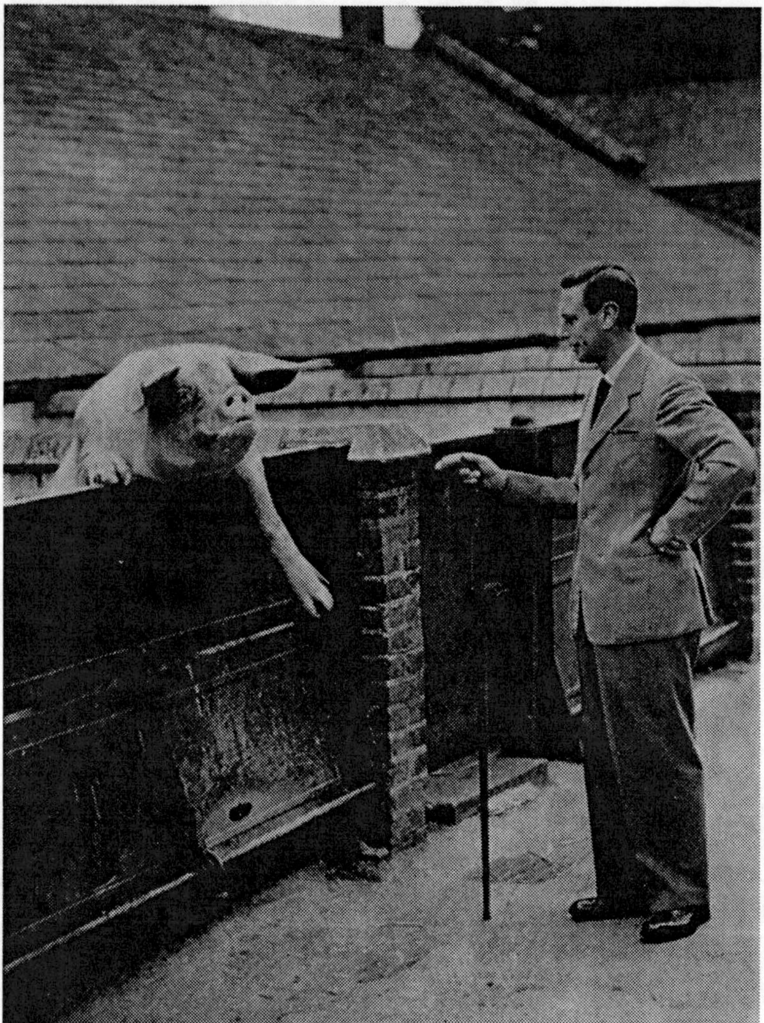

THE SQUIRE OF SANDRINGHAM—KING GEORGE VI

keeper, and a District Nurse. The estate, of which the Hall is the heart and the two sides of the village are the lungs, runs to two thousand seven hundred acres. The squire is a woman.

When Sir Everard ffolkes, the old squire, died the baronetcy went to a parson cousin. The estate, held by the family for three hundred years, came to "Miss Dorothy."[1] True, she married a peer who, on dying, left her with a title from a county a hundred miles away, but she is still "Her Ladyship, Miss Dorothy" to any gay young man over sixty-five who remembers her as a sprightly girl.

The squire has wise eyes, a slim figure, a gentle manner, and a purposeful tongue. Her life is dominated by a great sense of her duty to her own people and a never-ending self-analysis of what she considers may be her own failings towards them.

The hobby of this remarkable young lady of sixty-five is aviation. She can rattle off a perfect Who's Who of all the latest types of planes here and in Germany. Her business is corn, cattle, and woods. She farms four hundred acres, keeps her own farm and estate books, and administers the practical forestry of three hundred and twenty acres of woods and carrs. She loves land as she loves life. In the days of peace she grieved over dirty woodlands, thick hedgerows, choked drains, and weedy fields as other women grieve over laddered stockings and *démodé* hats. To-day the war has brought her land to life.

I thought of these things as the keeper and I stamped the mud off our boots and turned into the firelit bar of the ffolkes Arms. The Army and the village were gathered together, eight of them—two labourers, the cowman, two privates, a pilot officer, a W.A.A.F. girl, very rosy and self-composed, and Neil, the village postman. Neil also sells sweets and tobacco, buys and sells pigs, helps Drew, the landlord, unload his barrels of beer, and claims with an almost aggressive pride that he worked on the land when he was fourteen and left it as a horse-keeper, master of all its arts, when he was forty-two.

He won the D.C.M. in the last war, votes Labour, bitterly despises the leaflets of the Ministry of Agriculture, writes letters to the papers about farming, and ends every argument with, "Well, I'm only an old country boy, and I'm no schollard, but I'm the skilledest man of all on you—'cos I'm a farm labourer, ploughman, ditcher, hedger, cowman-horseman, and a little bit of a shepherd. Postmasterin' is easy after that. I'd like to have some of them Whitehall chaps for a day or two muckin' about in the slud helpin' me with my old boar. He'd learn 'em."

[1] Dorothy, Viscountess Downe.

I ordered a glass of Lynn port, for King's Lynn has imported port wine for men of discernment for two hundred years. I sipped and listened. The Parliament was in full swing.

Evacuees, ranker-officers, the Drainage Board, rabbits, pigeons and potatoes, air raids and invasion, pigs, pheasants, and the King. We ranged them all in an hour.

Hillington does not care for many of its evacuees. And Hillington is, of all villages, fair-minded. The village and the Army discussed ranker-officers with great candour. There had been two of them at the Hall with a previous unit—an ex-farmer and an ex-sergeant-major. The ex-farmer has local prestige, but was regarded with mixed feelings by the troops. They "think he would be better off on a hoss." He would certainly have been more in his element with a yeomanry regiment than with a searchlight unit. The ex-sergeant-major came off best of all; he is regarded as an excellent soldier.

The Drainage Board was damned for charging the same flat drainage on all land alike—bog or good farmland—and Whitehall, wrongly, is blamed for it.

Rabbits at 1*s.* 3*d.* a head were being sold by "Her Ladyship" and had solved the meat problem for the village, for meat was more difficult to buy there than in London.

Seven o'clock, and under the stars started the *thump-thump* of German aircraft passing overhead. The windows shuddered to the distant explosion of bombs.

"Them owd grunters are over agin," remarked the cowman, and spat into the fire. That is all the effect and the time that Germany's Luftwaffe claims.

The landlord lamented that no pheasants were reared that year. "We miss 'em peckin' about. Don't look like the old place at all."

A shepherd who had just driven down in a pony-cart from Sandringham way dropped in, bobtail at his heels.

"I see the King, come dinner-time," he remarked. "Walkin' up the street he were, gun under his arm. Bin a-shutin'. He's a rare nice young gennelman—give me the time o' day when I lifted my hat.

"I reckon he's a-gooin' the same way as his owd dad. That were a rare nice owd gennelman that owd King were—we cud du wi' a few more like him about. But this 'un's a-comin' on same as his dad. I 'ouldn't like to put in his day's work, bor! There aren't no trade union for he."

Under the stars on the crisp grass, with the 'grunters' still around, I stepped out for the tiny manor-house of Uphall, by the church, where lives "Her Ladyship Miss Dorothy," with her village maids and lurcher dogs. She would tell me, I knew, that she had just sold seventeen hundred pounds' worth of old timber at a good price and was putting the money into field drains and new fences.

The village huddled beneath the stars, alive and undismayed. England in little.

At Uphall Jim was bedding down the horses, snug in good stalls, the lurchers watching intently. The horse-box glimmered in a field across the road. Our pilgrimage was on yet another lap of its way, in the most English corner of all England. Overhead the plover called. An owl hooted to the climbing moon.

CHAPTER XIX

There is nothing grateful but the earth; you cannot do too much for it: it will continue to repay tenfold the pains and labour bestowed upon it.

LORD RAVENSWORTH

The King's Farms at Sandringham—Conservatism pays—Six Hundred and Eighty-eight and a Half Brace of Partridges in one Day—To Heacham, Home of the Hackney—Horace Callaby, a Sportsman of the Old Sort—The Heacham Harriers—The Greatest Farmer in all England—High Farming at Westacre High House—Major Birkbeck's Methods—A Ten-thousand-acre Estate—Rare Birds

FROM HILLINGTON IN ITS DELECTABLE VALLEY YOU CAN GO BY horse to a score of enchanted villages in that wide, windy country of North Norfolk. I went in the morning by way of Flitcham, Anmer, and Shernborne, three villages on the King's estate, to Sedgeford and thence to Heacham. A pleasant journey through a bold, rolling country of corn- and root-fields merry with partridges.

Big woods stood massed on the slopes. Lanes and fields were full of sunlight. Pheasants strolled by the hedgerows. Clouds of gulls, wheeling in from the sea, dappled the fields. Sheep were folded on roots. Stock-yards full of cattle, great flint-built farm-houses trim and clean, Shire horses and tractors side by side in the fields, the distant popping of guns out partridge-shooting—clouds of linnets and finches cascading up the hedgerows. All Norfolk on this bright morning seemed prosperous and at peace.

At Anmer we were in the heart of the King's fifteen-thousand-acre estate of Sandringham. Nearly three thousand five hundred acres of this is farmed by the King personally. Typical light Norfolk land, it carries good crops of barley and oats, several hundred acres of turnips, a certain amount of kale, large areas of sugar-beet, and a good deal of flax, in the growing of which the estate played a pioneer part.

Sheep are hurdled systematically. Without them this light land would be practically useless. It has been found that sheep hurdled on roots and brought out fat in the early months of the year pay very well, because the supply is always short of the demand. By keeping to the old way Sandringham has reaped the benefit and the estate has remained in good heart ever since it was purchased from the Hon. Mr Cowper, nearly eighty years ago.

At Wolferton the King maintains a herd of pure-bred Lincolnshire Red Shorthorns, which produce a good beef type. There is also a Red Poll herd at Sandringham itself which has won consistently in the show ring. A small herd of Jerseys supplies milk cream and cream cheese when the Court is at Sandringham. All the milking stock is regularly tested for tuberculosis.

The Shire stud at Appleton provides most of the horses on the estate and has bred a very useful type of heavy draught horse with a good many winners to its credit at the Shire Horse Show. Very few tractors were in use when I was there, and no attempt had been made at mechanized farming on a big scale. Indeed, the policy has been conservative throughout, the aim being always to put back plenty of natural manure into the soil, to grow corn and beet, breed sheep, and fatten cattle.

The flax crop does extremely well, since this part of Norfolk is similar in rainfall and soil to Belgium, where some of the finest flax in the world is grown. The crop is handled at a local plant on the estate and shipped to Northern Ireland, where the Ulster spinners are only too keen to buy good English flax.

I stopped at Anmer to hear the momentous news that a party of seven guns had just killed six hundred and eighty-eight and a half brace of partridges in one day. Shades of Lord Ashburton and Six Mile Bottom. Surely it is a record for England. It had been a remarkably good partridge season in that part of Norfolk. In the Broads district, near Rollesby, a party of farmers killed four hundred and fifty brace in a day on land which had never before been notable for heavy bags.

At Heacham, within sight and smell of the sea, I rode into the gravelled yard of Caley Farm to find that grand old sportsman, Horace Callaby, at home. Horace steps straight out of the pages of Surtees. A fine, broad-shouldered, blue-eyed, ruddy-cheeked Englishman with a crop of crisp grey hair, a hearty Norfolk voice and a handgrip that would hold a mule, he is the perfect picture of a sportsman of fifty years ago. Cutaway grey coat, blue bird's-eye stock with a magnificent horse-head tiepin, drab breeches, mirror-like boots, box spurs, and a hard grey felt hat, he looks the horseman born.

And, indeed, the horse world owes a good deal to Horace Callaby. He has helped to keep the grand old breed of Hackneys alive, those wonderful trotters which can look almost thoroughbred. Caley Stud Farm is a square, comfortable, Norfolk flint house with red-tiled roof and gay garden looking on to a gravelled yard surrounded by red-and-white loose-boxes, stalls, harness rooms, and the kennels of the Heacham Harriers, which should have been hunted by Jorrocks himself.

Horace Callaby can do anything with a horse from breaking and backing a colt to handling a team, riding to hounds, or judging at home and abroad.

I had a look at that grand thoroughbred sire, Solomon's Seal, a horse of great quality and character. A pat for Salmon Leap, a beautiful sixteen-two bay by Salmon Trout, and a nuzzle from the Arab stallion, Rafi, a beautiful golden chestnut, lovely in form and full of high courage, a true "drinker of the wind." Give me horses before most men's company.

"That horse's sire Akal," said Horace, in a voice like half a gale, "carried seventeen and a half stone for thirty-seven and a half miles in three hours, sixteen minutes. How's that for stamina?"

We went from the cheerful red-and-white boxes to tree-shaded paddocks through which runs a shining trout stream. There was a picture which would have delighted the heart of Alfred Munnings—who, by the way, is often at Heacham—or Lionel Edwards. That grand mare, Princess of Heacham, a great stone wall jumper who carried off the championship at Dublin, was at grass with a foal at foot by Spearwort, another Caley Farm sire, son of Spearmint, who won the Derby in record time in 1903. Spearwort stock so far have won well over £20,000 in some sixteen races.

We went into the house with its gallery of Herrings, Alkens, and Ferneleys, which were arranged and displayed by Munnings on one of his visits, to talk of Leopard. Leopard was Horace Callaby's best buy, one of the greatest Hackney stallions that ever walked. Horace bought him in 1910 for a thousand pounds. He turned out to be one of the greatest sires of the age and ended up in the South Kensington Museum, where he stands to-day as a model of the perfect horse.

Another great Hackney, Heacham Ripper, who stood sixteen hands, one and a half inches, was bred at Heacham, went to the Cape when he was nine years old, and won the championship in Johannesburg, where the reserve champion, Wykeham Squire, was a three-year-old, also from Heacham.

All the Leopard stock had great fronts and shoulders, dauntless courage, and tremendous leverage off their hocks. Horace told me that he had just broken a blue-and-white pony, thirteen hands, named Blue Belle by Don Juan, whose dam could trot sixteen miles an hour in harness, which reminded me of old John Tibbett, the breeder, who used to carry about in his pocket a cheque for fifty pounds to back his favourite to trot all comers from one mile to twenty miles. Horace may have similar hopes of the Blue Belle pony.

The Heacham Harriers are exactly what you would expect—a bold, varminty, mixed pack, who, I should say, would hunt anything on legs from a cat to an Income Tax collector. They were founded by the village baker, Mr F. C. Johnson, who got them together with drafts from the Arle Court and other packs. The whole turnout would have delighted Surtees, for the huntsman is also the stud groom; Mr Johnson, the baker, is field master and honorary secretary, and the hounds bundle out of the baker's van at the meet.

The van, with its bold inscription announcing bread and cakes and "families waited on daily," full of baying hounds, is exactly the sort of queer sporting conveyance that you feel fits naturally into the North Norfolk picture. So does Mr Johnson's grey cob. He carries his master out hunting twice a week, pulls the baker's van round the village with the early morning bread, and gallops to any local fire with the Heacham fire-engine at his tail. It is a pity there are not more Heachams and more Callabys to bring colour, originality, and good horses into the English picture to-day.

I left Heacham and rode back by Babingley, where the Hillington river, which here they call the Babingley Brook, runs hard by the house of Mr Billy Parker. Mr Parker is a remarkable man. Retiring and unknown to the general public, he is, I should say, the greatest farmer in England. He is a tenant on the King's estate and a great landowner into the bargain, although he neither lives in a mansion nor sports a park. His son told me in Lynn Corn Exchange that between them the Parkers, father, sons, and kin, farm forty thousand acres in England. Some is in Norfolk and some in Lincolnshire. More is in Leicestershire, where they have ploughed up the galloping grass in thousands of acres. May Whyte Melville turn in his grave! In Lincolnshire they had just bought from Lord Londesborough the 14,700-acre Blankney estate, immortal with its memories of Squire Chaplin and Hermit.

"We are farming fourteen thousand acres of it ourselves," said Mr Parker quite coolly. "The house and park and an odd farm are to be left undisturbed for the time being."

The Parkers have reduced farming on the grand scale to a methodical business not only of intensive cultivation but of careful book-keeping, big-scale buying and selling, and actual retailing. They own a chain of butcher's shops which sell their own meat. There is a plain lesson for farmers with capital who want to cut out the middleman. If it can be done with meat why not with vegetables?

Mr Parker is by no means the only big farmer in Norfolk. I often wonder indeed whether farmers elsewhere in England or one townsman in a thousand realizes the vast extent of the land and responsibilities of some of the great Norfolk farmers.

There is Mr Harry Thompson, of Middleton, near King's Lynn—'Rocky' to all Norfolk—who with his son Henry, of Dawsmere, farms about twenty thousand acres in a highly scientific manner.

Mr Mason, of Fincham Hall, a pleasant old grey flint house just outside the village, farms, so they tell me, about ten thousand acres, while the Keiths and Ringers both think and farm in units of thousands.

I left Hillington next morning to go and spend a day and night with Major H. A. Birkbeck at Westacre High House. Major Birkbeck is one of the biggest landowners and best farmers in Norfolk, a man who believes that "the master's foot is the best dung." I went by way of Congham Lodge, to look in on 'Sally' Clifton-Brown, and thence by Grimston, where the heather was in bloom, to Narborough, a truly lovely village, where trout were jumping in the little river beneath the bridge. There is a pretty little inn called the Ship, and a mill. At Narford in front of that excessively ugly Hall, where lives Admiral Fountaine, one of Norfolk's great characters, I stopped and walked down by the church to the great lake where you may always be sure of seeing rare duck including gadwall and garganey. The osprey has been seen there more than once, and the white-tailed eagle.

Then on through the village of Westacre with the ruins of its gaunt priory standing grey and bleached in the fields, until we came through a wide green park to Westacre High House, that great barrack-like eighteenth-century mansion which stands high in the heart of ten thousand acres of some of the best-farmed land in Norfolk.

A bold, rolling country. Fields of a hundred acres run to the sky-line. Tall woods stand magnificent. Ancient heaths, once the home of the great bustard, border the ploughland. The wind sings, and the air is sea-keen. It is a big land in which Westacre stands above its shining little river like a patriarchal fort.

Major Birkbeck is, in many ways, a model landowner. Although he is a banker part of the week, he none the less lives at home, farms practically the whole of his own estate, and administers farms, woods, flocks, herds, and labour directly by his own hand and eye. His estate is an example of how any landed property with working capital can be well farmed by the landowner himself, provided he is a practical farmer, a business man, and knows his men and enjoys their trust and confidence.

Major Birkbeck's first principle is the cultivation of the soil. He believes in muck, artificials and clover, and admits that he never knew the value of clover until he had none. In peace-time he reared a large head of game and found that, on balance, pheasants did quite as much good as they did harm. He is not a rabid anti-rabbit campaigner and points out that one hare will do as much damage as ten rabbits. As for partridges, Westacre has always been, and still is, one of the best shoots in the country, capable of showing bags of three hundred or more brace a day.

Each of his farms is run by a foreman answerable to the farm manager, Mr Thaxton, who takes his orders directly from Major Birkbeck each day. To show the variety of cultivation I found, in the course of a day's ride, five hundred and seventy-five acres of beet, one hundred and eighty acres of mangolds, eleven hundred acres of clover, one hundred acres of cabbages—prime Christmas and savoys—seventy acres of kale, seventy acres of swedes, twenty acres of parsnips, thirty acres of potatoes, one hundred acres of carrots, and fifty acres of peas.

He is a mixed farmer on a grand scale, employing over two hundred men, boys, and girls, and using seventy working horses and sixteen tractors with power-driven binders and tractor-drawn drills and rolls.

True to High Norfolk traditions he puts sheep on every acre of this light and loamy soil. There are four flocks of five hundred ewes in each flock, black-faced and first crosses by Cotswold and Suffolk rams. All the roots are fed off by the sheep and cattle. Of the latter there are two hundred and sixty beef shorthorn breeding cows, six beef bulls, four redpoll bulls, and thirty-five redpoll cows and heifers.

The result of this high percentage of live stock is that *every arable acre receives twelve to fifteen loads of farmyard manure every second year.* He has gone back to the four-course system because he believes that the land needs nitrogen from clover. In other words his motto is, "Farm light land with leys, sheep, and cattle." He ploughs a foot deep.

The practical results of this policy have been thirteen and a quarter tons of washed beet to the acre and eleven coombs of wheat.

I was shown one ninety-nine-acre field of beet which has been under beet and barley alternately since 1934. They got eleven hundred tons of washed beet off it in 1938 and thirteen hundred coombs of barley in 1939, following up the next year with one thousand tons of beet. The beet is sowed eighteen inches apart.

All muck carting is done by piece-work with a maximum of twenty-one loads a day. The result is that the men often finish by three-thirty and go home to their gardens and allotments. Some earn up to £5 6*s*. a week, topping and knocking and heaping beet at 52*s*. an acre, while quite a number of men on Soigne Farm earn £4 10*s*. a week and over. Girls, working on piece-work at topping, tailing, bagging, and tying white turnips, had earned as much as 18*s*. a day that year.

When I add that I found a flax stack in the park forty-two yards long, seven yards wide, and twelve feet high at the eaves you will understand that they do things in the grand manner at Westacre. The day for me, as an ornithologist, was crowned after dinner when my host handed me a Great Bustard's egg, taken on Ashe Breck on the estate in 1832. It is one of the few in England. Ashe Breck is now a wheat-field.

To show his faith in the future of land Major Birkbeck recently bought several hundred acres of rough, reclaimed land on the Wash, at an average of £54 an acre. It was under the sea less than ten years ago.

Westacre contains one of the best collections of stuffed birds I have seen anywhere. The great hall is lined from floor to ceiling with cases containing practically every British bird of prey, wildfowl, wader, game bird, and uncommon passerine. The Great Bustard, which was comparatively common on the estate early in the last century, is represented, although the specimens do not compare in interest with the family of cock, hen, eggs, and young which were unfortunately destroyed by fire when Congham House, Robert Elwes's place near by, was burned out a few years ago. The only private collection I have seen anywhere which can come near Westacre is that at Layer Marney Towers, in Essex, formed by Captain J. W. Campbell and containing a few of the late Dr J. H. Salter's birds.

It is always my fortune when in Norfolk, the county I love best in all England, to find good weather. Thus it was another of those bright blue mornings with a Norfolk sea nip in the air when I stuck my head out of the bedroom window to see cattle grazing right up to the walls of the house and be reminded, thereby, of Gerard Lymington's remark to me one night at dinner years ago, "Your true Tory squire doesn't live in a great Italian palace planked down in the English countryside with a miniature Versailles laid out in the gardens. He leaves that sort of house to the Whigs. He prefers to sit at breakfast with his cows poking their heads in at the windows."

After breakfast we were off by that lonely road across Massingham Heath where you feel that you are alone with prehistoric Britain. I could not help regretting that so much of the heath, untouched since the Stone Age, had been ploughed up. From here to Great and Little Massingham it is all Birkbeck country, owned by one or other of the family. Indeed, they say in Norfolk that if you are a Norfolk man you have not the slightest chance of getting into heaven unless you either know or are related to Birkbecks, Buxtons, Gurneys, or Lubbocks. They hold the four gates of heaven.

At Harpley I stopped for a midday pint at a charming little inn called the Crown. The landlord took me for the brewers' man and produced a glass of such excellent port that I stayed an hour to talk with a sporting blacksmith and a couple of farm labourers whose minds ran on horses and shooting. Part of the charm of North Norfolk—indeed, all Norfolk—is that every man, rich or poor, high or low, loves sport. If they cannot shoot they can snare rabbits and catch fish. If they do not ride a horse they take a rare pride in seeing a good one and can spot the faults and qualities of a horseman at first glance.

They talk of their squires and local peers possessively and by Christian names, as though they were of their own family. Thus it was that I heard how "our Oliver"—Mr Oliver Birkbeck, of Massingham House—had bred several good steeplechasers, and that "our Chummy"—the Marquess of Cholmondeley, of Houghton Hall—was the most dashing motorist for miles round.

An old woman came to her garden gate and, pointing to the horse-box, said, "Are them Newmarket hosses or huntin' hosses?" I told her. Next moment she was in the box, yelling for all her grand-children to "cum look at the huntin' hosses."

A pleasant midday hour, made pleasanter as we topped the rise, by the sight of Harpley Hall with its strange, straight-pillared front standing, framed in Scotch pines, in a little park, dappled with black-and-white cattle and piebald horses. At Harpley Dams over the hill live the Wilsons, who breed good horses, full of blood and fire, and who farm well. Gerry Wilson, that great steeplechase rider whose name is on the National roll for all time, was one of them.

And so, by Bircham Newton and Stanhoe, asleep in its dell, by Burnham Market, full of dogs and sunlight, to Holkham, the home of English high farming.

CHAPTER XX

Tradition said he feathered his nest
Through an Agricultural Interest
In the Golden Age of Farming:
When golden eggs were laid by the geese
And Colchian sheep wore a golden fleece
And golden pippins—the sterling kind—
Of Hesperus—now so hard to find—
Made Horticulture charming.

THOMAS HOOD

Holkham, the Home of High Farming—A Forty-three-thousand-acre Estate—Lord Leicester, a John Bull Englishman—Shooting at Ninety-three—High Wind in the East—On Savage Bulls—Sam Bone, the 'Fowler of Wells-next-the-Sea—Old 'Fowling Days—The Gun in the Closet—The Earl and the Queen—When he refused to be Shaved—A Royal Duke put to Flight

A COVEY OF PARTRIDGES WERE DUSTING IN THE ROADSIDE AS WE came in the afternoon sun by the park wall of Holkham Hall. That wall is nine miles long. It encloses a park of three thousand two hundred acres, twice as big as Hyde Park and Kensington Gardens. The estate runs to forty-three thousand acres. It includes towns, villages, and hamlets, a lake nearly a mile long, and a Palladian house which is three hundred and thirty feet long. Those bald facts give some slight idea of the magnitude of Holkham, greatest estate in all Norfolk and the birthplace of high farming.

I have known and loved Holkham for many years. It is historic in farming, in the shooting world, and among bird-lovers. For at Holkham corn, sheep, and cattle, game shooting, wildfowling, rare birds, deer, rabbits and hares, wild geese, and sea fishing all flourish on one estate. Holkham is one of the last remaining examples of beneficent large-scale landownership of the patriarchal sort.

Everything at Holkham from the house and its marble hall, seventy feet high, with wings and stables large enough to house a village, to the park, the farm buildings—you could put a whole regiment in the Great Barn—woods, lake, marshes, sandhills, and seascape is on the grand scale. It is the epitome of eighteenth-century solidity. Whig magnificence, which I do not pretend to like, is the keynote of its architecture. Its farming and forestry are the embodiment of quality. The shootings are among the first in the world.

It is their pride at Holkham that when a house or a farm building is put up everything, except iron, glass, and paint, is made on the place. Bricks, boards, mortar, tiles, chimney-pots, doors, floors, staircases, window-frames, mantelpieces, gates, hinges, posts, cupboards, boxes, mangers, stalls, troughs, and even weathercocks are made in the estate brick-kilns, lime works, carpenters' and wheelwrights' shops and forges. It is as near self-contained as any agricultural property can be.

And if you go into that red-roofed, sea-salty little town of Wells-next-the-Sea, which huddles round its quay and maltings at the head of a long sea creek, you will find that they talk of the Earl of Leicester, who is lord of Holkham, as children speak of a loved parent.

When William Cobbett, no lover of landlords, was in these parts a century ago he declared of Coke of Norfolk, Lord Leicester's ancestor, "Every one made use of the expression towards him which affectionate children use towards their parent." That is as true to-day.

So it was that when I had left the horse-box with that good sportsman, Mr E. W. Flint, of Manor Farm, who offered us stabling, forage, and beer in a breath, and asked of a farmer in Wells whether Lord Leicester was at home, the answer came pat, "Our owd boy's out a-shutin'. He's bin on the goo since eight this mornin'. He stopped me dinner-time and wanted me to have a goo at the puttridges with him, but I was tu busy. He's got Geoff Todd and three or fower farmers with him an' a couple o' young officers an' a parson, so I reckon you 'on't see much on 'em afore dark. He's like an owd steam-ingin when he git gooin'—that ain't so bad for ninety-three, is it?"

There you have a little sidelight on the character, the lovableness, and the amazing energy of that remarkable old man. He fought at Tel-el-Kebir and in Afghanistan, and for three-quarters of a century was the outstanding character in a county of characters and one of the best landowners this century has known in England. Alas, a full day's partridge-shooting in a downpour of rain which registered an inch and a half within eight hours—he kept going through it all without a coat or mackintosh—was the end of him within a few weeks of my visit. Otherwise, I do not doubt, he would have lived to a hundred. Cokes are long-lived. His own life and those of his father and grandfather totalled one hundred and eighty-seven years.

Lord Hastings, who was out shooting that day—the second of my visit—asked Lord Leicester if he ever knew such a blizzard in October. "Yes," said he, "I do. The year I came of age. We had to take refuge in a straw-yard. One of my sisters spread the lunch out on a heap of straw. We were just settling down to it when the lunch moved off. There was a pig under the straw."

He was a true John Bull Englishman. Every farmer, keeper, farm labourer, fisherman, and cattle dealer for miles round was his friend. He knew the soil and name of every field on his home farms and half those of his tenants. On shooting days or market days, at cattle shows or in the field, when his square ruddy face, white side-whiskers, bluff figure, and broad Norfolk voice were heard and seen, one would have thought that all this North Norfolk was one great family. He talked Norfolk, thought Norfolk, and thanked the cold Norfolk air for his long life. He was a practical farmer who could buy his own pigs and sheep, deal in cattle or horses, drive a bargain or direct the cultivation of his eighteen-hundred-acre home farm with the best of them. Not only North Norfolk but England has lost a grand, inspiring figure, a perfect example of a landowner who ran his estate for the benefit of those who lived on it and saw that its revenues were put back into the land and not squandered in London or the South of France. He spent £100,000 on improvements and upkeep of farms in the ten years after the 1914–18 war, although the revenue on an invested capital of about £1,000,000 was only just over 2 per cent.

He had the constitution of an ox. Out shooting he would march tirelessly all day, sometimes wet to the skin or in a bitter North Sea wind. He was the despair and admiration of the tenant farmers, London guests, village sportsmen, country parsons, keepers, and others who went out with him. His invitations to shoot were irrespective of class or wealth. If a man loved a gun and was a fair and generous sportsman that was enough. The broad manors of Holkham were open to the village tradesman or the son of a duke.

It was wild and red in the west when I saddled up in Mr Flint's yard to ride up to the Hall. Through seaward gaps in the narrow winding streets of Wells, where a wind always blows, I could see clouds of waders wheeling over the saltings. The far line of tawny sandhills where the sea groans ceaselessly were a savage yellow. The wind was rising. That eternal threnody of strong wind playing in tall firs, the everlasting undertone of Holkham, swelled like the notes of a Nordic harp. A rough night was blowing up.

The big Monson Grey, out for the first time on a tarmac road, new to streets and houses, reared and plunged. His great quarters, strong enough to carry a church, rippled with tremendous strength. Twice he stood straight on his hind legs, pawing the air like a charger on a Roman frieze. Jim, crouched on his back, looked like a mouse on a mountain.

"That feels like riding the Scots Express," he announced with a solemn wink.

By the time we had reached the park the wind was roaring in the pine tops, leaves blew like scattered butterflies, masses of black clouds drove up thunderously from the west. Fallow deer flickered through the bracken, darted ghostly beneath the shadows of great oaks.

The long lake, shining like a scimitar, wound into the hilly, farther wildness of the park. The obelisk to Coke of Norfolk stood grim and stark above the wind-rippled waters. Fleets of duck rode the lake in the sunset. Mallard were in scores. Early widgeon mewed like cats. Shoveller rose and grunted past on quick-cutting wings. Teal sprang and circled. Half a dozen pintail, most delicately beautiful of all duck, swam proudly, etchings in the sunset.

Beyond, a hundred black-necked Canada geese honked hollowly on the wind. A few trips and skeins of duck came overhead like bullets, landed with long, scuttering splashes. There must have been at least five hundred fowl on that end of the lake alone. A mere foretaste of the myriad which flock in when winter whitens the marshes and the North Sea wind groans in the pines.

We rode up to the estate office to have a word with Mr Turner, the agent, who knows Holkham like a book, and Mr Josiah Gunston, the farm manager, a practical man who writes on farming. There is a solid, eighteenth-century air about the estate office with its mahogany panelling and furniture, its tall desks and waiting-room for tenants, its leather-topped tables and portraits of bygone Cokes, of fat oxen, great rams, and mighty stallions. An atmosphere eloquent that here at Holkham land is the essential bank.

Above the lake the Hall, massive and grey, its long façade with the pillared doorway flanked at either end by square, squat, tower-like wings, stands brooding and immense. It is neither beautiful nor homely. Like most of Kent's houses it lacks grace and Englishness. None but a Whig could have built it. Indeed, it was erected first, like so many other eighteenth-century mansions, to house a collection of Italian sculptures and works of art.

Even so, it has somehow settled down, grey and sombrely magnificent, into its broad, wild park. Cattle and horses graze up to its walls and terraces. Sheep move before its windows. Deer glance by in startled grace. The cock pheasant struts its lawns, and wildfowl quack and whistle about its windows. It seems, somehow, a stern, grey, patriarchal fort, fatherly and protective, set down in this bitter-cold country of North Norfolk in lasting defiance of sea and north wind.

I rode across the park to the Palmer's Lodge for a word with old Moore, the tenant, seventy-four and still going strong.

"His looardship were by this mornin'," piped up Moore. "Didn't half pull my owd leg, tu. Ha towd me I were gittin' owd, an' that he'd hev tu run me half a mile for a quart o' beer to liven me up! Ha reckon I'm still a youngster!"

I went on down to Longlands Farm, galloping on the grassy verge of that long drive of great trees, almost royal in its scope and vista, to take a late cup of tea with Mr Gunston in his comfortable, book-lined cottage. The farmhouse was full of evacuees. They crowded with shrill Cockney curiosity round our horses.

"Coo! Look, he's got spurs on," shrilled one. "Stick 'em in, mister, an' make 'im run." I doubt if one of them had seen a man on a horse before.

In a wild and windy gloaming we rode back up the long avenue to the Hall. Rain pattered down. A sharp squall came like shot through the trees. The horses' flanks began to glisten with wet. High in the sky curlew skirled. Gusts of wind boomed in the woods. A sudden wild shaft of red light lit up the long lake. Pink-feet geese bayed overhead like hounds. A herd of deer bunched, startled and alert, on a grassy hillock. Cattle huddled under the trees. Somewhere a bull bellowed hollowly in the wet windiness. The rain came down in sheets.

I buttoned my coat to the throat, rammed down my hat, and urged Robert into a gallop. Flying hooves and sparkling raindrops. Startled scattered deer, glimmering palely under the trees. Cattle stampeding, horns clashing and tails up, eyes wild in the red glare of sunset. A rush of wings from the lake as geese, mallard, and widgeon thundered off the water in a cascade of spray and climbing pinions. The rain drove into our faces like stair-rods. The wind swooped and bellowed, and the smell of the sea came sudden, strong, and salt.

It was a mad gallop across that old wide park in the teeth of the tempest. A hundred yards from the Hall the great grey passed me like a thunderbolt, a momentary, mighty picture of action. Jim was hauling on his head like a sailor on a main-sheet. The grey ploughed on in a thunder of hooves, tremendous in strength and action.

They pulled up in the forecourt of the Hall, in a shower of gravel and stones, the grey rearing and pawing the air, nostrils distended, neck arched, mane and tail flowing. He looked magnificent, that great descendant of the mighty Marshland Shales with the desert blood of the Arab royal in his veins.

"Lor! I don't mind telling you this Smokey hoss nearly got away with me," Jim grinned, a little breathlessly. "That's the powerfullest hoss I ever straddled. Like ridin' a steam-engine. If he was a bit lighter in the bone I'd win the National on him. What a hoss! What a hoss! But he'll gentle all right."

A wet, wild ride back to Wells. The streets of that windy little sea-port glistened with streams of running water. Water ran down my neck and into my pockets. I sat in a saddle wet as a bowl. Water streamed into boots and ran out of shirt sleeves. The brim of my hat poured a constant gutter. Norfolk had broken its promise of kindly weather with a vengeance.

In the yard at the Manor Farm we unsaddled, rubbed down, and stabled them in homely, oak-built, cobwebby old stables that smelled half of horses and half of cows. An owl scrambled like a cat along the rafters in the lantern light. A half-bred terrier who made a snarling dive at our legs from a heap of straw collected a kick that sent him yelping into the night. A cat smiled sleekly from a wooden manger.

The head cowman leaned over a half-door and discoursed pleasantly on the ways of bulls. Bulls are my abomination. I have been hunted by horned cattle over marshes and through meadows until I am convinced that some evil spirit walks at my heels when a bull or a calfless cow is within sight.

"Our owd bull over the yard there nearly kilt me last autumn," confided he pleasantly. "I were leadin' him down the back lane with a bit o' binder twine on the ring in his nose when sudden he groaned at me, tarned round, and doshed me agin' the wall. That's an owd flint wall. I was right atween his horns. His eyes was up agin' mine like bike-lamps, an' his snout in me belly. That first dosh ripped all me clothes off up the right side. There I stud in me shirt with me britches down an' the bull gloutin' in me face, snortin' like a steam-ingin'.

"'Bill, yu owd b——r,' I hollered. 'Stop it, yu bloody owd fule!'

"Damn! Ha tarned round and dashed through a hole in the hedge arter the cows. That was my voice what done it, I reckon. Warn't that a funny job?"

"What did you do then?" I asked. "You must have felt pretty queer."

"Quare—I were half naked! He'd stripped me clothes off me. I stud in me shirt in the lane. I dussn't go home to the missus like that—so I went in the field arter the owd bull an' druv him back with the cows an' penned him. He went quiet enough."

"So," says I, "you were more scared of your wife than the bull?"

"Har! I couldn't go home like that, could I? An' I couldn't leave that owd bull roamin' the parish to do a mischief for summun else. But I were laid up for six weeks arterwards. When I did get back I found the owd bull penned where I'd left him. They'd fed him, but there warn't a man on the farm 'ud handle him."

It was this man who had a remarkable escape from being gored by a Jersey bull on the level crossing at Holkham station, where the single branch line to Wells runs through the fresh marshes. He was bringing the bull through the railway gate with a pole on its nose. As he turned to shut the gate the bull 'dunted' him. The pole was twisted out of his hand. Down went the cowman on his back between the railway lines. The bull charged, head down, to gore him as he lay. Luckily the pole twisted between its forelegs and halted it. There lay the cowman on his back with the bull half on its knees above him. Its eyes glared into his face not a foot away. Jets of steaming breath scalded his skin. Saliva dripped in great gobs into his nose and mouth.

Twisting, he freed his right arm, drew it back, and punched the bull smack on the nose! Up jumped the bull, tossing its head. The cowman leaped off the line into the ditch and through the wire fence. There, safe, he gathered a handful of stones from a platelayer's heap and stoned the bull down the line until it came to an open marsh gate through which it blundered. It is one of the most remarkable escapes from a bull I have so far come across. How many townspeople, particularly those who patronize the countryman as a bumpkin, ever realize the risks run by cowmen, horsemen, and pig men? An angry boar will bite half through a man's leg and rip up his stomach if it gets him on the ground.

Anyone who has been chased by a stallion, as I was once on a moonlight night, will not forget the nightmare of those bared teeth, flashing eyes, and blood-curdling screams. There have been horses which have knelt on men and kneaded them to death. Others, like Merlin, have got a man down and bitten half his face away. Years ago, at Wigborough, in Essex, out shooting early one morning, we found an old shepherd of seventy-three tossed up on to a half-cut haystack, dead. He had a hole in his ribs into which you could put two fists. The bull, hitherto as peaceful as a nannygoat, was grazing quietly on the marsh. We rounded him up with guns and drove him back to the yard. Nothing damps a bull's ardour so effectively as a charge of snipe shot in his rump.

When I was a boy we had a dangerous but valuable bull who could only be kept in order by a minute mongrel terrier named Floss. When the bull was sent to a farm near Ely or down to Barway he travelled with Floss perched like a jockey on his back. At the slightest sign of trouble Floss would hop down and nip his heels or pin him by the nose. To make doubly sure old Bob King, then the bailiff, always carried a little muzzle-loading pistol, charged with a clay pipe full of sparrow shot—"the bull tiddler," as he called it. When the bull was finally killed and cut up, the hide on his hind quarters was riddled like a pepper-pot.

Through the gusty darkness, from that farmyard with its smell of horses and cattle and tales of bulls, we walked back to the Buttlands for a bath and a change. I dined and went down to the quay, oil-skinned and rubber-booted, to seek, somewhere in the moaning buffets of the wind, a sight of Sam Bone.

Now Sam Bone has been a professional wildfowler in that tiny sea-port, where the whole business of man is the encompassing of wild geese and ducks, since the memory of man runneth. His father was a Holkham keeper. He is tall, thin, and grey. He has a hatchet face, a mild grey eye, a stooping walk, and a rare fund of 'fowling stories. His cottage, with its flint face set to the wet and windy street within stone-throw of the tide, is a meeting-place for wildfowlers from all over England. Sam has always a duck-gun to sell, a dog to swap, a pair of ducks to be bought, or a rare bird to be shown. His great canvas 'sidebags,' badge of the Norfolk wildfowler, have held in blood and feathers a medley of all the shootable birds that fly in England.

Sam will tell you on which stark pine the peregrine sits among the sandhills. He has seen the avocet stepping delicate as porcelain in shallow pools in the clear light of dawn. He has picked up the tiny snow bunting, huddled under the leeward crest of the sandhills, when snow flurries blew from the North. He has taken the wood-cock, luminous-eyed and weary, from its hiding-hole in the marram grass, a minute after it had flopped in over the winter waves, wing-tired from the woods of Norway. He has seen the Snowy Owl beat the marshes, a yellow-eyed, terrifying ghost. He has killed wild geese by the score at red dawn and moonlit midnight, shot into the widgeon as they mewed on the mud-banks, and watched the ruffs fight among the sea asters on East Hills.

Down a narrow, twisting lane between malt-houses where rats pattered and the smell of barley and brewers' grains was whisked on the shouting wind, I found an open doorway. A thin pencil of yellow light streamed into the wet blackness of sea and quay. Within, in a room cluttered with nets, corn sacks, trestles, and army blankets, sat Sam, glasses perched on his hawk-like nose, a pile of empty cartridge-cases at his feet. A tin of gunpowder stood on the table. A bag of shot spilled like caviare on the bleached wood. He was solemnly loading cartridges within a yard of the spluttering flames of a fire fed by the phosphorescent, salty timbers of an old boat. His sidebag hung on a hook. A pair of mallard splashed the table with blue, green, and grey. The long gun stood in a corner. Thus Sam, night guardian of the A.R.P. of Wells.

We sat and talked, the wind buffeting and roaring outside, the droning, double thump of German bombers overhead. Sam cocked his head sideways, peered upward like a spectacled old hawk. "There they goo. That's a fine set out. Progress! We're wusser'n our grandfathers were when they fought in the Crimea. Science and ingins—a rare lot o' good they brought the world. Listen to them b——rs up there now—there's ingins and science for you!"

The door burst open in a flurry of wind and rain. In stepped Geoffrey Todd, big, burly, red-faced, a solicitor who long years ago turned professional wildfowler. Geoffrey Todd is a philosopher and a good sportsman. He has found peace of mind in his farmhouse fronting the sea, with his gun to earn his dinner, his dog to keep him company, his books to lighten his mind. A simple happiness of plain values and quiet needs, of open-air pleasures and the sanctity of God's heaven above—that is the wisdom of Geoffrey Todd's life. I have known far less happy men, burdened with a hundred times more wealth, in the streets of London.

We talked of good sportsmen and naturalists, dead and alive. Of C. J. Cornish, that great countryman and naturalist whose books are an adornment to the mind and the library; Hugh Arthur Bishop, "Gentleman Arthur" as the fishermen called him, who was drowned punting on Blakeney Bar; Edward Valpy, that hero of my boyhood, restless, troubled, intrepid, a giant in body and mind. His huge four-bore is my dearest relic of a great-hearted man and explorer.

We remembered J. C. M. Nichols, always sketching and watching rather than shooting; K. K. Horn, quiet, deliberate, and indefatigable in all weathers; Beris Harcourt-Wood, Selby Bradford, and "Ginger" Dusgate, of Fring Hall, that gay trio. We mourned poor Tim Birkin, that dashing cavalier who lived for speed and thrills, and died before his time. For all his records on the motor-racing track he was happiest punting at the geese in Blakeney Harbour or standing in the tall reeds by Roy Pope's lagoons on Clay Marshes when the duck whirled in.

We smiled at the memory of old Calcutt, that restless gipsy of the gun who roamed all over East Anglia after the wild geese, from Boston to Whittlesey, from the Dog-in-a-Doublet to the Wells Marshes, a gay, amusing old man who dressed like a cross between a keeper and a bargee. He stepped, surely, straight out of the eighteenth century with his long guns, his brown buskins, his green cord jackets, red neckerchiefs, and vast stomach for steaks and beer.

We recollected how Valpy once killed four geese at a single shot with his great four-bore. We revived the morning when Cradock Nichols rushed on to the village green and shot geese down dead into the streets of the town as they flew cackling in at house-top level, bewildered by sea fog.

There were the Bird brothers, those young and delightful Canadians who lived all one winter in a tent on lonely Benbecula in the Outer Hebrides to study the wild geese undisturbed, alone with the seals and the booming Atlantic.

There was, too, that Jack-snipe which I shot one wintry morning among the railway wagons in the goods yard—a miraculous bird, for it was killed with No. 2 shot from a 4¼-inch double eight-bore, weighing seventeen pounds!

We recalled how Percy Barrett, that peerless little 'fowler, would, and can still, crouch in a mud-hole and whistle golden plover down from the clouds until they hang, bewitched, only six feet above his hat.

All these we remembered while the fire flickered, the wind roared in the chimney, and the bombers laboured overhead, high among the gusty stars. We remembered days and nights after geese; bitter dawns and nights when the hail stung like shot; nights when the snow fell softly, pitilessly, and there were seven miles to go, knee-deep in it, floundering through snow and soft sand in long water boots, lugging mighty goose-guns.

You will observe that Wells-next-the-Sea, like St Andrews or Newmarket or Cowes or the Elephant and Castle, is an eclectic spot, a hub of very particular gossip and highly varnished memories.

And when I walked back to Manor Farm for a final look at the horses and a toddy to see me home there were other memories. Mr Flint capped all the bull stories that ever were told, for he had known a Mexican in the 52nd Remount Depot at Market Harborough in the last war. This Mexican rode full tilt at a moaning, pawing bull, caught its tail under his saddle flap, turned his horse in a flash, and threw the bull!

They have coursed sixty hares in a day on Manor Farm using thirty couple of greyhounds not so many years ago, and it was on one such day that Mr Flint rode his horse straight into a wire fence without seeing it, was thrown, and dragged by the heel on his back for forty yards without being injured.

A little moon was creeping like a harvest-hook above a rift in the black clouds as I walked on to the gusty Buttlands, where once the town archers drew their long-bows. A voice hailed like a fog-horn in the half-light. Frank Cringle, that bold, buccaneering, devil-may-care fellow who, had he not been a keeper for Lord Leicester, might have made a good pirate captain or led a Commando raid, was standing on the doorstep.

"Heered yu was a-comin', sir! Seed yu in the park gallopin' on a hoss, but I couldn't get nigh yu. So I brought yu a little delicacy—shove it in yar pocket." He thrust a squashy, bloody mass, wrapped in newspaper, into my hand.

"Fawn's liver—shot it this mornin'. Get it cooked right, and that'll lay on your tongue like love. Light as dew. Come up, now; come up, now, to Cawdrons. Wells is damned short o' beer, baccer, an' matches, but I've got a pint on the hob for yu."

There, in that lamplit, smoky-blue bar where blue-jerseyed fishermen jostled keepers and farmers, where dogs wriggled between men's legs, where the talk was of farming and corn, of the mysterious explosives which had just blown up four dogs in a morning on a near-by marsh, of the early geese new in from the Arctic, Frank unburdened himself.

"Hosses! I hate 'em. Gimme a boat or a gun. Yu look as though yar owd hoss likes yu, but, damn, yu should a' seen me last week wi' my hoss!

"I borrowed one to go to Burnham for his looardship. The b——r wouldn't start! I put the helm down, but nothin' happened. I couldn't tack, and I couldn't go about. Blarst, I had to hev a tow in the end!"

You cannot be long in Wells or at Holkham before you hear tales of the late Lord Leicester or his father. That immortal old man was as obstinate as a pig, kind-hearted to a fault, and no respecter of persons. He lived for shooting, farming, and his tenants. He despised newfangled ideas and inventions.

Indeed, there is that lustrous tale of His Lordship and the Woodcock. It was the old man's custom, after breakfast, to collect his letters and the *Morning Post* and retire through the outside door of his study to a little wooden house of meditation, hidden in a clump of laurels. Each morning a light, double-barrelled muzzle-loader, newly loaded, was placed by the seat, ready to hand. This rite sprang from the day when his lordship raised his eyes from the *Morning Post* and saw a woodcock light slap in the path, not twenty feet away!

It was his habit to be shaved only twice a week. On those holy days the barber from Wells would set out solemnly with a little black bag of razors and brushes, and pedal up to the Hall. One day the news reached Wells, by stable gossip, that the Queen was to take tea at the Hall the following day. The barber, recollecting that his lordship would by then present a two days' crop of bristle, gathered his bag, mounted his bicycle, and pedalled away.

At the Hall he sought Lord Leicester. The old man glared at him. "Yu know very well this ain't my shaving day," he accused, in broad Norfolk.

"No, me Looard, but I did hare as how her Majesty the Quane was a-comin' tu drink tay along o' yu, so, thinks I, I'll take the razor to his looardship."

"Git yu on yar bicycle an' goo yu hum," roared the earl. "Wednesdays and Saturdays are my shavin' days, an' I don't alter 'em for anyone."

One assumes that the obstinate, lovable old man received the Queen, hospitable but bristled to the eyes.

When he (the late earl's father) could no longer shoot he would drive round the park in a little basket carriage drawn by two ponies, and stop behind each gun to appraise or criticize his performances. It was his practice to have a second line of guns, standing behind the first, to pull down the tall rocketers which they missed or stop any hares or rabbits that got by them. This second line almost invariably included many tenants, farmers, and local people.

One day a Royal Duke was out shooting. Behind him stood a young Holkham farmer. Time after time tall pheasants sailed over the Duke unmolested and came crashing out of the skies at the farmer's first barrel. The old earl sat in his little carriage watching. At last he could contain himself no longer.

"Thass right, bor," he roared. "If they can't shute du yu damn' well show 'em how!"

The Royal Duke, discomfited, never visited Holkham again.

That caustic criticism was, however, eclipsed by Thomas William Coke, who said curtly when George IV, as Prince of Wales, hinted that he might visit him, "Holkham is open to *strangers* on Tuesdays."

CHAPTER XXI

As one who is responsible for the exercise of control over a considerable area I say with conviction that a renaissance [of farming] . . . would have taken place if there had been no War Agricultural Executive Committees at all; and, conversely, that the W.A.E.C.'s would have accomplished very little but for the spirit which animates the farming community as a whole . . . planning and control do not count for nearly as much as most people seem to think.

LORD NORTHBOURNE, "Land Control After the War,"
in *Country Life* (June 19, 1942)

Reclamation of the Holkham Marshes—Seventeen Sacks of Wheat an Acre—Pasturing Beef Cattle on Sea Lavender—Coke of Norfolk and his Work—"The Father of English Farming"—The Quaker at Holkham—Air Raid at Stiffkey—The Sporting Grocer of Holt—And so Home

THREE DAYS IN THE SADDLE DID NOT COVER HALF THE FARMS ON the Holkham property. But I saw a lot. On the home farms within the park wall, some eighteen hundred acres, were good crops of wheat, barley, roots, and sugar-beet. They are big, pleasant fields, falling in gentle slopes to little valleys. Well-grown woods of oak, ash, beech, and firs crown the rises. Wild pheasants were plentiful, partridges as common as blackbirds. The methods of cultivation were conservative but practical. I saw steam tackle being used, the first for many weeks.

The Great Barn, where once the famous Holkham Sheep-shearings took place, gatherings to which came seven thousand farmers and landowners in one week, not only from all over England but from America, stood empty and deserted. The cattle-yards, pigsties, stables, and cart-sheds about it held only a few horses, basking in the sun after a tempestuous night of wind and rain. But if the Great Barn was idle not an acre elsewhere was wasted.

The Holkham principle is to put plenty of manure, chalk, and lime into the soil and maintain its colour and texture. Because this principle has been carried out for one hundred and fifty years the Holkham farms to-day are some of the best in the country. There is no question either of intensive soil exhaustion or the formation of 'dust bowls,' which will undoubtedly happen in some other parts of the country in years to come, as a result of the present exploitation of land by Committees and others in a hurry.

"Rich land," as Mr Gunston said to me, "is like a rich man. It can be killed easily." War-time methods of intensive farming are undoubtedly going to impoverish a great deal of land in England in the future. But at Holkham they have been manuring their land and caring for it for many years.

Compare the results of intensive farming to-day with those of well-manured land of ninety years ago. Holkham has records of these things. The results show that we are not so clever to-day as some of our so-called agricultural scientists and publicists would have the urban public believe. To quote Mr Gunston, "With all our new knowledge of fertilizers, machinery, and new strains of seeds, we can show hardly any gain in crop yields or quality."

Consider the yields on the home farm at Holkham when J. B. Lawes carried out his experiments in 1851. The result was from forty to fifty-four bushels of wheat per acre. How many modern 'scientific' farmers can show a result like that? The forty bushels was produced without manure and the fifty-four bushels with rape-cake at the time of sowing. "This gave a higher yield than two hundred pounds of sulphate of ammonia sown either in autumn or spring," said Mr Gunston, running his finger over the old records.

Rape-cake was one of the great secrets of success in those great days ninety odd years ago. It can still be used to-day.

Swedes averaged twenty tons to the acre in 1814, a yield which was got not only by careful manuring but by the spacing of rows and plants in a row. Twenty-seven-inch drills, Northumberland method, resulted in twenty-three tons to the acre in one case, while broad-casting the seed brought in only seventeen to nineteen tons.

In 1813 *the yield was fifty-six bushels of wheat an acre. Compare that with the average yield for Great Britain for* 1928–37, *which was only about thirty-two bushels!* In the same year fourteen hundred sheep and six hundred lambs were fed from March 26 to June 22 on two hundred and twenty acres of cocksfoot. We cannot do any better to-day.

Yet, to read and hear some of the pompous little professors and so-called agricultural scientists produced by the cheap and wordy educational system of to-day one would imagine that our grand-fathers were fools.

Various experiments on wheat in 1854 showed the bushel weight of grain for different types of manure. Farmyard manure came first with eighteen stone, four pounds, per four bushels. It gave the highest percentage of head corn.

A great deal of deep digging has been done at Holkham in the last few years, and lime and chalk, which are produced on the estate, are used extensively. Mr Gunston believes that early ploughing to expose the furrows to frost is almost as good as a fertilizer.

A miracle has been wrought on the famous fresh marshes reclaimed from the sea in the last hundred and fifty years. They have always been regarded as some of the finest cattle-fattening grounds in England. Equally they have been a winter sanctuary for thousands of pink-feet geese. To-day, hundreds of acres of those marshes between the pine-grown sandhills and the coast road have been ploughed up.

Mr Flint, who not only owns one of the finest Friesian herds in the kingdom but is a practical arable farmer, has got seventeen sacks of wheat to the acre from these marshes. So has Mr Arthur Ramm, of Wells. The yield has been astounding. Yet Mr Flint expects to get more. The soil, a rich alluvial, formerly salt marshes, is unbelievably productive.

Whether in the long run it will contribute more good as arable than as pasture remains to be seen. We are apt to forget nowadays that good old English pasture land, admitted to be the finest in the world, takes from ten to fifty years, and a lot of careful handling, to make it so. Tens of thousands of acres of such valuable old pasture have been ploughed up by the necessity of war. The time may well come when we shall need much of it back again.

Standing in the sea-holly on Gun Hill, that mighty, wind-tossed sandhill at the mouth of Burnham Overy Harbour, the immense, glittering loneliness of the North Sea behind, the cattle marsh in front, Mr Flint said, with a wave of his arm: "If it wasn't for the fact that I've been soaked of capital for the last twenty years and I dread E.P.T. I'd put all the money I'm making now into ploughing up these Overy grass marshes as well. I *know* they'd grow grand crops —but how can you do it with eighty per cent. of your profits swallowed up in tax?"

That is the rub. Nationalization is not the answer. The answer is to remit to the farmers a reasonable proportion of tax, on condition that it is re-invested in the improvement of the soil.

Mr Flint has done on these Overy marshes what I have seen no man do elsewhere. He pastures beef cattle with excellent results on salt-marshes, *where they graze on sea lavender*. When the marshes go under at spring tides the cattle make for the sea-wall, but at neaps they simply wade or swim from island to island. One or two have been bogged in the mud and had to be hauled out by tractor, but not one has been lost. There are thousands of acres of such saltings round our coast where cattle could be pastured, provided a boy was left in charge.

Mr Gunston is busy planting Spartina grass in the salt creeks to stop the scour of the tides and gradually reclaim more saltings. Time and progress, so far as farming is concerned, have never yet stood still at Holkham, the house which set the clock for English farming.

Now a word about Coke of Norfolk and the hey-day of Holkham in farming. Somewhere about 1759 Joshua Reynolds painted a picture of a little five-year-old boy, Thomas Coke of Holkham, as the young Hannibal. He grew up to be the Hannibal of agriculture.

When, some twenty years later, the Tories swept the country, Coke, who followed Fox, found himself without a seat in Parliament and with less interest in the social and political life of London. He had a large property in Norfolk, much of it let at eighteenpence an acre. It was so poor that Lady Townshend's remark about it to Mrs Coke has become classic:

"Going to Norfolk are you, my dear? Then all you will see will be one blade of grass, and two rabbits fighting for that!"

Coke determined to remedy this state of affairs. He had about three thousand acres in hand which grew no wheat, a little miserable rye, and about eight hundred half-starved sheep with backs like rabbits. Not an ear of wheat was grown for miles round. Norfolk farmers, poor as church mice, blamed the weather, the imports of foreign corn to Blakeney and Wells, and the poor, sandy Norfolk soil. "Muck is the mother of money," retorted Coke. "You must keep more cattle and better cattle."

He invited Robert Bakewell, the great Leicestershire pioneer of sheep and cattle breeding, to Holkham, took his advice, sucked his brains, and acted upon it. He tried Merinos and Southdowns, imported Shorthorns and Devons, experimented with bone-meal, and had deep pits dug in all his fields from which the subsoil, a rich marl, was spread broadcast.

He grew clover and good grasses, experimented with the drill, which was a new thing, and revolutionized the sowing of corn and grass seeds. He was the first to use oilcake and to grow swedes and potatoes. His neighbours said of the latter that "perhaps they would not poison the pigs."

He laboured in the fields in a smock frock like any of his men.

He was up with the dawn and out and about till the bats came out.

Finally, after he had experimented with cattle, sheep, corn, grasses, and manures he got on his horse and rode throughout England. He risked bad roads, highwaymen, dirty inns, wet weather, and ridicule. He discovered that Norfolk, at any rate, was no worse than many another county. He found, too, an appalling amount of stupidity, gross ignorance, and obstinate conservatism.

He records that in Yorkshire he saw grazing meadows more fertile than anything he had dreamed of. But there was only one donkey grazing in a score of them. In Shropshire he saw only two sheep in a ride of many miles. One was on the road, and the other was chained up in a field! He learned and profited from all.

In his lifetime Thomas Coke spent half a million pounds upon the farms, cottages, and buildings at Holkham. The result was that the rentals from the estates rose from £2200 a year to £20,000 in 1816. His rents were not high, but his leases contained management clauses. So prosperous were his tenant farmers that his detractors jeered that his farmers lived like gentlemen, drove curricles, and drank port wine.

In 1776 the population of Holkham was less than two hundred. By 1816 it had risen to eleven hundred. The two ale-houses in the village were shut up, and a local deputation suggested to Mr Coke that as the workhouse was always empty it had better be pulled down.

Few men in his day or since have equalled Coke of Norfolk. He did things in the grand way and benefited agriculture for all time. He was the father of modern English farming. He was recommended for a peerage six times to three Kings by five different Premiers and refused it each time. He finally accepted the honour the seventh time at the hands of Queen Victoria. But let it not be forgotten that many a lesser country gentleman throughout England followed in his footsteps and did great work for farming, even though on a smaller scale.

For a picture of this remarkable man I like best the plain, undecorated words of Jonathan Binns, the Quaker farmer of Lancashire who went on a visit to Holkham, and thus described it:

> Having borrowed a saddle and bridle I rode to Holkham and had the pleasure of finding Mr Coke at home & met with every civility and attention. Mr C. was engaged for the day; but directed his bailiff to show me round the farm in his occupation, consisting of 2000 acres. . . .
>
> Mr C. invited me to dine, but as I had ridden on horseback along

limestone, splashy roads and had no change of dress, intending to return in the evening, I could not accept the invitation. He would not hear of this, as he had arranged to ride round the farms with me next day, and he kindly said he would provide me with a clean shirt and what was necessary, and as his steward was away from home I might have his room, and I must stop two or three days, I could not see all in less time. Of course I had neither the power nor the wish to decline such unexpected hospitality.

I dined at Holkham that day. The company consisted of the Lady and two Miss Hunlokes, Lady and two Miss Fords, Mrs and three Miss Blackwells, Miss Coke, Miss Arbuthnot, Miss Anson, Sir Thomas Arbuthnot, Coll. Ponsonby, Coll. Cheney, Mrs Newcombe, Mrs Odell or Odie. I spent the evening most agreeably and never found less ceremony in any house that I ever was in.

The next morning I accompanied Mr C. on horseback thro' the parks and grounds . . . called on some of the tenants, the two Mr Moores.[1] He remarked to me afterwards that they looked too well, and that this was caused by their good living, and said he should like all his tenants to be able to drink their pint of wine to dinner and keep their hunter. . . .

Dined again at Mr C.'s and met nearly the same persons as yesterday. Mr C.'s friends come without invitation, his house being open to all; they went away also without taking formal leave; at the dinner table Mr C. noticed the newcomers and used to say Oh, such a one has left. Those who wished to leave before dinner had something provided for them in a room for the purpose, and anyone who wished to go out shooting had an early breakfast ready, they had only to help themselves.

Mr C.'s friends sat as long as each liked at the dinner table, and dropped off one by one to join the ladies. Tea and coffee were in the adjoining room and anyone that wished for it, went and took it; in the evening candles were brought into the next room and without the ceremony of taking leave you took one and retired to your bedroom. Thus throughout in this noble mansion, there was the greatest liberty, united with the greatest simplicity and liberality.

Mr Coke was a very handsome man of about 70. Some of the ladies at the dinner table were remarking on his fine handsome countenance in which not a wrinkle could be seen. He was desirous that a nephew should marry a daughter of the Earl of Albemarle and was recommending him to her, and she said she would rather marry him than his nephew. He took her at her word and they were soon married. This of course was since I was there. This lady brought him six children, sons and daughters.

[1] Ancestors of the present Old Moore, who lives at Palmer's Lodge in the park.

Holkham shooting needs no emphasis to the shooting man who knows his shooting history. Successive Lords Leicester have proved that it is perfectly possible to make good farming and game-shooting go hand in hand with mutual advantage. Well-farmed land is always good partridge land in any case.

That is why, on the Warham beat on November 7, 1905, eight guns set up, in twenty drives, a still unbeaten record of eight hundred and thirty-five and a half brace of partridges in addition to ten pheasants, twenty-six hares, two rabbits, and four golden plover.

Even better I like that old record of two hundred and thirty and a half brace *made with muzzle-loaders*, by the Hon. Edward Coke and the Hon. Thomas Coke on September 21, 1847. The present Lord Leicester discovered the record this year (1942) among his father's letters, and I take leave to reproduce it. Edward and Wenman Coke were brothers of Coke of Norfolk.

Holkham
21st Sept. 1847

Dear Wenny,

Well we have had our day's shooting. We went out yesterday I shooting on Bloomfield's farm and Tom on Hudson's and we succeeded in bagging two hundred and thirty brace and a half; not so bad was it? We were on our ground by 6 o'clock. I killed a bird before six and had killed 18 brace by 7 o'clock.

Tom killed about 12 brace more than I did, but he fired rather more than a hundred more shots than I did for we had our caps counted.

I missed about 80 shots and Tom missed about 180.

We had killed the largest bag that ever was killed in England or ever will be.

Your affectionate brother,

E. Coke

Some big bags of geese have been made on the fresh marshes. Five guns, including the late Lord Leicester, killed fifty-eight pink-feet, three duck, a snipe, and a curlew on December 26, 1870, while Lord Leicester killed seventy-three snipe to his own gun on the marshes in 1852. Nine guns on January 2, 1907, killed one hundred and fifty-eight mallard and one hundred and four pigeons in Obelisk Wood above the lake, which was frozen. Other records of sport at Holkham and Wells are in my book, *The Modern Fowler*.

Before I left Holkham I paid particular attention to the Spartina grass experiments which have been carried out there since Mr Gunston went to Holland in 1930 to study the subject. Spartina is the means by which we may reclaim thousands of acres of saltings from the sea all round the English coast. Experiments were carried out with it on Southampton Water in 1870, and I have seen hundreds of acres of tidal mud in Poole Harbour which have been reclaimed in the last few years from soft mud to comparatively sound, walkable land.

Briefly, Spartina grass will live and grow in salt water on mud where no other plant could exist. It binds the mud together and, if it is properly planted, reclaims it to solid land within five years. To do so about five thousand plants or cuttings must be put down per acre, three feet apart. The grass radiates just over a foot a year and grows best in mild districts. It raises the land level, and in Holland has been known to give a rise of twenty inches in three years. Planting is at the rate of one acre per man per day, and the plants cost between £3 and £5 per thousand. The cost at Holkham has been worked out to between £20 and £25 per acre, to include plant, transport, and wages; the cost of the sea-wall naturally varies according to length, site, and construction.

A good point about Spartina is that it makes good hay, equal to the best meadow hay. It can be used in its early stages for making silage, and it is, of course, well known for paper-making. Sheep, fed solely on it at Chelmsford Institute of Agriculture for two months, kept in perfect health. Whereas fifteen acres of saltings herbage will give a bite for a few sheep, the same under Spartina yields forty to fifty tons of good hay, provides several weeks of grazing for stock, and reclaims the land from the sea at the same time.

The famous pine belts along the coast at Holkham were planted partly as shelter belts for the reclaimed marshes, but mainly to bind the sandhills together and prevent a break-through of the sea. The second earl began the scheme in 1855, and it has been completely successful ever since.

Austrian pines seem to suit the more exposed places while Corsican pines flourish in the sheltered parts. Maritime pines did not come up to expectations. Scotch pines have done, on the whole, quite well but they are more suited to the sheltered sides. Practically all the trees were raised from seed in nurseries on the estate. The original cost was about a pound an acre, and on balance the Corsican pine has proved to be the best all-round tree as it thrives anywhere, on pure sand or not. The Austrian pine is, however, the hardiest and more suitable for the seaward slopes.

The trees were widely spaced to begin with, from four yards to eight yards apart, and this has allowed full development. The

Holkham pine belt, which extends for miles, is one of the great sights of the North Norfolk coast and an object-lesson which the Government might do well to copy at such places as Horsey, if further inundations of the sea through unprotected sandhills are to be prevented.

Holkham, indeed, has shown the way in a hundred different aspects of farming. It is a perfect example of the great good which can be done by a responsible landowner who puts his heart and soul into agriculture and the welfare of his tenants. It is a perfect vindication of individualism, and it provides all the answers to the would-be land nationalizer and to those slick, modern, agricultural publicists who try to tell us that they are so much cleverer to-day than the 'old-fashioned' farmers of yesterday.

One can say of Lord Leicester to-day as White, the Norfolk historian, said of his ancestor in 1836: "He has contrived to fertilize the soil, while drawing from it the most exuberant supplies. . . . His farms are let at moderate rents, on long leases, and liberal covenants, affording every encouragement for the employment of capital and industry."

I cannot see, however, that the present-day Government treatment of the landowner, whereby Lord Leicester and others receive a fraction over 2 per cent. on their outlay of capital and the invested brains and goodwill of their ancestors, "affords every encouragement for the employment of capital and industry."

The present Lord Leicester, I am sure, will be the last to complain. He, like many another landowner, is content so long as he can see his land in good heart, his tenants well housed, his farm buildings in good repair, and himself able to afford to live in a few rooms of his house on his own Norfolk acres.

But what shall we have to say of the system of death duties if one day it causes the break-up of such an entirely beneficent estate, as it has broken up hundreds of others in Britain? We cannot go on killing all the geese which lay the golden eggs all the time. The landowner has been badly treated for years. The best of them have hung on and done their job. They must be given more security when peace comes to maintain farming in the great tradition which is their heritage. Death duties must be revised as Lord Eltisley suggested—payable on sale and not on death.

I left Holkham and Wells with real regret. On the coast road to Stiffkey, with the sea lonely on the left, plovers and partridges busy in the fields on the right, an air-raid warning went. Distant sirens wailed. There were we, trundling along a lonely road in a great black-and-white horse-box, the sort of thing which makes an ideal target for the tip-and-run German raiders of our East Coast. We looked sufficiently like a Red Cross ambulance to invite their machine-gun bullets. I loaded the huge 4¼-inch eight-bore with five ounces of S.S.G., the twelve-bore with three ounces of B.B., and gave the little gun to Jim.

We rumbled on. Three minutes later Jim suddenly said, "Look up, sir. Here he comes! Straight up the road—head-on for us." An aeroplane was flying directly along the coast road at us, not sixty yards up.

"Quick! Stop. Out you get and into the ditch. Wait till he's almost on you, give him a good lead, and shoot the pilot in the face."

Out we bundled into the ditch on either side. The plane roared over, four barrels swinging on it ready to rip half a pound of buckshot into the cockpit. Only just in time did we see that the markings were British. But I still cherish the beautiful thought that it would have been easily possible to have shot an enemy machine down at such short range with goose-guns.

Beyond Morston partridge-shooters lined the roadside hedge. Machine-guns blazed off in the sky above the sea. Aeroplanes swooped in and out of the clouds. A ragged line of schoolboy beaters advanced through a root-field. The guns waited by the hedge. Rural England was going about its normal business.

One gun, huge, craggy-faced, waved an enormous hand, grinned as we passed by. It was Peter Ackroyd, foxhunter and wildfowler. The last time I had seen him had been two months before when we were both convalescent at Windsor, he scarce able to walk, on sick leave from the Guards Depot. Here he was shooting partridges in Norfolk with machine-gun bullets ripping through the air. Unchanging England!

In Blakeney, at midday, I forgathered with Peter at the White Horse, that grand inn in the steep, cobbled little main street above the harbour where Charlie Long, coxswain of the lifeboat, draws beer and talks 'fowling.

A quick word with Roy Pope, that good man with horse or gun, at the Manor House and then on by Cley and Salthouse, where the seaward marshes, immortal home of rare ducks, ruffs, avocets, Caspian terns, Sandwich terns, godwits, and golden plover, were fenced off from the road by a mighty barricade of barbed wire, anti-tank defences, iron girders, and concrete posts.

There a storm of wind and rain struck us. A full gale blew off the sea. Spume and spray whirled by in dizzy eddies. The North Sea rose and lashed itself white. In a minute the sky and countryside changed from green and blue to black clouds and steaming rain. The horse-box rocked under the tremendous buffets of the wind. That gale must have blown a full seventy miles an hour.

In Holt, after we had climbed in a burst of sunshine through the wet and glistening loveliness of Salthouse Heath, glowing with broom and heather, we halted for a last horn of ale. Alas, they were shut. Returning to the horse-box, we found a middle-aged gentleman with a fiery face and a judicious eye, contemplating the horse-box. He swivelled benevolently on us, and proceeded to talk horse.

"I've not ridden a horse for a year or two, but I keep some rare good 'uns, and I drive the missus in a smart little trap. It does me good to see you on the road with a couple like this. Gentlemen, do me the pleasure of taking a drink."

I pointed out gravely that we had just trodden a half-mile of Holt streets and returned heavy with defeat. He winked solemnly: "Come you with me. Uncle Roland knows the way." We followed.

At a demure, old-fashioned little pub on a corner, with white dimity curtains in the window, he tapped thrice, unconcernedly and as though by accident, as he passed. We went round by the back door. We entered.

In the parlour, by a cheerful fire, sat two charming old ladies. One wore a white lace cap. The other had a bow of black ribbon at her throat. Both were small, demure, and frail. They were like old china. They belonged to *Cranford* or Mr Trollope, these faded rose-leaves of the village past. Their knitting needles clicked. Their two cats purred. Their eyebrows were raised demurely. We drank.

Then, by little back streets, we followed Uncle Roland to stables, old, small, sweet, and clean. They were swept and garnished. A beagle bitch with a lame foot limped to greet us.

"I stable a few hosses here," said Uncle Roland modestly. "We've got the Essex chaps not far off at the minute. A good sportin' regiment, if you know Essex at all. They ride an' they hunt. And they've got a few couple o' beagles with 'em. They're out huntin' the hare at this moment. Does my old heart good to see a hoss an' a hound again."

We left Holt with a memory ineffaceable of Mr Roland B. Lee, the fiery-faced, sporting grocer of that fine little Norfolk town. And so, regretfully, summoned by more urgent business, began the long run back to Colchester.

Half Suffolk and all East Norfolk were left unexplored. There were farms at Herringby and Acle I should like to have seen. There were fishermen at Waxham and Palling to be remembered, old friends at Mannington Hall and Martham, in Yarmouth and Orford. There was wonderful farming, good horses, and grand cattle that should have been seen at Sudbourne and Bawdsey, good farmers about Woolverstone and on the high lands above Erwarton and the broad Stour. Half East Anglia lay untouched. The rest of England beckons.

On another day, when war allows, I shall put my foot in the iron, hear the saddle creak, and go forth again on the timeless bridleways of England.

This is my stedfast creed, my faith and all my trust;
That in the heavens there is a God, most mighty, mild and just;
A God above all Gods, a King above all Kings,
The Lord of Lords, chief Governor of Heaven and earthly things.

THOMAS TUSSER, *One Hundred Points of Good Husbandrie* (1557)

INDEX

Abberton Manor, 66, 67, 68
Abbots Hall, Wigborough, 28, 29
Abdy of Albyns, Sir Thomas, 19, 22–23
Ackroyd, Major Peter, 166, 243
Adders, anti-snakebite serum from, 33, 34; dangerous habits of, 194
Adeane, Robert, of Babraham Hall, Cambridgeshire, 126, 161, 166
Adventurers' Fen, 170
Allen, Ted, the "Essex Marshman" of the B.B.C., 31, 32 *et seq.*, 35–36, 49
Allingham, Margery L., at D'Arcy House, 18
Allington, Sir Giles, 124
Allix, Squire C. P., of Swaffham Prior Hall, 159
Ambrose, Cole, of Stuntney Hall, 159
Amos, Bert, innkeeper, 39
Anglo-Saxon Chronicle, 75
Anmer, 212, 213
Appleton, Shire stud at, 213
Arch Hall, mystery of, 39
Ashley-Dodd, Major, squire of Croxton, 189
Aspland, Isaac, 159

Badcock's Hut, the sick child at, 170–171, 173
Badgers, 73
Bailey, Bert, fenman, 171, 172
Bailey, John 'Bunyan,' 172
Baldwin of Bewdley, Stanley Baldwin, first Earl, 29, 103
Barnwell Priory, 128–129
Barnham Heath, 186
Barton Mills, Bull Inn at, 180
Beak, Major-General W. D. M., V.C., and Malta, 120–121
Beaumont-cum-Moze, 27
Beckingham Hall, 69
Bedford Level Board, 155
Beeleigh Abbey, 85
Bensusan, S. L., 100
Berechurch Hall, 68
Bigod, Hugh, 188
Binney, Squire Thomas Godfrey, 29, 58
Birds, 20–21, 101, 125, 156, 158, 160 *et seq.*, 170, 186–187, 194, 195, 206–207, 212, 216, 224, 243; and the soldiers, 27, 207–208; a Great Bustard's egg, 218; stuffed, collection of, 218
Birds through the Year (Wolfe Murray), 164
Birkbeck, Major H. H., banker and farmer, 216–218
Birkbeck, Oliver, 219
Bishop Stortford, 121
Blackwater, river, 19, 28, 56–57, 69, 74, 84
Bledisloe of Lydney, Charles Bathurst, Viscount, and direct marketing of farm produce, 88
Bloomfield, Robert, Suffolk plough-boy poet, 182
Blumenfeld, R. D., at Muscombs Farm, 122
Bohuns Hall, 79
Bone, Sam, wildfowler, 228–229
Boreham House farms, 85–86, 88 *et seq.*, 94, 110
Borrow, George, 200, 203; quoted, 201
Bos urus, the great ox, skull of, dug up, 169
Boswell, Mr, farm manager, 89, 90–91
Bottisham Hall, 155
Bradwell-juxta-Mare, 54, 67; King's Head inn at, 83
Brampton Park, 145
Brandy Hole Creek, 28, 101
Braxted Park, 94
Brentwood Grammar School, boys of, and Wallasea harvest, 104
Brickwall Farm, 66, 70
Bridgemarsh Island, 28
Brooks family, the, of Childerley Hall, 148

Brown, Bob, 38–40
Browny Boy (horse), 72
Bruntisfield, Sir Victor Warrender, Baron, 38
Buchanan, Hector, 142
Bunting, Jack, 78
Burnham Overy grass marshes, cultivation of, 236
Burnham-on-Crouch, 27, 67, 102
Burrows, George, Pin Mill harbour-master, 51–52, 53
Burwell Fen, 159, 161, 162, 163, 165; skull of the *Bos urus* found in, 169
Butterman's Bay, 51
Buxton, Captain Aubrey, 163

Callaby, Horace, Master of the Heacham Harriers, 130; his stud farm, 212–214
Cambridge, 153; inns of, and their customers, 127–130
Cambridge Revisited (Gray), 173
Cambridge University, 152
Cambridge University Air Squadron, 152
Campbell, Captain J. W., stuffed bird collection of, 218
Campbell, Lorne, 119
Canewdon, 66, 101
Canvey Island (Connos), history of, 106
Carlingford, Chichester Parkinson-Fortescue, first Viscount, 29, 32
Castle Hedingham, 122
Cattle, narrow escapes from, 226–227, 228, 231; grazing land for, 236–237
Cedd, Bishop, 54
Chamberlain, Right Hon. Neville, 50
Champion de Crespigny, Sir Claude, 32, 48, 58, 69, 74, 94
Champion de Crespigny, Victor, 76
Charles II, 100, 175–176, 180, 184, 186
Charrington, brewer, 82
Chelmsford Museum, 58
Chickens, war-time restrictions on keeping, 140–141; catching and plucking competition, 190
Childerley Hall, Dry Drayton, 148
Chivers, Messrs, factory and farms of, at Histon, 133–136; their Percheron stud, 134–135
Cholmondeley, George Cholmondeley, fifth Marquess of, 219
Cholmondeley, Richard, 149
Churchill, Right Hon. Winston, Prime Minister, 23, 47, 68, 89
Clarke, "Jumping Jack," 83
Cobbett, William, 12, 13, 75, 76, 222
Cock-fighting, 129
Cockup Bridge, 161, 169
Coke of Norfolk, Thomas William, and George IV, 233; life and farming activities of, 237–240; brothers of, 240
Colchester, 25, 57
Colchester Castle, remains of Roman temple in, 39
Colne Engaine, fox at, 70
Cottis family, of Lambourne Hall, 101–102
Cowlard, Frank, keeper, 147
Cowley, policeman, 175
Cranworth, Bertram Gurdon, second Baron, 142
Cressing Temple, manor farm, 91
Crisp, Charlie, sportsman, 174
Cromwell, Henry, Lord Protector of Ireland, 175–176
Cromwell, Oliver, 21
Crouch, river, 28, 101
Croxton Park, 137, 191; destruction of rabbits at, 138, 147. *See also* Eltisley, Baron
Curzon, Ralph Nathaniel Okeover, 166

Danbury Hill, highwaymen on, 99
D'Arcy, village of, 18
de Boys, John, 11
de Grey, Hon. Richard, 195
Dean, Basil, 122
Death duties on land, effect of, 16, 143–144, 242
Defoe, Daniel, 75
Dengie Hundred, the, 28, 100
Devitt, Major Sir Thomas Gordon, Bart., 121
Dewsbury, Bert, skater, 177
Dhuleep Singh, Prince, 187

Diesel tractor, the, 23, 115, 116–118, 138–139
Donyland, 31
Downe, Dorothy, Viscountess, 206, 209, 211
Duberley, Major Hugh, of Great Stoughton Manor, Huntingdonshire, 146, 148
Dunmow, 121, 122
Dunn-Gardner, Cyril, 178
Dunraven and Mount-Earl, Windham Henry Wyndham-Quin, Colonel the fifth Earl of, and his yachts, 74

East Donyland Hall, 37
East Essex Hunt, the, 22, 67, 69
East Horndon Hall, W. Goodchild's house, 109, 111
Edward VII, King, 148
Elmsett, fox at, 68
Eltisley of Croxton, George Douglas Newton, Baron, and direct sale by producer to consumer, 86; scientific farming of, 137 *et seq.*, 145; and restrictions on keeping of live stock, 141; on death duties on land, 144, 242
Eltisley, Lady Muriel, 139
Eltisley, Leeds Arms inn at, 148
Elveden Hall, 187
Elwes, H. J., of Colesbourne Park, 108
Elwes, Robert, of Congham House, 218
Ely, Cutter Inn at, 175
Ennion, Dr E. A. R., ornithologist, 163, 166
Essex, and the World War, 45, 46, 50 *et seq.*, 76, 80, 81, 82, 83, 95, 96–97; families, 78, 81; farms, ancient names of, 79
Essex and Suffolk Hunt, the, 67
Essex Farmers' Foxhounds, the, 67, 100
Essex Union Hunt, the, 67
Euston Hall, Suffolk, 178, 180, 181 *et seq.*
Evadne, yacht, 49

Fairey, Sir Richard, 49
Fambridge Ferry, 28, 101
Farley, Reuben, 147
Farm labourers, living conditions of, 92; wages of, 86, 87, 92, 141, 177; objection of, to income tax, 92, 141–142; objection of, to unskilled labour on the land, 93; Irish harvesters, 108–109
Farming, and the Government, 16–18, 29, 89–90, 91, 103, 139 *et seq.*, 143–144, 176–177, 210, 242; the small farmer, 143; crop yields, 235, 236
Faulkbourne Hall, 94
Felix Hall, 94
Fens, the, draining of, 154, 166–168, 177; the people of, 156, 159, 171; flooding of, 157–158; oak of, 180; reclamation of, 180
Finch, H. M., "the Fighting Barrister," 174
Finchingfield Manor, 67
Fingringhoe, 28, 31, 37, 39
Fisher of Kilverstone, Cecil Fisher, second Baron, 189
Flax, growing of, 218; at Sandringham, 212, 213
Flint, E. W., of Manor Farm, Wells-next-the-Sea, 222, 223, 226, 231, 236
Folly Faunts Manor, 79
Food, cheap imported, demand for, 16, 17, 39, 91–92; home-grown, health value of, 17–18; direct sale of, to consumer, 86, 88
Ford, Henry, 85
Fordham Abbey, 178
Fordson Estates, Ltd., 85; organization of, 86–88
Foulness Island, 28, 108, 109
Fountaine, Vice-Admiral Charles Andrew, 216
Fox, Sir Gifford, M.P., 151
Foxes, ways and adventures of, 67 *et seq.*, 150
French, Arthur, 79
Freshwater Sand and Ballast Company, 37
Friday Wood, 66
Friedberg, Mrs W. L., 71–72, 113, 124
Fuller, Robert, 142, 176, 177, 188
Furneaux, Colonel Claude, 37

GALITZINE, PRINCE NICOLAS, 128, 130, 166, 194
Galitzine, Prince Yurka, 82, 127, 130, 194
Gallyon, gunsmith, 151
Gentle, Sir William, of Ford Place, 191
Gentlemen Adventurers, the, and the draining of the fens, 154, 155, 156
George V, King, 206, 208, 210
George VI, King, 210
Ghosts and witches, 26, 35, 43, 105–107, 128–129, 174, 186, 188–189, 204, 205
Godolphin Arabian, 125
Gog Magogs Park, 125
Goldhanger, 69, 78
Goodchild, William, 103, 109–110
Gordon-Dickson, Colonel D. J., 82
Gorst, Sir John Eldon, 174
Gosfield Park, 67, 122
Gough of Goojerat, Punjab, and Limerick, Hugh Gough, fourth Viscount, 32
Grafton, Charles Alfred Euston Fitzroy, tenth Duke of, 178, 181, 182 *et seq.*, 189
Gray, Arthur, Master of Jesus College, 173
Great Canfield, 121
Great Illusion—Now, The (Angell), 76
Great Totham, Cricketers inn at, 74
Great Yeldham, the White Hart inn at, 122–123
Green, Basil, birds observed by, 163
Green, Daniel, yeoman, 37
Greville, Hon. Maynard, 122
Guedalla, Philip, 122
Guisnes Court, 28, 29, 58
Gunston, Josiah, manager of Holkham farm, 224, 225, 235, 236, 237, 240
Gwynne, H. A., former editor of the *Morning Post*, 122

HALL, MISS, rabbiter, 15
Harding, Colonel Walter, 149, 150
Hare, Sir Ralph, Bart., of Stow Bardolph Hall, 195
Hastings, Albert Astley, twenty-first Baron, 222
Hatfield, 67, 111, 121; Eight Bells inn at, 113–115
Hathaway, Mrs Sybil, Dame de Serk, 93
Havengore, 28, 108
Hawker, Colonel Peter, 81
Hazeleigh, 100
Heacham, 130, 213–214
Heacham Harriers, founding of, 215
Heathland, reclamation of, 182–183
Heckford Bridge, 73; Angel inn at, 73–74
Heckstall-Smith, Tony, D.S.C., 82, 166
Hedge End, Walton Backwaters, 28
Hempstead, Arthur, oysterman, bomb experience of, 48–49
Herm, island, 93
Hertford, 121
Hillington estate, 206 *et seq.*, 212, 215; inn on, 209; and present war, 210
Histon, 133–136, 182
Hinchingbrooke Castle, 145
Holbeach, 196; potato-growing in, 198
Holbrook, Commander Norman, V.C., 50
Holder, Nigel, 161, 163, 165, 166
Holkham Hall and farm property, 218, 220 *et seq.*, 234, 237; shooting at, 240; pine belts along the coast, 241–242
Hooley, Terah, his herd of Large Blacks, 148
Horn, Major K. K., of Thurlow Park, 166
Horse-box, the, description of, 70 *et seq.*
Horseheath, 124, 125
Horses, 179, 181; traffic in, 107–108; use of, on farms, 117, 139; narrow escapes from, 226–228, 231. *See also under* names and breeds
Horsey Island, 28
Hosier's Farm, 123
Houston, Lady, D.B.E., 93

JAMESON, DR AND MRS, ghostly experience of, 188
Jellicoe, George Jellicoe, second Earl, 166
Jenkins, T., farmer, and the foaling of Marshland Shales, 200–201
Jenyns family, of Bottisham, 126, 155
Jermy, Sir Henry, 174
Johnson, Fred, of Wicken Hall, 159
Jolliffe Tufnell family, 85

KEEBLE, FRED, marshman, 105
Kenyon, Lloyd Tyrell-Kenyon, fifth Baron, 85

Keynes, John Maynard Keynes, Baron, and compulsory saving, 87
Kimbolton Castle and village, 145, 146, 147
King's Hard, the, 65
King's Lynn, 204, 206, 210

LAND, death duties on, effect of, 16, 143–144, 242; nationalization of, 40, 236, 242; as the Fourth Fighting Service, 144; arable, uncultivated, 157; the richest in England, 196
Landowners, the best type of, 132 *et seq.*
Langenhoe Hall, 28, 29, 31, 32, 39
Langford, 85, 94
Latchingdon-cum-Snoreham, 79
Lawes, J. B., experiments of, in crop yields, 235
Layer Brook, 67
Layer Marney, 11
Layer Marney Towers, 58, 61; collection of stuffed birds at, 218
Leach, 'Chub,' 166
Leach, Felix, 166, 179
Lee, Roland B., sporting grocer of Holt, 244
Leeds, Dukes of, at Gog Magogs, horses of, 125
Leez Priory, 67
Leicester, Earls of, 222, 223, 232–233, 240, 242
Lincolnshire, old language of, 126; farming in, 196–199
Linnett, Walter, fisherman-fowler, 55–56
Linton village, 124
Lloyd of Dolobran, Alexander Lloyd, second Baron, 166
Lloyd George, Right Hon. David, his Budget of 1910, 16, 23; and agriculture, 176
Londesborough, Ernest Denison, sixth Baron, and sale of Blankney estate, 215
London, 46–47, 65; Railway Tavern ("Charlie Brown's") at Limehouse, customers and curiosities at, 112
Lord of the Harvest, the, 14, 117
Lucas, Dr, of Burwell, 159
Lucas, Major Sir Jocelyn, Bart., M.P., 115, 119, 161, 163, 166
Luddington, James, of Wallington Hall, 195
Lymington, Gerard Lymington, Viscount, on the Tory Squire's house, 219

MACDONALD, RIGHT HON. RAMSAY, 29, 103
McKinnon, Alastair, 194
Macmillan, J. A., 168
Machinery, agricultural, 22–23, 29, 196–197; the John Deere tractor, 197
Madingley Hall, 148; gardens at, 149; visitors to, 151
Maeldune, epic battle of, 75, 77
Majendie family, the, 122
Maldon, 14, 66, 74, 76, 82, 84, 94, 98; inns of, 75, 79, 80–81, 99, 104
Manchester, William Drogo Montagu, ninth Duke of, 145–146
Mandeville, Alexander Drogo Montagu, Viscount, 145–146, 147, 161
Mann, Tom, yeoman, 21, 22–23, 143
Manningtree, 67
Marks Hall, 94
Marmansgrave Wood, 187
Marshland Shales, 200–201
Martin, Alfred Herbert, labourer, his story, 105
Mason, Mr, of Fincham Hall, farmer, 216
Massingham, H. J., cited, 133
Massingham Heath, 219
Mersea Island, 18, 19, 29; bombing of, 24, 42, 48–49; the Strood, 25, 26, 66; Old City of, 41; war casualties of, 45; inns of, 47, 56, 57, 64, 83; its mud, properties of, 66
Milgate, Ted, oysterman, 48
Milgate, Zebedee, 58–59
Modern Fowler, The (Wentworth Day), 240
Monson, Squire Claude, horse- and dog-breeder, 200 *et seq.*; and Tamzen, 203
Monson Greys, 205, 223–224, 226
Moore, Squire, of Coney Weston, 190
Moyns Hall, 67
Much Hadham, 121

Munnings, Alfred J., R.A., 214
Mussett, 'Duck,' 60
Mussett, Jim, boat-rigger, 44
Mussett, Whitey 'Swan,' 45, 60 *et seq.*
Myddleton, Sir Hugh, and London's pure water-supply, 156
Myers, F. S., the "Caterpillar King," 196–197

NATIONAL TRUST, the, 144, 158, 162
New England, Essex, 22, 108
Newmarket, 177, 179
Newton, Sir Isaac, 144, 187
Norfolk, the people of, 202, 219; county of, 205–206; old families of, 205
Norfolk, West, 205; villages of, and their inns, 194; squires of, 195–196, 200
North Foreland, 66
Northey Island, 28, 76–77

OLD ENGLISH HAWKING CLUB, members of, 195
Old Hall Marshes, 18, 58
Old London Bridge, stones of, 58
Olding, Jack, 67; demonstration by, of farming machinery, 111, 113, 115 *et seq.*
Olsen, Mr, pig expert to the Danish Government, 90
Onions, sale of, at controlled price, 197
Orwell Park, 51
Osea Island, 77, 78, 82, 83, 97
Othona fort, 54
Ouse Drainage Board, the, 156, 157
Oysters, 44, 66, 104

PACKING HOUSE ISLAND, 65
Padney, 175, 176
Paglesham Creek, 105
Pansies, growing of, for munitions, 24
Parker family, Heacham, land farmed by, 215–216
Parker, the Misses, of Woodham Mortimer Place, 100
Parr, Ernest, keeper, 166
Pease, Sir Alfred, Bart., and the fox, 68
Peldon Rose inn, preservation of, 24 *et seq.*
Penney, Gerald, 50
Percherons, 134–135
Perry, Percival Perry, Baron, 93, 115; and Boreham House, 85, 86–87; on fruit-growing, farming, etc., 89–91, 92, 142
Philipson, Major George, 178
Philipson, Mrs G., 178, 179
Pigs, feeding of, 86, 90–91, 141; farms for, 90; farrowing of, 91
Pin Mill, and the Butt and Oyster inn, 51
Pitt, Ernie, fowler, 81
Plummer, Dick, of the *Daily Express*, 123
Pods Wood, 74
Potatoes, mechanical digging of, 197; growing of, in Lincolnshire, 198–199
Potton Island, 28, 105, 108
Prehistoric man, remains of, found in peat, 169
Pretyman, Mr, of Orwell Park, 51
Proctor, Harold, his house and farm, 36–37
Pullen, Ivan, 26 *et seq.*
Pullen, Mrs Jane, 25–26
Purleigh, 100
Pyefleet, creek, 25, 31

QUORN, THE, 68
Quy, 154, 179

RABBITS, destruction of, 138, 147, 189–190, 217; sale of, 210
Ratcliff, Stanley, farmer, 30, 99
Ray Island, ghostly inhabitant of, 43
Rayleigh, Robert Strutt, fourth Baron, farming of, at Terling Place, 94
Raypits, 101
Reach, 159, 160, 165, 166
Rebell, Jack, and his family, 104
Red deer, the Easton herd, 122
Rimington-Wilson, R. H., 32, 67
Rivenhall Place, 94
Robert (horse), 71, 72, 79, 202
Robertson, Mr and Mrs Douglas, of Brickwall Farm, 70
Rodd, Jim, 12, 58, 60, 67, 68, 70, 71–73, 190, 203, 224, 226, 243
Rodd, Maurice, 67
Round, Charles, 22–23, 30

Round, Charles James, Squire of Birch, Father of the House of Commons, 22, 29, 32
Rouse, Dr W. H. D., 131
Royal College of Surgeons, Museum of, midwifery instruments found at Woodham Mortimer Hall deposited in, 100
Royal Commission on Historical Monuments, 25
Royal Harwich Yacht Club, 51
Rue, Larry, of the *Chicago Tribune*, 119
Ruggles-Brise, Archibald Weyland, 108
Ruggles-Brise, Colonel Sir Edward, Bart., M.P., 30, 108
Rushley, 108
Russell, Colonel, brewer, 19
Russell family, the, and fen drainage, 155, 156

St Paul's, Dean and Chapter of, as landowners, 100
St Peter's Lodge, by Walpole Highway, 200, 201 *et seq.*
St Peter's-on-the-Wall chapel, oldest 'cathedral' in Britain, 54, 55
Salcott, 18–19, 20, 25, 58
Salisbury, James Gascoyne-Cecil, fourth Marquess of, his farms, cultivation of, 117
Salt marshes, grazing of cattle on, 236; reclamation of, sowing of Spartina grass, 237, 240–241
Salter, Dr J. H., 18, 58, 74, 218
Sandringham, farming at, 206, 212, 213
Sandwich, 77
Sark, island, 93
Sawbridgeworth, 121
Selborne, Roundell Cecil Palmer, third Earl of, 115, 119
Sempill, William Forbes-Sempill, nineteenth Baron, 115, 119, 166
Sexton, Jimmy, 102
Sheep-counting, old style, 126–127
Sheep-stealing, 159, 160, 177
Shrimp ale, 19
Smart, 'Fish,' champion skater, 177
Smith, Charlie, and the bombing of his smack, 95–96
Smugglers, tales of, 19, 25
Soham, 175
Soham Mere, 157
Soil fertility, 135–136, 142–143
South, Bob, boat-rigger, 44
South Fambridge Hall, 101
South House Farm, 37
Southend Bypass, 111
Southminster, 100
Spalding, land about, value and farming of, 196, 198, 200
Spartina grass, cultivation of, 237, 240–241
Spinney Abbey, 165, 174, 175, 176
Spinney Fen, freezing of, 177
Sportsmen and naturalists, well-known, recollections of, 229–230
Stamp, Charlie, wildfowler, 106–107
Staples, Luke, of Landwade Hall, 160
Steeple, 79
Stephens, Alfred, 100
Stephenson, Moray, 118
Stoker, Charlie, marshman, 69
Stoker, Mrs Sydney, 42
Stowell, E. F., Assistant Editor of the *Daily Telegraph*, 119
Strafford, Thomas Wentworth, first Earl of, 184–185
Sugar beet, 39–40, 85, 86, 90–91, 212, 217, 218
Swaffer, Hannen, 120
Swaffham, Cambridgeshire, 154, 179
Swaffham, Norfolk, 192, 195
Swaffham Fen, prehistoric remains found in, 169
Swan Mere, 161, 163, 165, 167
Sycamore, Captain, 44

Takeley, 121
Thetford, 180, 187–189; Bell inn at, 189
Thompson, Harry, of Middleton, farmer, 216
Thorn Fleet, 43, 45
Thorn Hall Farm, 176
Thorney Abbey, 154–155
Thoroughbreds, 214–215
Tillingham, 100
Tiptree Heath, 74
Todd, Geoffrey, 229
Tollesbury chaps, the, 19

Tollesbury Fleet, 58
Tolleshunt D'Arcy Hall, 11, 12, 13–14; panelling of, 15, 16
Tothams, the, 69
Townley family, of Fulbourn Manor, 126
Turnor, Christopher, pioneer of direct sale by producer to consumer, 88

ULTING, 85
Upware, 173; inns of, 159, 173–174

VERMUYDEN, SIR CORNELIUS, engineer, 156
Via Devana, Cambridgeshire, 124, 125, 127
Vikings, the, 77
Virley Hall Farm, 21

WALLASEA ISLAND, 28, 102 *et seq.*, 108
Walsingham, John de Grey, seventh Baron, 194
War Agricultural Committees, 22, 30, 39–40, 139–140, 146, 155, 183
War Birds (E. W. Springs), 166
War evacuees, conduct of, 178, 179, 210, 225
War Office, land bought by, 38
Ware, 121
Warner, Dick, thatcher, 107–108
Warrender, Sir Victor—*see* Bruntisfield, Baron
Warwick, Frances, Countess of, 121
Wash, the, 66
Washington, Lawrence, of Maldon, ancestor of George Washington, 98, 99
Watson, Tommy, 119
Wells, H. G., 121
Wells-next-the-Sea, 222, 223, 226, 231
Wentworth, Sir John, 122
Wentworth, Thomas D'Arcy, 11
West Mersea Hall, 54
Westacre, farming at, 216–218
Weston Eve family, the, 12, 14, 15, 16
White, Mr, estate man, 148, 149, 150
Wicken, 173, 176; first policeman at, murder of, 160, 179
Wicken Sedge Fen, preservation of, 158, 170; shooting on, 162; birds on, 165; draining of, 166–168
Wigborough, 24, 28, 67, 228
William II, Kaiser, 220
Willis, Dr, of Soham, 171, 172
Wilson, Gerry, steeplechase rider, 220
Winner, Eric, of Beachamwell, airman, 192, 193
Witham, 94–95; inn at, 92
Wolfe Murray, David ("Fish-Hawk"), 82, 163, 164–165, 166
Wolferton, herds at, 213
Wolmer, Lord—*see* Selborne, Earl of
Woodford, inn at, 111–112
Woodham Mortimer, old houses in, 99–100
Woolton, Frederick Marquis, Baron, 89; and the small business man, 133
Wyatt, Captain Bill, boat-builder, 43, 45, 46–48, 53, 58–60

YEOMAN, the, definition of, 109, 131–133
Young, Arthur, 14, 75, 76

Other titles in the Equestrian Travel Classic series published by The Long Riders' Guild Press. We are constantly adding to our collection, so for an up-to-date list please visit our website:

www.thelongridersguild.com

Title	**Author**
Southern Cross to Pole Star – Tschiffely's Ride	Aime Tschiffley
Tale of Two Horses	Aime Tschiffley
Bridle Paths	Aime Tschiffely
This Way Southward	Aime Tschiffely
Bohemia Junction	Aime Tschiffely
Through Persia on a Sidesaddle	Ella C. Sykes
Through Russia on a Mustang	Thomas Stevens
Across Patagonia	Lady Florence Dixie
A Ride to Khiva	Frederick Burnaby
Ocean to Ocean on Horseback	Williard Glazier
Rural Rides – Volume One	William Cobbett
Rural Rides – Volume Two	William Cobbett
Adventures in Mexico	George F. Ruxton
Travels with A Donkey in the Cevennes	Robert Louis Stevenson
Winter Sketches from the Saddle	John Codman
Following the Frontier	Roger Pocock
On Horseback in Virginia	Charles Dudley Warner
California Coast Trails	J. Smeaton Chase
My Kingdom for a Horse	Margaret Leigh
The Journeys of Celia Fiennes	Celia Fiennes
On Horseback through Asia Minor	Fred Burnaby
The Abode of Snow	Andrew Wilson
A Lady's Life in the Rocky Mountains	Isabella Bird
Travels in Afghanistan	Ernest F. Fox
Through Mexico on Horseback	Joseph Carl Goodwin
Caucasian Journey	Negley Farson
Turkestan Solo	Ella K. Maillart
Through the Highlands of Shropshire	Magdalene M. Weale
Wartime Ride	J. W. Day
Across the Roof of the World	Wilfred Skrede
Woman on a Horse	Ana Beker
Saddles East	John W. Beard
Last of the Saddle Tramps	Messanie Wilkins
Ride a White Horse	William Holt
Manual of Pack Transportation	H. W. Daly
Horses, Saddles and Bridles	W. H. Carter
Notes on Elementary Equitation	Carleton S. Cooke
Cavalry Drill Regulations	United States Army
Horse Packing	Charles Johnson Post
14th Century Arabic Riding Manual	Muhammad al-Aqsarai
The Art of Travel	Francis Galton
Shanghai à Moscou	Madame de Bourboulon
Saddlebags for Suitcases	Mary Bosanquet
The Road to the Grey Pamir	Ana Louise Strong
Boot and Saddle in Africa	Thomas Lambie
To the Foot of the Rainbow	Clyde Kluckhohn
Through Five Republics on Horseback	George Ray
Journey from the Arctic	Donald Brown
Saddle and Canoe	Theodore Winthrop
The Prairie Traveler	Randolph Marcy
Reiter, Pferd und Fahrer – Volume One	Dr. C. Geuer
Reiter, Pferd und Fahrer – Volume Two	Dr. C. Geuer

The Long Riders' Guild

The world's leading source of information regarding equestrian exploration!

www.thelongridersguild.com

CPSIA information can be obtained at www.ICGtesting.com
Printed in the USA
LVOW13s2216031213

363723LV00001B/195/A

9 781590 480397